A Life in Code

A Life in Code

*Pioneer Cryptanalyst
Elizebeth Smith Friedman*

G. STUART SMITH

McFarland & Company, Inc., Publishers
Jefferson, North Carolina

Library of Congress Cataloguing-in-Publication Data

Names: Smith, G. Stuart, author.
Title: A life in code : pioneer cryptanalyst Elizebeth Smith Friedman /
    G. Stuart Smith.
Description: Jefferson, N.C. : McFarland & Company, Inc., Publishers, *Apr. 28,*
    2017 | Includes bibliographical references and index.
Identifiers: LCCN 2017016179 | ISBN 9781476669182 (softcover : acid
    free paper) ∞
Subjects: LCSH: Friedman, Elizebeth, 1892–1980. | Cryptographers—
    United States—Biography. | Women—United States—History. |
    World War, 1914–1918—Cryptography. | Cryptography—United
    States—History.
Classification: LCC D639.C75 S65 2017 | DDC 652/.8092 [B] —dc23
LC record available at https://lccn.loc.gov/2017016179

British Library cataloguing data are available

ISBN (print) 978-1-4766-6918-2
ISBN (ebook) 978-1-4766-2816-5

Front cover image of Elizebeth Smith Friedman
© National Security Agency

Printed in the United States of America

McFarland & Company, Inc., Publishers
* Box 611, Jefferson, North Carolina 28640*
* www.mcfarlandpub.com*

For Chris, Vanessa and Eric

Table of Contents

Preface

When I was a teenager my parents handed me a well-worn copy of a 1937 edition of *Reader's Digest*. They said it was mine to keep and preserve. In it was an article about my great aunt, Elizebeth Smith Friedman, titled "Key Woman of the T-Men." I read the article with the semi-interest a 14-year-old boy has about a relative he had never met, then put it aside to pursue other interests. About three decades later, I got a call out of the blue. The voice on the phone said, "You don't know me, but I'm your second cousin." John Friedman, the son of William and Elizebeth, had moved to Sanibel Island, Florida, near where I was working as a TV reporter in Fort Myers.

John invited me for lunch at his home and proceeded to tell me about his mother and father. At first I was most interested in William Friedman, who broke the Japanese cipher "Purple" before World War II. John told me that upon hearing the radio report about the Pearl Harbor attack, his father said, "But they knew, they knew, they knew." With a deep interest in World War II history, and a reporter's sense of a good controversy, I never forgot that.

While always working on other projects, I kept the code couple in the back of my mind, waiting for an opportune time to research them. I was working on a documentary in 2006 and while returning home decided to stop by the National Cryptologic Museum just outside the National Security Agency headquarters in Maryland. I was surprised to discover that William and Elizebeth Friedman rated their own display. He was billed as the "Dean of American Cryptology," but both were enshrined in the "Cryptologic Hall of Honor." When I finished the documentary, I decided to pursue a project about the code couple.

William already had a book about his accomplishments; I also discovered while doing more research that everything that seemingly could be investigated about the controversy over what the government knew about Japanese intentions before Pearl Harbor had already been written by historians, military theorists and conspiracy junkies.

Elizebeth, however, was a totally different matter. As one of the most publicized federal agents in Prohibition and with information about her World War II work just being declassified, Elizebeth also seems highly deserving of a book. Yet one cannot talk about Elizebeth without also including William as well. They truly were a code couple. In the middle of their careers, they labored separately, but at the start, and to a degree at the end, they were major collaborators.

Getting information for the book has sometimes been a challenge—especially specifics on Elizebeth's World War II work. I have made numerous trips to the National Archives in College Park, Maryland, Washington, D.C., and New York City; I searched the British National Archives online and in person at Kew as well as the Canadian archives in Ottawa; I have filed a dozen Freedom of Information requests with the NSA and FBI; I have reviewed the Friedman papers at the George C. Marshall Library twice. Elizebeth wrote memoirs of her Riverbank and Prohibition years, but just a few lines about her secret work between 1940 to 1945. I have had to rely on information about her Coast Guard unit that was declassified in 2008 to extrapolate from that as to what Elizebeth achieved during the war.

I would like to thank several people for their help in the process of researching and writing this book. First, I need to thank the late John Friedman. Without his call many years ago, I might not have been tipped off to the importance of his parents' accomplishments. I called on John a few times before his death in 2010 for more information. After he died, I also tracked down his sister, Barbara Atchison. I interviewed her in person and on the phone several times before her death in 2014. Her son, Chris, also has been a great help, offering information and encouragement—not to mention a place to stay while interviewing his mother. It also has been a pleasure getting to know these members of my extended family.

Others who have been of great assistance include Paul Barron and Jeffrey Kozak at the George C. Marshall Research Library at Virginia Military Institute, where the Friedmans donated a trove of cryptographic literature and their own papers. Commander Michael Bennett of the Coast Guard has also been a giant help. He began his research of the World War II "Guardian Spies" of the Coast Guard well before I decided to dip my toe into the water. He is the one who first gave me a clue about Elizebeth Friedman's important role in breaking German spy codes during the war.

The historian at the Bureau of Alcohol, Tobacco, Firearms, and Explosives, Barbara Osteika, has been of great assistance as well. There are many at the NSA's Center for Cryptologic History who have lent advice and encouragement including Betsy Smoot, Rene Stein and Dr. David Hatch. Thanks also go to Dr. David Sherman of the NSA, who I understand led the charge to declassify and release the Friedman papers in 2015. Colonel Rose Mary Sheldon, Gail Heiser, Chris Christensen, Bob Hanyok, David Kahn, Sandra Jacobs and Deeg Mitchell also lent advice and support. Steve Thomas, one of my distant cousins, also supplied some background on Elizebeth's family ties. Many at the National Archives in both College Park and Washington have been a great help when I visited. Unfortunately, I do not know all of their names, so I hesitate to name only a few.

Writing this book certainly would not have been possible without Elizebeth Smith Friedman's help. Though I never met my great aunt, I feel I have come to know her. Fortunately, she left pages and pages of memoirs that chronicle her romance with William, raising their two children, and the intricate details of many of the high profile cases that she helped solve. She also wrote of the troubled times in Prohibition, the Great Depression and the period leading up to World War II. Her papers have become my most valuable resource.

Thanks to Hofstra University for defraying some of my research costs by issuing me several faculty research grants.

Finally, my wonderful companion, Pam Deitrich, has assisted me in the research and was the first to critique my writing.

I set out to write about Elizebeth Smith Friedman, not a code breaking manual. In doing that I also had to delve into the world of cryptanalysis and cryptography—fields in which I have absolutely no expertise. I have used examples of many of the codes and ciphers that Elizebeth solved, but attempted to simplify them so that almost anyone could understand the cryptanalytic process. If there are mistakes—or oversimplifications for those who desire more cryptographic detail—the fault is solely mine, and I apologize.

Prologue

The illuminati of federal law enforcement gathered in June 2014 to give Elizebeth Smith Friedman a belated recognition. Even though she had never worked for the agency, the Bureau of Alcohol, Tobacco, Firearms and Explosives (ATF) held a ceremony 34 years after she died to name its headquarters auditorium for Mrs. Friedman. Speakers called her an "American hero" and "pioneer" in the field of cryptology. A slide show that outlined her accomplishments described her as the "tip of the spear of law enforcement."

Elizebeth Friedman was an unlikely hero. She wasn't a spy. She wasn't a gun-slinging federal agent. She was a pert lady who became famous during Prohibition for busting rum runners smuggling alcohol from foreign countries. Her background made her an odd candidate for hero worship. She was raised on a farm far from the smugglers' coastal havens, wore her hair in a bun and relaxed with her favorite pastime, gardening.

Yet she "mastered the tradecraft in cryptology," Coast Guard Rear Admiral Christopher J. Tomney remarked at the ATF ceremony. Her early 20th century work became the model for law enforcement and anti-terrorism operations in the 21st century. Today law enforcement and security personnel are building on Elizebeth's ground-breaking work in which intelligence drove the operations to round up and convict gangsters. "Her legacy has become the benchmark for our efforts in directly supporting law enforcement operations to counter illicit activities on the high seas," said Admiral Tomney, the assistant commandant of Coast Guard Intelligence and Criminal Investigations, "while also supporting critical national security efforts around our coasts and globally around the world."[1]

In Prohibition and in later drug smuggling cases, Elizebeth made the key breaks for many federal law enforcement operations. This diminutive woman sat behind a desk, analyzing words that appeared to be mere gobbledygook to most people. In the skilled hands of Elizebeth Smith Friedman, however, the decrypted jumble of phrases proved time and again, first to investigators and later to judges and jurors, what liquors the rum runners had on board, where they were likely to drop the illegal cargo and who the gangsters were behind the felonious enterprises.

It was an age when America's greatest national security threat came from organized crime—largely bootleggers and rum runners abetted by an alcohol-thirsty public. In one of Elizebeth's most famous cases, the Coast Guard sank a rum runner flying the Canadian flag; many irate Canadians called it an act of war. But the Coast Guard's chief intelligence officer concluded that Elizebeth's code breaking launched an investigation that put the Canadian government in an "awkward" position.[2]

Government detectives did a lot of legwork in the case, but breaking those rum runners' secretive communications ultimately saved the United States government more than $300,000[3] in reparations to the Canadians.[4]

That investigation, and many others in which she testified against rum runners as well as narcotics smugglers in both the United States and Canada, made Elizebeth Friedman not just one of the nation's best known female public servants, but one of the most publicized law enforce-

Elizebeth leaves her northwest Washington, D.C., home to testify in a federal smuggling case. Date of photograph uncertain (National Security Agency).

ment agents in the country. That was a result of her specialized niche that seemed to fascinate the public: breaking the secret codes and ciphers used by criminals trying to circumvent the law. In an era when many of her fellow agents were gunned down by gangsters, her specialized niche also put Elizebeth at risk from mobsters seeking to avoid a trip to prison.

Her career was ground-breaking in two respects: she was a professional woman successfully navigating a man's world, and in that world, the just-developing field of cryptanalysis, Elizebeth Smith Friedman was a pioneer. "There was a lot of prejudice against women doing intellectual work, despite Madame Curie and all that," *The Code Breakers* author, David Kahn, observed. Elizebeth Friedman "showed women could actually do this too."[5]

Friedman's resume boasted that she was "the first woman and one of the first persons in the United States to engage in cryptanalysis" as well as the "first person in the United States to apply cryptanalysis to solution of smugglers' communications (1924–1927)."[6]

Organizing law enforcement operations around intelligence gathering—in Elizebeth's case, breaking smugglers' codes and ciphers—was a ground-breaking concept at the time. "She was using the law enforcement tools of the day and combining that with the direction finding and the radio communication monitoring and intercept which was predominantly being done by the Bureau of Prohibition and Coast Guard and the forerunner of the FCC," according to ATF historian Barbara Osteika. "And she was turning all of that intelligence into nowadays what we call actionable intelligence."[7]

That is the major reason that ATF officials see her as the "tip of the spear" and why they named the agency's auditorium in Washington, D.C., for her. The ATF grew out of the Bureau of Prohibition, where Elizebeth did some of her early work, so the officials in the modern agency claim her as one of their own.

"She had an impact on intelligence-driven law enforcement," ATF Director B. Todd Jones said in remarks at the auditorium-naming ceremony. "She is the Mother of the Fusion Center."[8] The Department of Homeland Security (DHS) reports Fusion Centers developed after the 9/11 terrorist attacks. The DHS website describes Fusion Centers as focal points for federal, state and local law enforcement and public safety agencies to "conduct analysis and facilitate information sharing, assisting law enforcement and homeland security partners in preventing, protecting against, and responding to crime and terrorism."[9] Though they were not known as Fusion Centers in Elizebeth Friedman's day, Jones said that they were "pioneered by this wonderful woman."[10]

Elizebeth Smith Friedman blazed her career path with help from

Elizebeth's grandchildren, Chris Atchison, Eric Sky and Vanessa Friedman, unveil her portrait at the ceremony naming the ATF auditorium in her honor (Photograph by the author).

another cryptographer who eventually gained even more fame than she did, her husband, William Friedman.[11] They both got their start at Riverbank Laboratories. It was a "think tank" of the era. The estate's eccentric founder tasked the as-yet-unmarried couple with helping to prove through analyzing supposed codes in the literature that Francis Bacon was the true author of William Shakespeare's works. That inquiry evolved into code breaking by the couple for the U.S. Army in World War I. Then the code couple's paths diverged: William stayed with a career in the U.S. Army— where he led the team that broke the Japanese diplomatic cipher "Purple" just before World War II—and eventually helped merge America's cryptographic functions in the National Security Agency (NSA).[12] After World War I Elizebeth spent a few years compiling codes for the Army and Navy[13] before discovering that the nation's 18th Amendment prohibiting the manufacture, transport and sale of booze required a person with her skills to help enforce the unpopular social experiment.[14]

Then an even bigger national security threat in World War II put demands on Elizebeth to create a code system for the agency that would become the Office of Strategic Services (OSS),[15] the forerunner to the Central Intelligence Agency, train FBI cryptanalysts,[16] and decipher messages that helped break up German[17] and Japanese spy rings.[18]

Courses for the career which she eventually pursued did not even exist in college. "The title by which I am known now was not at that time in the language," Friedman wrote in her memoirs. "The terms 'cryptanalyst' and 'cryptanalysis' were yet to be coined."[19]

Elizebeth had a natural interest in secrets from her college studies. "I first got interested in codes and ciphers when I was a student in Wooster College, Ohio, majoring in English Literature," she told an NBC radio interviewer in 1934. "I became intrigued with that controversy over whether or not Sir Francis Bacon wrote Shakespeare's plays and whether he concealed his authorship in cipher, and decided I'd try my luck at the mystery. So I began the study of cipher analysis."[20]

As a result, at a young age, and without a text to help, Elizebeth Smith delved into the principles of cryptography. Basic cipher analysis requires one to know the difference between a code and cipher. In his seminal work *The Code Breakers*, David Kahn takes care to explain the intricacies of cryptographic vocabulary to readers.

Kahn notes that there are two basic transformations in cryptography: transposition and substitution. A transposition jumbles the letters of the plaintext. For example, he writes, the word "secret" might be *transposed* as "etcrse." In substitution, words, numbers or symbols *replace* the plaintext meaning. In this example, Kahn writes, the word "secret" could be substituted with a series of numbers such as "19 5 3 18 5 20."[21]

In addition, substitution systems are usually more complicated than transpositions. This is where a cipher comes into play. A cipher alphabet can be used to create secret messages. For example, ABC could be represented by QDF, or ABC might also be represented by TMA. What is needed is a *key* to the system. The key, which explains what terms were used to encipher a message, allows the receiver to easily read the message. Those without the key will need to resort to cryptanalysis to decipher— or break into—and understand the message. Codes, on the other hand, usually employ groups of numbers or letters to substitute for whole words or ideas. For example, the numbers 1563 could mean the word "employ," or 8808 could mean "enable," in a code group.[22]

Mathematics enters into cryptanalysis as well. A well-documented fact is that the letter "e" is the most frequently used in the English language; the letter "t" is the second most-used. Other letters also have documented frequency counts. When they don't have the key to read a cipher, cryptanalysts will count an encoded message to see which letter, number or symbol appears most often—a frequency count.

"I look carefully through that jumbled mass of letters to find two letters that are used together most," Elizebeth told an interviewer who inquired about the subject. "Suppose they are RC. That pretty well establishes for me that in this particular secret cipher the letters RC are really TH. Then I look for the letter used after the letters RC most. Perhaps that gives me a combination of RCX, which tells me that RC and X in this code represent the letters THE. With that established, I go through the rest of the jumble of letters, applying the same principle, and that's how the secret message is deciphered."[23]

Often, however, it takes not just one, but multiple messages for a cryptanalyst to discern the frequency count of the letters in a particular cipher and then break into the secret messages.[24]

It is, admittedly, an arcane, complicated and esoteric subject. Its difficulties even perplexed an expert like Elizebeth: "Cryptanalysis has its dull moments, and even despairing ones," she professed in her memoirs. "On the other hand, when I have struggled for long, weary hours (which sometimes stretch into weeks) on a problem that has appeared utterly hopeless and then suddenly burst through to light and a successful solution, then the work has its thrills."[25]

Even though codes and ciphers had been around for centuries, the Friedmans came along just as this *science* of cryptography and cryptanalysis were in their nascency. Elizebeth was, as was her husband, self-trained in the field. "She had, like her husband, precious little mathematical grounding," a friend of Elizebeth's said at her 1980 memorial service. "Her gift was God-given, and that is the most wondrous thing about it; God-given however each of us differently conceives of God."[26]

Because of that God-given talent at ferreting out hidden messages and the troubled times, Elizebeth became a star witness in some high profile Prohibition cases and a minor celebrity. "I never thought of my job as terribly unusual until the newspapers stumbled upon what I do for the Government," she said on NBC.[27] Elizebeth eventually tired of the publicity and came to despise many of the journalists who wrote about her.[28]

Yet when Prohibition ended, her career took a new direction as the world faced another war. Now, instead of being in the public eye, Elizebeth

Friedman's work had to go underground—deep underground. The code breaking had always been secretive, but often became public when cases went to trial. Now she had to double down on secrecy with friends and family. Her daughter, Barbara Atchison, was in college during World War II, but lived at home during the summers. "I knew that she was in codes and ciphers because of what she had done in the 30s. But she never really talked about it [the war work]," said Atchison. "I didn't know about it until after."[29]

The government has volumes of information on Elizebeth Friedman's work in the Prohibition years, but scarcely mentions what she did in the Second World War. Her NSA biography online extols her code breaking in World War I and the work busting rum runners, but it remains strangely silent about her World War II work. There is a paragraph explaining how she helped bring a Japanese spy to justice. But nowhere does the government write about Elizebeth's war contributions with a secret Coast Guard unit that helped track and break up German spy rings in the Western Hemisphere.[30] An official NSA memorial article following her death in 1980 just brushes past Elizebeth's war duties: "Mrs. Friedman served the U.S. as a cryptologist in both World Wars, and in the period between she won distinction for work on international drug and liquor smuggling cases." Even as the government started declassifying World War II cryptography secrets in the 21st century, no additional information was added about what she did during the war when the memorial article was republished in 2006.[31]

Because of the drain upon manpower in the military services in World War II, there was a tremendous need for qualified personnel in both the Army and Navy. As "Rosie the Riveter" did on the industrial front, women helped fill the void behind the scenes in secret code breaking jobs. "Thousands of women helped to win World War II through their cryptologic efforts," declared a 1998 NSA article about women's contributions to code breaking during the war. Many of those positions—though classified secret—were clerical and technical in nature. Yet the article fails to mention one word about Elizebeth Friedman, whose war work included not only breaking enemy codes, but managing a major cryptanalytic unit.[32]

Even 30-plus years after her death and seven decades after completing her war duties, the secrets of Elizebeth's work have been difficult to dig out from government records. Many of the official cryptography documents from World War II have recently been—or are in the process of being—declassified. Those who participated in cryptography and cryptanalysis for the government in World War II were required by presidential order to sign a secrecy pledge that had no end date.[33]

"That's when we hit the brick wall," remarked Colonel Rose Mary Sheldon, an expert on intelligence at Virginia Military Institute (VMI). "We know she was involved in OSS, we know that one of their biggest cases was broken because of her, but we can't seem to declassify or find any evidence of what she did."[34]

What is known is that as the war loomed, the Coast Guard cryptanalysis unit that Elizebeth created in 1931 was absorbed by the U.S. Navy's communications and intelligence operation, OP-20-G.[35] With the nation in crisis, Elizebeth swallowed whatever trepidations she had and accepted the wholesale movement of Coast Guard Unit 387 from the Treasury Department to the Navy.[36] A major accomplishment of Unit 387 during the war was breaking Enigma cipher machine codes used by the German intelligence agency, the Abwehr. Because it dealt with counterespionage and double agents, an NSA historian concluded that the unit was "probably even more secret than other Comint [communications intelligence] operations."[37] Indeed, an NSA report that describes how the Coast Guard solved German agent messages in South America has 35 of its 38 pages redacted, even after it was declassified in 2009.[38]

After the war, with Congressional investigations of the Pearl Harbor attack and whether the United States had foreknowledge of Japanese intentions, William Friedman's fame began to exceed that of his wife. A book, *The Man Who Broke Purple*, was written about his life and cryptography accomplishments, which were considerable for the man who came to be called the "Dean of American Cryptology." Where William's career largely focused on military applications that continued to be highly valued in the Cold War, Elizebeth was more like a utility player for government agencies, moving from place to place, wherever her services were needed. That half of the code couple was downsized from her government job as Americans weaned themselves from a war economy and the government began doing away with code breaking units in multiple agencies, concentrating its cryptography efforts into a single entity, the NSA.[39]

Elizebeth spent a few years after the war compiling codes and setting up a secure communications system for the newly created International Monetary Fund.[40] But in retirement she returned with her husband to the mystery that brought the code couple together in the first place, examining the suspected Baconian codes in Shakespeare's plays. Their professional paths merged once again to write the definitive book on the topic, *The Shakespearean Ciphers Examined*.

"Possessing uncanny skills for making and breaking codes, the Fried-mans dedicated their lives to public service and America," remarked VMI historian Colonel Sheldon at an event in 2015 noting the declassification and release by the NSA of more than 7,000 files compiled by William Friedman.[41] Because of their ground-breaking work, both Friedmans are enshrined in the inaugural class of the NSA's "Cryptologic Hall of Honor,"[42] and also share a joint exhibit space in the National Cryptologic Museum, just outside of the secure NSA compound in Maryland.[43]

Elizebeth devoted the last 11 years of her life to compiling the couple's papers, with an eye toward preserving the legacy of the American cryptology dean. As she promoted her husband's reputation, she also began writing her memoirs in an effort to cement her own legacy as a pioneering cryptanalyst. Cases in which she became a star witness for prosecutors, already had given her a stellar reputation in the cryptologic community. Since her death, based on what she had accomplished before 1941, cryptographers in and out of government noted that Elizebeth Smith Friedman "was truly a legend in her own time."[44] Now with new 21st century threats to deal with, modern law enforcement personnel are extolling Elizebeth Friedman's work as a model for fighting organized crime *and* terrorism.

New information seeping out from what had once been top secret World War II files only enhances Elizebeth's "tip of the spear" reputation.

William and Elizebeth Friedman, photographs top left, were inducted in the inaugural NSA Cryptologic Hall of Honor in 1999 (National Security Agency).

≡1≡

The Imperious Patron

When Elizebeth Smith graduated from Hillsdale College in 1915, little did she know that a year later a poorly dressed, multi-millionaire twice her size would pin her against a window and thunder at her: "WHAT DO *YOU* KNOW?"

After college Elizebeth spent a year working as a principal at a high school in Wabash, Indiana,[1] but was dissatisfied with the teaching life. She wanted to find a job that would better utilize the skills she had learned in college. "I thought of myself as sitting down at a desk or two or three desks in front of me and working away at research or something like that," Elizebeth told an interviewer a number of years later.[2]

She went to the Newberry Reference Library on Chicago's north side looking for a job. The library had a Shakespeare folio, which was a passion for Miss Smith. "My first sight of an original 1623 Shakespeare folio gave me something of the feeling, I suppose, that an archaeologist has when he suddenly realizes that he has discovered a tomb of a great pharaoh," Elizebeth later wrote.[3]

A Newberry librarian referred her to a position on the 600-acre estate of a very wealthy man about 25 miles away in Geneva, Illinois. "It was something so startling that I could not grasp it all at once," Elizebeth wrote in her memoirs. The work would be to investigate the biliteral cipher writings of Sir Francis Bacon that were said to prove that Bacon was the actual author of William Shakespeare's plays.[4]

The librarian called about the position, "and before you could have hit a button," Elizebeth recalled, "here was this limousine pulling up—a big limousine with a driver. And in came this storm, this huge man, and his bellowing voice, you know, could be heard all over the library floor."[5]

All of a sudden this large, bearded man Elizebeth described as having a "dashing imperious manner,"[6] stepped over to her, "towering down like ...

like a windmill." He invited her to the estate immediately, saying: "Will you go out to Riverbank and spend the night with me?"[7]

"I was a bit taken back, because in my youth and innocence, and small-town origin and habits, this kind of thing seemed a bit startling to me. But he was the kind of man who did not take no for an answer."[8]

The owner of Riverbank Laboratories was Colonel George Fabyan, a wealthy industrialist who had retired from the cotton trading business to focus his energies on studying a variety of subjects on his property.[9] He wasn't a real colonel; the title was honorific, conferred by an Illinois governor for Fabyan's participation in the 1905 peace commission that ended the Russo-Japanese War.[10]

Fabyan whisked Elizabeth to his waiting car and chauffer. "'Come on!' he said. And he just practically lifted me by one arm, you know, under one elbow and he stiffened my body so that he just carried me like that, swept me out of there." While driving to the Chicago and North Western railway station,[11] Fabyan "talked about everything under the sun except the possibly forthcoming position, until we got to the train and sat down. Then after a very few moments he turned to me, sitting next to the window, and shouted 'WHAT DO _YOU_ KNOW?'"[12]

Elizebeth remembers that she was dressed in a grey faille dress with a white Peter Pan collar, a simple style of clothing with an even simpler, un-permanented hairdo and unassuming hat. "I was realizing by this time that I probably appeared a demure little nobody to him," she wrote. "Although I had had a reputation for volubility in college, I certainly was anything but that in the presence of the awesome person, about who [sic] I had up to that moment, not formed any very favorable opinion."

So before responding to Fabyan's question about what she knew, Miss Smith leaned back against the train window—as far away as she could get from him—then said in a low, but very firm tone: "That remains, sir, for _you_ to find out."[13]

Dealing with imperious men was nothing new to 22-year-old Elizebeth Smith. Her father, a Civil War veteran, dairyman, banker, county commissioner and Republican stalwart in Huntington County, Indiana, was cut from the same cloth as George Fabyan. Though coming from an anti-war Quaker heritage, Elizebeth's father, John Marion Smith, enlisted in Company D of the Indiana 130th Infantry Regiment in 1863, just two weeks shy of his 16th birthday. During the war Smith's unit saw action in Tennessee, Georgia and South Carolina before he mustered out of the service as an 18-year-old veteran in Charlotte, North Carolina, in December 1865.[14]

John Marion Smith was irascible and didn't like women says Elizabeth's daughter, Barbara Atchison.[15] She attributes his curmudgeon-like character to chronic stomach problems that he developed as a prisoner during the war,[16] though his service record does not confirm his status as a prisoner. His irascibility seemed to overshadow his relations with his youngest daughter. According to Barbara, Sopha Strock Smith, Elizabeth's mother, had to protect the frail girl with a weak stomach[17] from an abusive father. But Sopha, too, had her own idiosyncrasy about the youngest of the couple's ten children.[18] When born on August 26, 1892, she named Elizabeth with an e between the z and b instead of an a because Sopha did not want her daughter to be called "Eliza."[19]

Growing up on that northeast Indiana farm had limitations for the aspiring adolescent. Elizabeth set her sights on attending one of two Quaker colleges, either Earlham in southeast Indiana or Swarthmore outside of Philadelphia. Elizabeth was proud that one of her ancestors had come from England in 1682 with William Penn and settled north of Philadelphia near Wrightstown. That ancestor, William Smith, had converted to the Quaker religion before coming to America from Yorkshire.[20] "I had felt that my many generations of Quaker ancestry on my father's side should have brought the compulsion on the part of my father, although he was no longer a practicing Quaker, to see that I got to a Quaker college," Elizabeth notes in her memoirs. "But he was uninterested in my going to college anywhere."[21]

After applying, and being rejected, for a scholarship to Wellesley College near Boston, Elizabeth settled for a school closer to home, The College of Wooster in Ohio. But since her father would not fund it, Elizabeth had to borrow the money from him at six percent interest to pay for her college education. At least she was admitted with advanced credit for her five years of high school studies in Latin and another four years of German.[22]

Defying her obstinate father must have gratified the young Elizabeth. An entry in her diary during college confides an independent streak: "I am never quite so gleeful as when I am doing something labeled as an 'ought not.'"[23] Yet paying for her independence with a $600 college loan—instead of her father paying for her education outright—ate at Elizabeth throughout her life. It took years to pay off the debt. When Elizabeth discussed the loan with her daughter, she always expressed her resentment in words and gestures: "I remember Mother shaking her finger, 'Six percent interest!'" Barbara recalls. "She would kind of jab her finger, not at me, but at him [John Marion Smith]."[24]

Two years after starting at Wooster, Elizabeth transferred to Hillsdale

College in Michigan. There she was literary editor of the *Collegian* and won second place in an oratory contest. She also pledged the Pi Beta Phi sorority in her junior year.[25] She graduated with a degree in English literature from Hillsdale.[26]

Then, in June 1916, she found herself on a train, transferring to the Riverbank estate by limousine, ready to tackle one of Colonel Fabyan's pet projects. He hoped to become "known to posterity," said Elizebeth, as the man who proved that Francis Bacon was indeed the author behind Shakespeare.[27]

That project was just one of dozens that Fabyan underwrote at Riverbank, a property cut into two pieces by the Fox River. One side of the estate contained Fabyan's home, swimming pool, and stables, the other side the working laboratories. Fabyan himself never was seen on horseback, but always seemed to be wearing riding clothes.[28]

The eccentric millionaire used his wealth to hire people to investigate a number of topics. "Some rich men go in for art collections, gay times on the Riviera, or extravagant living," said Fabyan, who came from a wealthy Boston family. "But they all get satiated. That's why I stick to scientific experiments, spending money to discover valuable things that universities can't afford. You never get sick of too much knowledge."[29]

"It was very much like what we would call in the Renaissance a villa," is how Renaissance studies professor Bill Sherman described Riverbank. "It's an agricultural and recreational complex with a serious almost college structure attached to it with departments and deans and what the letterhead called a standing faculty."[30]

The estate reflected Fabyan's quirky character. It had a Dutch windmill that he bought in Holland and reconstructed on the property.[31] Another landmark was a lighthouse that flashed a Morse Code message, "2" then "3," followed by the letters "s-k-i-d-o-o," a popular phrase of the time.[32] His employees studied the acoustic property of sound waves and planted oats at night to see if different moon phases affected their growth. The grounds were decorated with a Japanese garden and the main house was inhabited by a monkey named Pansy[33] that roamed the residence freely.[34] When some of the exotic animals, such as bears and peacocks, from Riverbank's menagerie died, the Fabyans stuffed them and kept them on display in their home called Engledew.[35]

Colonel and Mrs. Fabyan also had a penchant for suspending all of their furniture by chains from the ceiling.[36] One of those pieces of furniture was a wicker arm chair swinging from a tree limb. Those working for Fabyan dubbed it the "hell chair."[37]

"If anything displeased him, he would stand the offending person up before the hell chair and literally give him hell," Elizebeth recalled. "It was never spoken of in any other way."[38]

Elizebeth's introduction to Fabyan's estate came after a mile and a half drive from the Geneva railroad station down the Lincoln Highway. Fabyan's first stop for his potential employee was the building where Elizabeth Wells Gallup worked, The Lodge.

Gallup had convinced Fabyan of the validity of the Shakespeare project. She based her theory, circulating among the literary world at the time, that buried within the Bard of Avon's writings were

Colonel George Fabyan, the Friedmans' "imperious patron," in the infamous "hell chair" at Riverbank (courtesy George C. Marshall Foundation, Lexington, Virginia).

secrets, that once unlocked, would lead everyone to the conclusion that Shakespeare was the *nom de plume* of Francis Bacon. The genesis for that was the fact that in 1623 Bacon had invented what came to be known as a biliteral cipher. In this scenario the letters "a" and "b" would be used in a combination to represent the entire alphabet. In other words, in the Bacon biliteral cipher, "aaaaa" stood for the letter "A," "aaaab" would represent the letter "B" and "aaaba" meant "C" and on down the line.[39]

With her decryption method, in 1899 Gallup had published an article reporting hidden messages by Bacon in "Shakespeare's First Folio." One of the deciphered messages read: "Queen Elizabeth is my true mother, and I am the lawful heir to the throne. Find the Cypher storie my books contain; it tells great secrets, every one of which, if imparted openly, would forfeit my life. F. Bacon."[40]

A background in English literature would be a natural fit for someone working on the Shakespeare investigation. Thus Elizebeth spent nearly three hours finding out more from Mrs. Gallup in their introductory meeting. Elizebeth described Mrs. Gallup as "elderly," but with an "aristocratic appearance." Miss Smith deduced from the conversation that Gallup would associate professionally only with "those who agreed with her premise" and that she had little personal contact with those who did not believe in Bacon's authorship.[41] Gallup was searching for assistants, according to Elizebeth, who would repeat the hunt for the Baconian codes and "prove that her decipherments were correct."[42]

Before returning to Chicago the next morning, Elizebeth was requested to dress for and stay for dinner that evening at Riverbank. The closet in her guest house bedroom, she discovered, had been stocked with a semi-formal dress and sleeping apparel.[43]

That evening she met a young man working on the estate who made an immediate impression as he strolled up the steps to The Lodge: "I'll never forget his appearance," Elizebeth wrote about William Friedman. "He was kind of a Beau Brummel; he was so beautifully dressed and so there was no country informality about his attire at all. He was dressed as he would have dressed going to a very well-to-do home in a city house."[44]

The year before, Fabyan had hired Friedman, who had been a graduate student assistant in genetics at Cornell University, to help improve Riverbank's crops. When Friedman asked Fabyan what he raised on the estate, the colonel replied, "I raise

Elizabeth Wells Gallup worked at Riverbank trying to find codes in William Shakespeare's works to prove someone else wrote the Bard's plays (courtesy George C. Marshall Foundation, Lexington, Virginia).

hell."[45] Friedman, whose Russian parents brought him to the United States as an infant,[46] located his genetics lab in the Dutch windmill.[47]

Elizabeth doesn't say whether it was the charming young Mr. Friedman, or the research challenge that Colonel Fabyan offered, that ultimately led her to accept the position at Riverbank. She does admit being skeptical about the Fabyan/Gallup investigation: "It's always puzzled me why can't they let Shakespeare write Shakespeare—what's wrong with that?" Nevertheless, she was soon analyzing Shakespeare's text looking for indisputable proof that would lead them to Bacon's authorship. She mastered Gallup's methods within a few months of arriving that summer.

When Fabyan invited scholars from around the country to come and view the work, Elizabeth now was expected to introduce them to Gallup's findings and help them understand how the Shakespeare texts were deciphered to make a Baconian conclusion. Some visitors not only challenged that conclusion, but were hostile to the idea.[48]

Friedman also was busy with more than crop research. "Fabyan found William Friedman so useful because he was a wonderful photographer," Elizabeth recalled, "and could [do] anything with a camera that he was requested to do and so Fabyan consequently just made him enter into everything that went on there."[49]

Fabyan decided it would help Mrs. Gallup analyze Elizabethan texts if Friedman would photograph and enlarge them. Looking at the blown-up typefaces should surely help prove the Baconian Theory, the reasoning went.[50] The English literature major also convinced William "that he could have more fun solving the Baconian mystery than charting the family trees of fruit flies," as a magazine article two decades later put it.[51] When Elizabeth introduced the geneticist to the cryptanalytic methods utilized in Gallup's pursuit, William seemed to take to it extremely well. Soon he was spending more time on this new code work than he was in the fields and his genetics lab. As a result, Elizabeth writes, the young couple's intense work on the Shakespeare inquiry "threw him and me together a very great deal in and out of social hours."[52]

In their first day working together, William passed a scribbled note to the young Miss Smith. It said, "My dearest—I sit here studying your features. You are perfectly beautiful!!"[53]

With only a few other young people on the Riverbank campus, William and Elizabeth soon became an item. William played tennis, a sport which Elizabeth admits didn't suit her skills. Yet, "We both got bicycles and would ride around the countryside."[54]

The Hoosier farmer's daughter and the Russian-born Jewish immigrant found a mutual attraction working and playing side-by-side. "She was quite beautiful," the Friedmans' first child, Barbara, says of her mother. "She had a gorgeous figure and she had brown, wonderful naturally curly hair."[55]

The couple, while still single, got accustomed to living on a multi-millionaire's estate. "We always had pitchers of ice water and fresh fruit with fruit knives by our bedside when we went to bed. And we really lived the life of what you might call the minor idle rich," Elizebeth later gushed about the experience. "But he [Fabyan] paid almost nothing."[56]

Just as they were becoming well-acquainted, however, tragedy struck Elizebeth's family back in Indiana. She returned to Huntington in the winter of 1917 to be at her mother's bedside during a severe illness. Correspondence between the couple indicates a growing bond and reliance on each other, as well as a penchant for terms of endearment. "Dear Billy Boy, I'm in some need of comfort and 'rocking,' so I'm bothering you as usual," reads Elizebeth's first letter to William from her parents' home. It closed, "I'm missing my Comforter. Always, Elsbeth."[57]

Follow-up letters from Elizebeth kept William abreast of her mother's condition, but also indicated she continued to have a battle of wills with her father.[58] Despite her despair, Elizebeth's letters over the next week also encouraged William to continue their work in her absence: "Billy Boy, like me just a little bit always. I want you for the dear good friend you are, if nothing more. Work hard with the letters. I want, oh, so much, for us both to 'achieve.' If I could feel that I had helped a little, I should not feel so 'what's the use?'"[59]

Elizebeth was also feeling the pressure to continue producing for Riverbank while she was helping her family. "I shall write to Col. Fabyan this afternoon, explaining as much as possible the situation," she wrote. "If I can do my work here—part of it—I shall. If Mother is to live only a few weeks or a few months longer, I think my place is here. Of course, I cannot afford not to be making at least a little money."[60]

Sopha Smith, the mother who insisted that her daughter not be called Eliza and protected her from a strong-willed father, passed away on Valentine's Day.

Elizebeth's letters refer to William as a "dear good friend." Yet the crisis in her family seemed to draw the couple much closer than that. Within a few months of Elizebeth's return to Riverbank, they were married. "This young man was the antithesis of Colonel Fabyan," Elizebeth wrote years later. "He was gentle, considerate, polite, very handsome always immaculately dressed, whether it was tennis dress, laboratory costume or social affairs, dinner dress, whatever."

To mark the occasion of their marriage, Elizebeth gave her new husband a photo of them together inscribed on the back in her handwriting: "My prayer—that Divine Fire may always be a living flame—to you!" After their wedding on May 21, 1917, the couple took up residence in the upper floor of the estate's landmark, the Dutch windmill.[61]

There was surprise about the mixed-religion marriage from both sides of the family. Elizebeth's father described the event as "very sudden." Her new Jewish mother-in-law collapsed on hearing the news that her son was marrying what she called a "shiksa."[62] Yet the Friedmans' romance carried on until William passed away in 1969. "Every wedding anniversary he sent her a dozen long-stemmed roses,"

William and Elizebeth Smith Friedman's 1917 wedding photo at Riverbank Laboratories, where the "code couple" met (courtesy George C. Marshall Foundation, Lexington, Virginia).

says their daughter. He would also bring his wife chocolate and other unexpected gifts. "He was always very romantic and he was always proud of her."[63]

But after more than a year of working at Riverbank, the honeymoon with Colonel Fabyan was wearing thin for the Friedmans. Elizebeth reminisced,

He gave orders on every phase of life, even dictating what sort of clothes I should wear and where I should buy them, angering me somewhat by this because what resulted was that I spent more for my clothes than I could afford. But if I ever raised my voice, and complained about this, he always reminded me to hush.

There were a great many features of luxury with the life there but there was also a good deal of the feeling that we couldn't go in any direction we wanted to. Whatever we did we were expected to come to a conclusion, somewhere along the line, that would be beneficial to whatever George Fabyan wanted. That was the kind of thing he wanted out of his workers there.[64]

Fabyan's nature soon brought him into conflict with William and Elizebeth, who did not have the unquestioning attitude about the Shakespeare project that their employer had. Their backgrounds in genetics and literature gave them an unbiased perspective; now, with a good grounding in ciphers, they soon came to have major doubts about the validity of Gallup's theory which, to buy into, required more personal judgment than science. "I can state categorically that neither I nor any other one of the industrious research workers at Riverbank ever succeeded in extracting a single long sentence of a hidden message," David Kahn quoted Elizebeth as saying in his opus, *The Code Breakers*, "nor did one of us so much as reproduce, independently, a single complete sentence which Mrs. Gallup had already deciphered and published."[65]

Questioning Gallup's methods never got very far, Elizebeth noted in her memoirs: "When the two of us or either of us alone attempted to raise any question with Col. Fabyan, we were shouted down: we were not there to question but to follow his lead and to convince the academic world of the authenticity of the work."[66]

With the European continent aflame in the Great War since 1914, even more conflict was in the Friedmans' future at Riverbank. In April 1917, just a month before William and Elizebeth's wedding, the United States had entered the war. Seeing a national security crisis unfolding before him, the eccentric millionaire with the honorary officer's title forecast his country's urgent need for experienced cryptographers. George Fabyan, in a patriotic bid to help the nation's war effort, would demand that his Shakespearean code couple turn their attention to military ciphers to fill the void.[67]

=2=

The World War I
Transformation

Colonel George Fabyan's actions before, during and after World War I would steer the code couple to the path their celebrated careers would take for the rest of their lives. But it would also leave the Friedmans disenchanted with and embittered about their patron.

William and Elizebeth Friedman entered the war as novice code breakers. At war's end they were becoming two of cryptography's brightest stars, masters of this new and esoteric field that the United States, now an acknowledged world power with secrets to keep as well as uncover, was eager to embrace. Elizebeth never was paid by the government for her service during the war, yet when the armistice was signed, was recognized for helping the United States military negotiate this new maze of secretive communications: "By the end of the war she probably knew as much about military code making and breaking as a division signal corps headquarters," a magazine article said of her.[1]

Less than two decades into the 20th century, the world was still learning how to use radio in many ways. "The invention of radio had a profound affect on World War I military operations and in all conflicts since 1901," a National Security Agency study reports.[2] Military services found it faster and more convenient to send their messages over the air waves instead of by written correspondence. Since anyone with a receiving set could pick up a radio signal, that required those messages to be coded if the military wanted to maintain any kind of secrecy. Thus countries that wanted to send secret messages trained their radio operators in preparing codes and ciphers; those who wanted to discover their enemies' secrets also began training their personnel how to break them.

In this new era of decrypting secret communications called signals intelligence or SIGINT,[3] the imperious Colonel George Fabyan was the key to William and Elizebeth's transformation from literary to military code breaking. Elizebeth remembers Fabyan being good at foretelling things: "He seemed to know months and months before we were into the war that we were going to get into the war. He kept coming down to Washington to talk with the higher-ups here, there and everywhere. He persuaded them that they didn't have a cipher bureau, they didn't have anybody who knew anything about ciphers and that was true."[4]

"U.S. government cryptology 100 years ago was quite a small thing," remarked Betsy Rohaly Smoot of the Center for Cryptologic History. "There was no U.S. intelligence community, no equivalent of NSA, no coordinated system to collect communications and break coded and ciphered messages."[5]

With such weaknesses in mind, Fabyan led Riverbank Laboratories to become a military testing ground. The War Department experimented with everything from hand grenades to trench warfare techniques on the estate.[6] Fabyan also figured that his Shakespeare code breaking unit was way ahead of what the Army's staff could accomplish. For the first year of the war, until the Army created its own Cipher Bureau, Riverbank was the only organization in the country "capable of working out secret messages." Thus Fabyan offered the services of his code couple to the government for free.[7] The government accepted the offer, but did not buy the name that Fabyan wanted to call it—the Deciphering Bureau.[8]

Yet the Friedmans felt unprepared for the cryptanalytic challenge. "The great drawback was that there was no way of acquiring any knowledge of the subject, for military ciphers were so little known in this country, that the people best informed about them had the merest smattering of knowledge," Elizebeth recollected.[9] "Literary ciphers may give you the swing of the thing, but they are in no sense scientific. There were no precedents for us to follow. We simply had to roll up our sleeves and chart a new course."[10]

When the U.S. declared war on Germany, Fabyan established a school to train cryptanalysts at Riverbank with the Friedmans as its instructors. He got the Army to send him two brief training pamphlets, *Manual for the Solution of Military Ciphers,* and *An Advanced Problem in Cryptography and its Solution.*[11] Fabyan tried to convince people in Washington "that he could in no time flat, have an office full of people who could translate other languages and solve the ciphers," Elizebeth recalled in an interview. "We learned as we did it.... We had to learn it by working the things out."[12]

"It was the succinctness of Parker Hitt's manual [*Manual for the Solution of Military Ciphers*] that caused us much work and perspiration in our self-training at Riverbank," William Friedman declared in one of his lectures on cryptography published by the NSA, "but we later came to know and admire its author."[13]

Two Army Signal Corps officers, the training manuals' authors, Captains Hitt and J.O. Mauborgne, came to inspect Fabyan's Illinois training center to see if it would help the war effort.[14] They gave the go-ahead. Captain Mauborgne's memo noted that Colonel Fabyan was a "gentleman of means" with a "force of eight or ten cipher experts." The memo noted the Riverbank facility had vaults to protect secure messages and the grounds were "patrolled against intruders." Thus, Mauborgne recommended that the Justice and War Departments "utilize Col. Fabyan's laboratory to the fullest extent, for the solution of difficult ciphers."[15]

Fabyan put William in charge of the Riverbank military operation; Elizebeth was second-in-command. "Fabyan got him translators and we translated and deciphered volumes, literally volumes of messages that passed between Germany and Mexico, for example," she said about the newly-formed venture.[16]

Soon the Riverbank cryptography unit was handling the codes and ciphers forwarded to it from the War, Navy, State and Justice Departments. The unit at one point had 30 people working on the codes.[17] The section set up to train Army officers was in a nearby hotel where Fabyan paid the bill to house and feed some 80 trainees.[18] One day at the hotel the Friedmans posed a group of the Army trainees for a group photo. They were facing different directions to create a biliteral cipher in a statement attributed to Francis Bacon.[19]

In a classified lecture more than 40 years after the photo, William Friedman told a military audience that he, Colonel Fabyan and Elizebeth along with the trainees were posed to form a specific message: "If this chap hadn't goofed you'd never suspect that there was a cipher message. But the cipher is involved in whether the officers are facing straight forward or with their heads turned to either the left or the right. So that the message spells out 'Knowledge is power.'"[20]

The volumes of messages coming to Riverbank from various agencies included some from Hindu groups in the United States. Under influence from German agents, they were conspiring to undermine British control of India, which violated U.S. neutrality laws. Letters delivered to the Friedmans by either Scotland Yard or U.S. censorship officials had a cipher consisting of groups of three numbers such as 26–2–39 or 4–1–7.[21] Even though they were brand new to this kind of code breaking, Elizebeth noted that several times the correspondents had repeated short sequences of numbers.[22] She reported that she and William determined the key for the cipher "was a type of book the Hindus and Germans could carry about on the person, and not arouse suspicion."[23]

It was most likely a book on German political science. The first number in the cipher represented the page, the second number the line and the third was the number of the letter in that line. The Friedmans could "state with authority" that on page 7, line 3 would be the word "constitution." It was "an extremely laborious type of encipherment," wrote Elizebeth, "and the only reason that anyone would use such a method would be the for the purpose of eluding censorship."[24]

The Friedmans got Fabyan to cable stores all over the world seeking a book that the Hindus had used for the key. Still, as the conspirators' trial neared, the couple could not determine which book the conspirators had used, something that would be needed to convince a jury. The government called William to testify at the conspirators' federal trial in Chicago. Elizebeth reports that just before testifying, her husband rummaged about a bookshop on Clark Street "and miracle of miracles" came across the book they were looking for to unlock the conspirators' codes. William's testimony helped convict about 50 German and Hindu conspirators.[25]

Several weeks later, when William was called to testify in another conspiracy trial in San Francisco, the Friedmans were still at a loss to find a different book that could be used as a cipher key. A friend in Berkley suggested that he go to a nearby book cooperative, where he once again found the key manuscript, a dictionary dating to 1880.[26] "He just had a touch somehow, he had some luck," Elizebeth said of her husband.[27]

"It was a matter of considerable regret to me that I could not accompany Bill to San Francisco or that I had not been summoned as a co-witness with him," Elizebeth wrote, "since we had completed this task completely alone, but someone had to stay behind and sort of oil the machinary [sic] at Riverbank."[28] By staying at home, Elizebeth missed the trial's dramatic climax. One of the Hindus who had become a witness for the prosecution was gunned down while on the witness stand by another Hindu who was in the public gallery. Again, all the defendants were convicted.[29]

To see just how much this Fabyan-financed group was capable of, Army officials sent Riverbank's neophyte military code breakers a problem to solve on a British-made cipher device. It was called a Pletts Cryptograph. No one in the British, French or U.S. military had been able to break the ciphers that came out of the device.[30] The British and Americans planned to use some of the 11,000 devices manufactured to communicate securely between the new allies as they maneuvered on the battlefield.[31]

The military code experts thought the device was invulnerable to cryptanalysis. Elizebeth reported the Riverbank code breakers received five short messages to solve from the Pletts Cryptograph: "We had never seen the small device, but we knew the principle on which it worked."[32] It had an inner mobile wheel and an outer disc that each contained the alphabet. The mechanism regularly altered the scheme of the cipher so that the first time an "a" might come out as an "f," but the next time the "a" might turn up on the cipher as an "r."[33] A person with the proper key could use the device to code or decode messages. "We had no knowledge or even a wild guess as to the sequence of letters on either of the two alphabets," said Mrs. Friedman.[34]

"My husband lined up the five short messages and began to puzzle them out," she continued. Within a few hours William had worked out the key for the device's outer disc—the word "cipher," but still did not have the key to make the inner disc work.[35] William said he tried every combination of word along with cipher to figure out, the second part of the key: cipher alphabet, cipher device, cipher polyalphabet. "Finally, I came to the end of my rope," William told a class years later, "and said to the new Mrs. Friedman: 'Elizebeth, I want you to stop what you are doing and do something for me.'"[36]

"I was sitting across the room from him very busily engaged on something else," Elizebeth continued the story. "He asked me to lean back in my chair, close my eyes and make my mind blank." At that point William sprung a word-association exercise on his wife. "I was not to consider the reply to any degree, not even for one second, but instantly to come forth with the word which his question aroused in my mind. I proceeded as he directed. He spoke the word 'cipher,' and I instantaneously responded, 'machine.'"[37]

That proved to be the proper keyword. It took the Friedmans only three hours to solve all five messages. The first of the five messages they broke read: "This cipher is absolutely indecipherable."[38]

Elizebeth writes that those who developed the cipher disregarded an absolutely sacred principle of cryptography: never choose a keyword or phrase that is associated with the subject of the message. William got stumped, writes Elizebeth, because of the psychology of it: "It did not occur to his meticulous mind to use the word machine. Nevertheless, 'machine' it was."[39]

William, on the other hand, said, "You see my male mind didn't regard this thing as a machine at all; but the female mind is, as you know, a thing apart."[40]

When the novice Riverbank code breakers sent the decrypted solutions back to Washington, according to Elizebeth, "the waiting military authorities British, French and American, who had expected to install this device on the Western front as a means of communication in the front lines were constrained to cancel those plans."[41]

After that successful cryptanalysis assignment, the Riverbank unit kept training U.S. Army cryptographers in six-week sessions.[42] In addition, they kept getting more and more messages from the government to solve. "We were driven to produce right from the start," Elizebeth told an interviewer years later. "Washington would send messages to Riverbank, we'd solve them, then send them back. The messages were picked up out of the air mostly, or subpoenaed from Western Union or cable offices. We had a pretty systematic inflow of messages the government felt weren't plain English."[43]

Some of the messages Washington sent to Riverbank came by mail. Those deemed more urgent came by wire. Most were important to the war effort. But some turned out to be less so. The post office, which was responsible for wartime censorship, sent a suspicious-looking letter to the Friedmans. Elizebeth reported that she worked on the missive for hours and finally determined that the message wasn't code; it was just a note in Czechoslovakian from a young man to his girlfriend.[44]

Yet after doing this for nearly a year, officials in Washington found the process of transmitting the messages to Geneva, then sending them back to Washington was too slow and taking up too much time and space on the telegraph wires. So, in January 1918 the Army established its own Cipher Bureau in Washington and asked Fabyan to transfer the Riverbank staff en masse. "George Fabyan never told us about that," Elizebeth remarked. "We had to find that out after the war's end."[45]

Within a year of the start-up Riverbank cipher bureau, Elizebeth credits her husband with developing "methods of decipherment in systems which had hitherto been considered completely indecipherable." Together the pair wrote a brochure, "The Solution of Running Key Ciphers," the first of a series of brochures they co-wrote at Riverbank.[46] But Fabyan "loved power so much that he was utterly unwilling for any author to have his name appear as author of any text produced on any subject at Riverbank," Elizebeth declared. So under his own copyright, Fabyan self-published the brochures. "There was only a letter of transmittal in the beginning of each brochure from my husband, a more or less tangible evidence of authorship but the appearance of his name on any title page or elsewhere as author, was not permitted by Fabyan."[47]

Keeping Washington's offers secret and taking credit for their work were not the only instances of subterfuge that Fabyan visited on the Friedmans to keep control of his innovative code couple. Early in the war, as they prepared to set up the cryptography school at Riverbank, Fabyan took William to visit U.S. Army officers, including Captain Mauborgne, in Washington. Mauborgne asked if Friedman would be interested in a commission in the Army. Friedman responded positively and Mauborgne said that he would follow up with a detailed letter when William returned to Illinois. Elizebeth wrote the Navy Department to see if they needed her skills in military intelligence as well.[48]

The letter from Mauborgne never got to William. As a result, Elizebeth began to suspect that Fabyan was reading and censoring the couple's mail.[49]

The Friedmans kept at their work of training cryptographers and breaking codes for the government. But they began to feel extremely uneasy. Elizebeth said her husband especially became agitated: "He felt like a draft evader, he was embarrassed." By now William had learned about the offer of a commission from the Army that Fabyan had purloined. "He kicked up a fuss," and was sent to a nearby induction center for a physical, but failed because of a heart murmur.[50]

"We became suspicious that Fabyan would doctor the documents, whatever they were, which is exactly what happened," Elizebeth told an interviewer many years later. They discovered that Fabyan's sister was married to an Army officer at the camp where William received his medical exam. "When we insisted on my husband having a thorough physical examination and not by an Army board but by experts on the outside, they found nothing wrong." In the end, William received a commission as a first lieutenant, lower than the rank he might have received on the earlier offer from Captain Mauborgne. "And that was Fabyan's doing," Elizebeth concluded.[51]

Nevertheless, William Friedman was soon on his way to American General Headquarters in France. Though Billy, as his family and friends called him, was doing his patriotic duty, the separation was difficult for the newlyweds. He wrote one love letter to Elizebeth while visiting his parents in Pittsburgh en route to New York for embarkation to the front. "Oh, Dear Sweetheart be brave Darling and trust your Lover to come back to you," Billy wrote. "May God keep you and protect you while I'm away.

And may He watch over both of us and bring us into each other's arms soon again."[52]

The night before he boarded a ship for Europe, Billy wrote another long letter to his bride: "Dear Heart O'Mine, Sweet Elsbeth Love, think of your boy quite often but don't grieve. I'll be coming back soon to my Own, and what a reunion it shall be!" He concluded, "Good night, Dear One, My Own True Love. I kiss you over and over again. Utterly, Your Billy."[53]

When he arrived with the other doughboys, Friedman served with the Radio Intelligence Section helping to solve German ciphers and codes.[54] Besides his military work, he also had to continue dealing with George Fabyan. Colonel Fabyan sent a letter to "Dear Billy" on August 8, 1918, chatting about what was going on back at Geneva and his work with Army officials in Washington. Fabyan wrote that he would like Friedman to arrange a dinner for the officers who trained at Riverbank "and I want the bill for it."[55]

Even though her husband did eventually receive a military commission, not even a request from American commander General John J. Pershing could break a military taboo in Elizebeth's case: "There was a letter requesting my services at General Headquarters in the A.E.F. [American Expeditionary Forces]," she told a radio interview two decades later, "but there was a ruling about women serving near the front, so my husband served on the other side while I remained here."[56] A few months before the war ended, Elizebeth did receive a response from the Navy. It indicated that if she knew Spanish or German there might be a position for her; the response asked her to correspond further; a lack of any more letters on the subject, however, may indicate that Fabyan was purloining those letters as well.[57]

Elizebeth remained at Riverbank running the estate's remaining code breaking tasks for only a few months after her husband went to France. As most of the operations had been transferred to Washington, she says, the operation began to die slowly as young people working on the estate went to more lucrative and busy jobs. Elizebeth also was becoming disillusioned with working on the Shakespeare project and with Fabyan himself: "Col. Fabyan's deceptions while posing as a great benefactor to us in our individual lives had caused me to lose my taste for connection with this institution."[58]

When the armistice came in November 1918, William remained in France to write his unit's history. As the war was drawing to a close, Mrs. Friedman decided against moving to Washington to work in the government Cipher Bureau. "I returned, therefore, to my hometown, where my

father was living in our home with a housekeeper after my mother's death."
While caring for her father, who had suffered a stroke, she took a job at a
library to pass the time until her husband came home. "I felt that for the
short time that my husband remained in France, I could give some attention to him, although my father had been a character somewhat like
George Fabian [sic] in his rigid requirement of running everyone's personal
life."[59]

Even a state away, however, Elizebeth had to deal with Fabyan's
demands. "I'm expecting two students within a week or ten days and I
want to rush them through the course at the earliest possible moment
and will be glad to have your assistance," Fabyan wrote Elizebeth just
before the armistice. "We are getting out a number of pamphlets and I
would very much like to have you do the proof reading."[60] A few days later,
Fabyan wrote again, thanking Elizebeth for offering to do the proofreading,
but telling her it would "be necessary for you to be at Riverbank" to complete the work.[61]

Elizebeth adamantly refused to return to Riverbank. She had her husband's backing on that. Within weeks of the war's end, Fabyan was trying
to get his code couple back under his wing. Elizebeth had forwarded one
of her husband's letters to Fabyan. That teed him off in this response to
Elizebeth shortly after New Year's Day 1919: "I have evidently been labor-
ing under a misapprehension. Having read the letter carefully and noted
the fact that he signs his full name and a formal manner in place of 'Billy,'
I feel that the whole matter is rather up in the air." Fabyan noted that
William left for the Army with the intent of returning to work for him.
"Correspondence is rather unsatisfactory at best and when the mails
require two months or more, it is almost prohibitive so far as arriving at
conclusions. I naturally desire to make some definite plans and if you and
Billy do not intend returning to Riverbank, I would like to have the infor-
mation as early as possible."[62]

Elizebeth replied to Fabyan immediately, making her point very
clearly: "As it is quite impossible for me to come to Chicago at present, I
deemed it unnecessary to wire you, as you suggested. I am inclined to
agree with you that in most cases, correspondence is rather unsatisfactory.
But with you I confess it has some advantages—for, you see, in conversation you insist upon doing all the talking! Now I suppose you're going to
retort, 'This, from a woman?'—or perhaps, 'C'est la guerre?' [It's the war?]."

On the matter of returning to Riverbank, Elizebeth left the door
open just a bit: "I don't mind reminding you of what you must naturally
understand, that if we do return to Riverbank, it must necessarily be on

altogether different terms than those of our former stay. If, therefore, you are unwilling to consider that fact, there is no use in going into the matter further."[63]

While dealing with Fabyan's machinations, the Friedmans continued their romantic correspondence. In one billet-doux William lamented that the process of bringing the troops home was taking too long: "Traffic conditions are in a very bad shape. There either aren't enough facilities or else the French want to keep us (and our money) here a little longer." He also noted that the couple had skipped one tradition when they remained at Riverbank after their wedding a year and a half earlier. "You Love-Girl! As for that honeymoon: we are going to have it, that's settled!" He wrote that a fellow officer had offered them a summer cottage where they could spend their honeymoon when he returned—whenever that would be.

In closing, Billy once again expressed how much he missed his new wife. "Yes, Dearest, the pictures of you are my great billet attractions now. And never a time I light my lamp or blow it out but I'll kiss you and whisper to you—oh lots of things!"[64]

Then, instead of love letters, Elizebeth began receiving telegrams: William would return to America in March 1919.[65] She met up with him in New York; they traveled to Pittsburgh to see Billy's family and began discussing what to do in the next phase of their lives. The Army had offered William a salary considerably more than he had been making at Riverbank. They also offered a position to Elizebeth at half the salary proposed for her husband.[66]

Neither desired to return to Geneva, Illinois. "We were determined that we would not go back to Riverbank. We were sick and tired of Fabyan's scheming and dishonesty although he was generous and we lived rather luxuriously, at his expense. It just didn't go down to be treated like chattels," Elizebeth stated in her memoirs. But Colonel Fabyan kept sweetening the pot, offering the Friedmans double the amount that the government put on the table.[67]

After William explored other job opportunities, the Friedmans did return to Riverbank despite their reservations about Fabyan and the work on the Shakespeare ciphers. This time, however, instead of living on the estate, they rented a house where the Friedmans began entertaining friends. "It was a sweet little cottage and we were really quite happy there," wrote Elizebeth.[68]

Yet before long, Fabyan proved that his stripes had not changed. For one, Fabyan failed to double the Friedmans' pay as he promised. Their pay remained the same as it had been, $30 a month.[69] Then, when William

Elizebeth behind the wheel of a Scripps-Booth auto in 1919. Both she and William complained in correspondence about the difficulty of keeping their old cars running (courtesy Steve Thomas).

finished writing another ground-breaking cryptographic article, again Fabyan refused to give him credit. "Fabyan always came out ahead," according to Elizebeth. "And we always came out at the other end."[70]

Enough was enough. Working for George Fabyan became unbearable. An official letter arrived at Riverbank for Fabyan; the Army asked for the Friedmans' help in breaking the enclosed coded material. In reality, the code was an offer for the Friedmans to go to work for the Army—a ruse to slip through Fabyan's censorship noose.[71]

The Friedmans surreptitiously negotiated contracts to begin working with the War Department on the first day of 1921. An official noted that Fabyan had been trying to find out what was going on: "the old gentleman seems to be smelling a rat," wrote Signal Corps officer J.O. Mauborgne, who had been promoted to major since first working with Riverbank at the start of the war.[72] When they notified Fabyan—just a day before they scheduled their departure[73]—Elizebeth notes he was not very gracious, but accepted his fate.[74]

As they put the Riverbank experience behind them, William Friedman was forced to leave an important manuscript with Fabyan.[75] This was *The Index of Coincidence and Its Applications in Cryptography*, which later was recognized "as the most important single publication in cryptology."[76]

"My husband was left to wonder a long time what had happened to this important piece of scientific analysis. Finally a long, long time after we had taken up residence in Washington, two bound copies came from Col. Fabyan." Elizabeth explains that Fabyan had indeed placed William's name on the title page, "however, as time went on this proved to be another example of Col. Fabyan's deceptions."[77]

Fabyan had the publication printed in English in France to save money. But a French military officer translated it, post-dated it and took credit for it.[78]

The Friedmans learned of this deception two or three years later. The copies of *The Index of Coincidence and Its Applications in Cryptography* sent to William in English with his name on the title had been printed for him alone so that he would not discover that Colonel Fabyan had the pamphlet printed in France without any indication of its true authorship. This was contrary to an agreement the Friedmans made with Fabyan when they returned to Riverbank after the war. They were to receive publication credit for anything they wrote while employed at the estate.[79] William was reluctant to confront Fabyan, but Elizabeth did and forced him to republish it with the proper attribution.[80] When William's authorship of the seminal work was rectified, it established him as a pioneer in crypto-mathematics.[81]

The Riverbank years allowed both William and Elizabeth to learn and grow in the cryptographic community. "The Friedmans were on the leading edge of modern cryptology," said historian Betsy Rohaly Smoot.[82]

Yet when the couple moved to Washington in late 1920, Elizabeth was being overshadowed. "By the end of the war I was more or less known as a military cipher expert, but I was better known as the wife of my husband who, having been persuaded by me to forsake Genetics for Ciphers and Codes, had gone to General Headquarters, A.E.F., (where I, a mere woman, could not follow to pursue my 'trade') and made a reputation so startling that I regarded the task of catching up to him as being altogether hopeless."[83]

Elizabeth Friedman would discover in the coming years, however, that her reputation would not only begin to match her husband's, but her cryptographic accomplishments would soon be legendary.

=3=

The Prohibition Years

The 1920s ushered in a new challenge for America: how to enforce the social experiment of Prohibition. Elizebeth Friedman would play a key role in enforcing the unpopular law, but first she would continue to employ her expertise with military codes and ciphers.

When World War I ended, the War Department wanted to continue its code breaking success in peacetime. On May 16, 1919, the Army intelligence unit, G-2, recommended that $100,000 be budgeted for a cryptography operation. The Army funded $60,000 of the operation and the State Department $40,000. William Friedman's history of that era noted that instead of using existing Washington government buildings, $3,900 of the budget was earmarked for rent, light and heat for a New York office "with a view to hiding its existence." The chief of the bureau was H.O. Yardley, later to be discredited for revealing the United States' cryptographic secrets in his book *The American Black Chamber*.[1]

Yet when the Friedmans arrived in Washington to start working for the Army in 1921, cryptanalysis was starting to lose its cachet with the brass. As officers who had benefited from code breaking during the war moved on to other assignments, the cryptography coffers that had once been full started to dry up.[2]

Nevertheless, there were full-time jobs for William and Elizebeth with the Signal Corps. They had made the arrangements to start in Washington while still at Riverbank. A memo from Major J.O. Mauborgne dated November 30, 1920, stated: "it is requested that immediate steps be taken to place an order with Mrs. W.F. Friedman" for "services in connection with the reconstruction and revision of a confidential staff code and the construction of three field codes." Elizebeth was to be paid $900 per year for the preparation of manuscripts and codes and proofreading them after everything was set in type. "Inasmuch as this is a matter of urgency,"

Mauborgne's memo continued, "it is requested that the placing of the order be expedited as much as possible."[3] Yardley, the head of the so-called Black Chamber, received a salary of $6,000, more than six times as much as Mrs. Friedman.[4]

With his background serving in the Great War, the Signal Corps paid William twice the salary that his wife received. Elizebeth never complained about the pay disparity in her memoirs, explaining that her husband was the pair's key innovator when it came to breaking codes.[5] She also once noted to a magazine editor that even though she had been offered a job with the notorious Black Chamber, she refused to accept the position.[6]

The understanding with the Army was that William would not only develop new codes, but also try to develop devices or machines for using the ciphers in the field. As the code couple worked on these assignments, they incorporated lessons they had learned during the war: that the codes needed to be in two distinct parts, one for ciphering when sent out and another for deciphering on the receiving end. They also developed a variety of codes, utilizing the maxim that the codes would need to be changed often to make it harder for an enemy to break them. "For one year I worked with William Friedman on this phase of employment with the Signal Corps," wrote Elizebeth.[7] That would be the last time that the Friedmans collaborated officially on military cryptography.

Before taking another full time job, Elizebeth started writing a children's book, which she apparently did not finish. She also worked sporadically on projects for both the Army and Navy.[8] But 12 months after leaving the full-time Signal Corps position, a job for cryptanalyst building "secret codes and ciphers" opened up with the Navy. "The work requires thorough training in english [sic] and mathematics, coupled with a thorough understanding of the principles of code and cipher building and analysis, which can only be obtained by long study and training," proclaimed the memo describing the position. It also noted that a Navy cryptographer had resigned the $1,600 position to take another in a commercial cipher company that paid twice as much. It also reported that the Signal Corps was paying $4,500 a year for "a cryptanalyst engaged upon duties very similar to the duty required in our Code & Signal Section." The conclusion was that the Navy needed to pay its cryptographers more to remain competitive in the field.[9]

Elizebeth took the Navy position at $1,900 per year, starting in February 1923. "The codes and ciphers involved are used in the preparation of all secret communications transmitted by the Navy," read the official job description. "These messages necessarily contain military and diplomatic information of a most secret nature and the position is one of high responsibility." It also had the proviso that she "give a course of instructions to Naval Officers" in the Office of Naval Communications.[10]

The oath of office that Elizebeth signed, swearing to "support and defend the Constitution of the United States against all enemies," had her name typed incorrectly as "Elizabeth." That was something that official government documents would continue to get wrong for the rest of her career.[11]

Within two months of starting the position, the director of the Naval Communication Service recommended to the secretary of the Navy a $240 "Congressional bonus" for code builder Mrs. E.S. Friedman.[12]

But as the Friedmans prepared to start their family, Elizebeth quit her Navy code job after only five months. As he recommended approval of the resignation to the secretary of the Navy, the director of Naval Communications wrote: "The employee above mentioned is being separated from the service without delinquency or misconduct."[13]

Settling into Washington seemed to be far harder for the Friedmans than performing their official duties. Elizebeth remembered, "Housing was very scarce, in fact unobtainable. As was proved by the fact that we had been in Washington exactly one year before any apartments in any part of the city became available, although it was a pursuit of mine daily to cover the field for available living quarters."[14] They finally found and rented an unfurnished apartment on S Street on a triangle of land facing Connecticut Avenue.[15]

Elizebeth had not been to the nation's capital before and found it "exciting." Having grown up in rural Indiana, Elizebeth admits that she was "starved for theater." As a result, the couple initially attended one kind of performance or another "at least three times a week."[16]

The Friedmans seemed to make friends fast in their new home. They formed a quartet that performed in their apartment. The members included Major Mauborgne, who played violin; Elizebeth played piano, another Army officer the cello, while an acquaintance from Illinois that they had run into joined them on the cello. "We used to have crowds below, on the street [listening], when the windows were open," Elizebeth remarked. "Well, that was great fun."[17]

A year later, however, after keeping her eye on the newspaper classifieds, Elizebeth found a better apartment. They moved to Park Road and 17th Street, the end of the Mt. Pleasant streetcar line. It was the only apartment she found that had a fireplace.[18] The Friedmans' search for the perfect spot in Washington would continue for another few years; while visiting her sister in Detroit, Elizebeth wrote Billy that she had seen a "darling" apartment there: "Would give anything if I could find one like it in Wash [Washington]. Has two huge windows <u>each</u> on the north and west in the living room which is beautifully large and light therefore the kitchenette is as large as three of ours. And Ruthie has a huge five-room and sleeping porch apt for $60! Wash. is a century behind the times in apartments."[19]

The young couple kept moving around the area looking for accommodations that better suited their needs. They moved for a few years to the Bethesda suburbs in a house they called Green Mansions. "We learned ... that anyone who has a country place or a watering place never becomes lonely," Elizebeth wrote, "because everyone who drives for entertainment in passing of time on weekends and summer evenings, invariably drops in on you. We ... entertained more people at an outdoor cook out supper in one year there than we would have in five years or perhaps even ten in a city house."

The Friedmans' first child, Barbara, was born in 1924 while still residing at Green Mansions. Now with a daughter, the Friedmans acquired help to run the household. "Our beloved Cassie, an extraordinary fine person and marvelous cook and housekeeper had been with us since the birth of our first child and had always lived in our house except for her days off," Elizebeth wrote.[20]

Then, in 1925, Billy and Elizebeth built a home on the pleasant, tree-lined Military Road in the District of Columbia near the border with Chevy Chase, finally settling for two decades to raise a family.

Cassie roomed on the third floor of the new home. The family pet didn't make the transition as easily. The Friedmans brought their Airedale, Crypto, to Military Road, but found that he was more suited to Green Mansions. "Crypto was so used to being unrestrained in the country," wrote Elizebeth, "that he roamed and not always thoughtfully in the proper places on neighbors [sic] property, tearing and trampling upon flower beds and plantings." They ended up trading Crypto to their gardener for landscape services.[21]

Despite being occupied as a mother, Elizebeth did freelance code work on the side. The publisher of the *Washington Post* contracted Billy and Elizebeth to compile a private code for him. "I spent approximately six months with my husbands [sic] help in evenings when he was at home in preparing a ten thousand group private code for the purpose demanded," she wrote. After finishing the work, it took the couple two years to collect the money owed them on the contract. After their experience with George

Fabyan at Riverbank, Elizebeth noted: "we were becoming weary of very wealthy men and their dealings in money matters."[22]

Some government agencies also continued to call for Elizebeth to do code and cryptanalysis work since "few indeed of that peculiar genus exist," she wrote. She found that she was on "almost constant call" for her expertise. "Some of the queer consequences of following such a strange calling are requests to read illegible shorthand notes, forge[d] signatures, and even perform magic tricks!"[23]

Soon she would be called on to perform some serious magic for the U.S. government. Her "peculiar genus" of work was about to take a turn that would make Elizebeth Smith Friedman famous.

The United States had outlawed the manufacture, sale and transportation of alcohol on January 16, 1920. But *drinking* liquor remained legal.[24] The moral crusade against alcohol had contributed to ordinary people openly flaunting the law and creating illicit business deals that could turn dangerous. Some actively worked to undermine the law as evidenced by marine engine companies offering free machine guns to rum runners who purchased their engines.[25]

By the middle of the decade liquor smuggling had become big business. "The risk in breaking the law remained with the seller. As America's thirst for alcohol grew, so did the numbers of those willing to supply it," a Joint Military Intelligence College analysis summed up the problem decades later. "Manufacturing and importing alcohol immediately became a very lucrative business." Smugglers with safe havens in foreign ports—especially those in British and French colonies in the western hemisphere—began to exploit the largely unprotected U.S. coastlines of the Atlantic, Pacific, Gulf of Mexico and the Great Lakes.[26]

United States law enforcement agencies, with a deluge of liquor pouring into the country illegally, were desperate to find better measures to enforce the Volstead Act, which gave force to the 18th Amendment that mandated Prohibition. The Coast Guard found its search and rescue duties now complicated with the burden of enforcing the new law. With 12,000 miles of shoreline to patrol, the Coast Guard had only 75 vessels, most of which were ill equipped for law enforcement duty. The Coast Guard commandant, Rear Admiral Frederick C. Billard, described the challenge of enforcement as "the greatest and most difficult task that has ever been imposed upon any of the floating forces of the United States in time of peace."[27]

Most of the rum runners, or blacks, as the Coast Guard called them since they ran the seas at night without lights, used radio to communicate ship-to-shore and vice versa. They developed complex codes—many of them developed commercially and sold to smugglers[28]—to make sure that official eavesdroppers couldn't steal information about secret rendezvous points and bust up their operations. A Center for Cryptologic History article concluded that the "radio operations of the rum-running organizations were, in fact, comparable in terms of size, technical skill, and organization with the radio operation which would be conducted by enemy agents in World War II."[29]

William Friedman was well entrenched in his duties at the Army Signal Corps at this time. Elizabeth wrote that her husband "had gone far beyond anybody else of the day in the cryptanalytic side of cryptology, that is, the solution of 'enemy' codes and ciphers." The Army resisted the Coast Guard's efforts to enlist William Friedman full-time in the battle against liquor smuggling, preferring him to stay on the career path of military cryptography.[30]

Since the Army wouldn't let loose of William, the Coast Guard sought Elizabeth's help. "It was only a very short time after we had moved into the Chevy Chase house that I was called by Captain Charles Root, a Coast Guard officer who had the title of Intelligence Officer for the United States Coast Guard. He was extremely interested in developing an anti or counter-intelligence work by the Coast Guard in its duties as one of the law enforcement agencies of the Treasury Department."[31]

Root had organized the Coast Guard Intelligence Section in 1924[32] and began intercepting rum runner radio transmissions in December 1925.[33] "He maintained a wallchart at Headquarters with the name and noontime position of all suspected rum runners and he disseminated this information back to the fleet via 'Intelligence Circulars,'" according to a 2001 monograph, *Intelligence in the Rum War at Sea, 1920–1933*, published by the Joint Military Intelligence College. That report credits the creation of the Intelligence Section as "the turning of the tide in [the Coast Guard's] favor in the Rum War."[34]

But the mere creation of a unit for intelligence was only half the battle. Root had called on the Navy to help solve the rum runners' intercepted codes. That resulted in one successful interdiction, but the Navy balked at doing any more code breaking since military forces are forbidden to do law enforcement work. So the Navy suggested that the Coast Guard create its own decrypting unit.[35]

Thus Elizabeth Friedman's full-time adventure into the world of law enforcement code breaking came at the behest of the Coast Guard, but was funded by a different agency. The Internal Revenue Service, also operated by the Treasury Department, appointed her a Prohibition Investigator at a salary of $2,400 in December 1925.[36]

With Elizebeth and a stenographer now working under the auspices of the Coast Guard, the Intelligence Section grew to five people. The Coast Guard repair depot, with the assistance of the War Department, created a wooden deciphering machine to aid in Mrs. Friedman's work. Captain Root outlined the function of this new unit: "It solves all enemy cryptograms and problems of like nature received from the forces afloat or afield and handles problems of like nature, received from other bureaus of the Treasury, as a matter of cooperation."[37]

An April 1927 memo from Captain Root about Mrs. Friedman noted that before beginning her full-time work with the Coast Guard she had "courteously given her services in emergencies for the solution of the complicated codes and ciphers, exhibiting much shrewdness in the breaking down of enemy ciphers and in enciphered codes." The memo further extols her unique abilities for the cryptanalysis position since "she has a good working knowledge of the Latin languages which at this time are more or less used by the enemy."

Root concludes: "This office knows of no available person so well fitted for this duty as is Mrs. Friedman. Sh[e] has at her command highly confidential and secret methods of solving ciphers, which methods were developed by Major Friedman [her husband] and are not generally known by others. It need hardly be stated that in this game of wits in which we are now engaged, the breaking of the enemy's communications is not only of great importance but is probably the most efficient single operation in which we can engage, and in such an operation the cryptanalyst holds the key position, and the most skillful is none too good."[38]

Though technically employed by the Bureau of Prohibition or the Customs Foreign Service at various times,[39] Elizebeth was appointed a Coast Guard special employee. She wrote that her title and duties had benefits for her as a new mother: "A special agent is someone who does not have to conform to the requirements of office hours and the like, but is expected to go wherever and be wherever his scent nose leads him in pursuit of the investigation which he is engaged. For this reason, it came about that I was able to do the work for which I was requested at our home. In other words, I went to Captain Roots [sic] office, collected materials, took it home and when solved the material was returned."

As the bureaucratic shuffle among Treasury Department agencies continued, the Civil Service Commission in 1927 recognized a new position for Mrs. Friedman, an appointment as "Crypt Analyst" in the Bureau of Prohibition at a pay grade of CAF-7. Her salary continued at $2,400 per year.[40]

Barbara was just one year old when Elizebeth began working with the Coast Guard. Another child, John, was born in 1926. The Friedmans hired a nurse for the children, Carlotta, a "lovely fine girl" who, according to Elizebeth, got along "beautifully" with Cassie.[41] Mrs. Friedman organized an entire week's menu for five-course meals for the family and Cassie prepared them.[42] Carlotta worked from 7 a.m. to 7 p.m. as Elizebeth performed her official duties.[43]

Having help at home must have been a crucial family decision to help Elizebeth work with the Coast Guard. There was an "enormous number" of encrypted rum runner messages—hundreds—stacked up in the Intelligence Section waiting to be solved in the spring of 1927. But within two months Elizebeth and her clerk had eliminated the backlog.[44]

Elizebeth summarized her first months of chipping away at the hundreds of coded messages: "This traffic covered a period of more than a year, was from many different sources both on the Atlantic and Pacific Coasts, and the volume was increasing daily. Upon the first date above

Elizebeth with her children Barbara and John. Barbara was born in 1924 and John in 1926 (courtesy Chris Atchison).

[April 1927], work of solution was begun upon the hundreds of messages on file. Within two months a great mass of the accumulated traffic was reduced from unknown to known."[45]

Smugglers attacked weak points on the United States eastern frontier from ports in safe havens such as Belize, the Bahamas, Havana and up to Newfoundland. Though the smuggling routes along the eastern seaboard extended throughout the Gulf Coast up through Maine, she remarked that the codes encountered on the west coast were "of a different class"—in other words, more complex—than those used on the Atlantic coast.[46]

"I recall a single long message which had come to the United States by telegraph from Havana, Cuba. It, when examined by me, revealed itself as a transposition cipher. Since this was the only communication I had between these correspondents, there was nothing to do in my attempt to solve it except in trial and error."

Elizebeth recalled a young officer, inexperienced in cryptanalysis, who suggested that if she could guess a keyword for the cipher, the problem would be simplified and that it might be the only method of ever solving the message.

> In his innocence, the young man suggested that probably the keyword Havana had been used as a method of transposing the columns in the message. I laughed at him, saying that no one in his right mind would ever use as a keyword the name of the city from which he was sending a message. However, the young man was proved right and I wrong because after I had worked a long time going through the trials of solving the message by analysis, I did try the word Havana and found that indeed it had been used as a key word. I decided right then and there that I would not permit my mind to become so rigid as to exclude the obvious but that hereafter, I would try first that very supposition and thus clear away the possibilities that the sender of a secret message had been so foolish as to employ a tool of the naïve practices.[47]

Elizebeth's solution of some cryptographic puzzles was aided by the Coast Guard's occasional capture of a list of codes and their keys. One such case was the code used by rum runners off New Jersey in October 1929. It is a list of jumbled letters starting with C, M or O. The list then has the actual meaning of the otherwise incomprehensible letters. For example in the codes starting with C: CABZA means *account*; CADIR means *afternoon*; CAGJE means *bring*. Others include: MOBAT for *engine oil* and MOORM for *Fire Island Light Ship*. OGVAB is decoded as *patrol boat is following me*. OGWAC means *put running lights off*.[48]

The rum runners soon grew wise to the ways of their official adversaries. "As the means of communication between mothership, supplier, and customer grew more sophisticated, so did the types of codes and ciphers used," *Intelligence in the Rum War at Sea, 1920–1933* noted. "Whereas in 1927 only two general systems were in use, changing only every six months, [by] mid–1930 practically every rum boat on the Pacific Coast had its own code or cipher." To combat that, the Coast Guard doubled the number of radio operators listening to the rum runners at key interception times each day.[49]

In another measure, to protect all of the country's sea approaches from liquor smuggling, along with the main office in Washington, the Coast Guard established subsidiary intelligence units in New York, Mobile and San Francisco.[50] The system allowed "systematic sampling of known black frequencies while still maintaining continuous coverage of Coast Guard operational frequencies." Yet the system also overloaded the cryptanalytic unit in Washington. So in July 1928 the Coast Guard sent Mrs. Friedman to San Francisco to train selected prohibition agents in the science of cryptanalysis.[51]

"I proceeded to California stopped first at San Pedro where I obtained from the Coast Guard a mass of information extremely useful in solving the secret systems in use," Elizebeth wrote in an official report. "From there I proceeded to San Francisco, where it was agreed that Mr. C. A. Housel, of the office of the Coordinator of the Pacific Coast Details, should be instructed in methods of transcribing the traffic from code and cipher into plain language. Mr. Housel proved to be of a very industrious and painstaking disposition and soon showed capability for the work of transcription."

In the 21 months ending in January 1930, the San Francisco station intercepted 3,300 messages between four or five shore stations and 25 different vessels at sea. The interceptions discovered nearly 50 distinct secret systems of communication, some of them with up to five subsystems of ciphers or code. Elizebeth concluded, "Although to date Mr. Housel's aptitude for this work has not reached the point of solving a new system, his powers of inference and his sources of information have been of great benefit and usefulness in the pursuance of the work at headquarters."[52]

In 1930 the Army Signal Corps did consent to William Friedman working with Elizebeth and others in the Coast Guard to develop an HF/DF capability on a fleet of 75-foot cutters. William spent a two-week stint aboard the cutter CG-210 in the New York area. It had high-frequency receivers and direction finders (HF/DF) that allowed cryptanalysts to not only break rum runners' codes, but direct law enforcement vessels to the exact spots where the illicit cargoes were to be dropped. "The resulting confusion to this group of rum ships was more than all the efforts of the destroyer force and the other units combined have been able to effect in months," the head of the intelligence unit, Lieutenant Commander Frank J. Gorman, wrote of the operation.[53] Modern-day Coast Guard officials credit this operation as the first *tactical* law enforcement use of COMINT (communications intelligence) in U.S. history.[54]

The cryptanalysis unit of the Coast Guard examined about 25,000 messages each year. As a result of her efforts, in her first three years, Elizebeth Friedman was credited with solving more than 12,000 messages.[55] "A 10-year-old boy could write a single message that the most highly trained expert could not decipher," Elizebeth said in an interview. "But it is another matter when it comes to devising one that can be put to everyday use."[56]

One successful decryption involved an intercepted message intended for the *Corazel*. On September 29, 1930, a shore station in Vancouver, British Columbia, radioed the rum runner operating in the Gulf of Mexico this code:

HAWSE	HARRY	BONES	RADIO	SPURN
HENCE	PYGMY	WHITE	SNIFF	SHREW
ABRIA	BRIT	RIGHT	SHEUO	APHIS
SPRIG	LOUIS	WITCH		

The plain English solution read: "Harry cannot take goods now. Proceed 50 miles east Briton Island and give to Louis when he comes." The cryptanalytic unit sent the decrypted message to the Coast Guard commander in the Gulf to take action.[57]

Smugglers kept seeking more elaborate ways to disguise their messages as they discovered the Coast Guard breaking their codes. "Some of these are of a complexity never even attempted by any government for its most secret communications," wrote Elizebeth. "At no time during the World War, when secret methods of communication reached their highest development, were there used such involved ramifications as are to be found in some of the correspondence of West Coast rum running vessels."[58]

As a result of the increasingly sophisticated cryptography employed by the smugglers, and the sheer volume of messages, Elizebeth told her superiors in a seven-page memo in November 1930 that it would take more than just her and a clerk to make the cryptanalysis unit productive enough to have much impact on the rum running. "It may be stated that every system employed by the smuggling interests has been solved but in no case has it been possible to read all of the messages in view of the large amount of labor involved and the lamentable lack of personnel to accomplish the work."[59]

Elizebeth complained not just about the lack of personnel, but shoddy work by some of those at the head of the chain created to wreak havoc on the smugglers' operations. In a memo to the head of the intelligence unit, she urged that "operators intercepting [radio] traffic take more care in recording the stations sending messages." A large percentage of the radio traffic had not been transcribed she said, and some that were did not indicate whether the message came from a boat or a shore station. "Also it is important to know the locale of boats operating. For instance, in working upon the system which employs the letter-numeral code groups (B 512, N 337, A363, and the like) this office has no idea whether these boats are operating off the coast of Maine or of New Jersey." She also remarked that inexperienced radio operators who were making assumptions about intercepted codes were hampering cryptanalytic efforts and suggested that "the radio personnel ... 'stick to their specialty' and let us stick to ours."[60]

These conditions indicated a sense of futility—a morale problem—spreading among those tasked with bringing the rum runners to justice after a full decade of Prohibition.[61]

At the suggestion of her boss in the Intelligence Section, Mrs. Friedman laid out a plan for the minimum number of personnel to decipher encrypted messages collected from the airwaves. Her memo listed five positions with seven people for the upgraded cryptanalytic unit. There would be one cryptanalyst in charge, an assistant cryptanalyst, one senior cryptographic clerk, one cryptographic clerk and three assistant cryptographic clerks. The cryptanalyst in charge of the unit would be rated P-4 in the Civil Service with a salary of $4,000; the assistant cryptographic clerks would be paid $1,620. The seven salaries for the unit totaled $14,660.

"The expenditure of the foregoing amount of money in the manner outlined in solving secret communication systems would accomplish vastly more concrete results than many times that sum spent in equipping and maintaining Coast Guard vessels engaged in a more or less blind search for smugglers." Without sufficient cryptanalysis the Coast Guard seizing rum runners' vessels would be "almost purely a matter of accident," Elizebeth argued. "With a properly functioning unit for reading the Blacks' secret systems of communication, the Coast Guard vessels can be informed both as to the time and place of contact. This known, the Coast Guard can first of all prevent the contact; or if they choose to allow the contact to be made, the Coast Guard vessel can then locate itself in such a way as to seize the returning liquor-laden speed boat, either within or without the twelve-mile limit; and lastly, with the approximate available landing points known, every effort can be exerted to prevent the landing."[62]

Without the increased help in the cryptographic unit, Mrs. Friedman predicted there might be more missed opportunities to capture smugglers. She cited a case off Long Island that, because of the inability to decrypt the black's messages in a timely way, the smugglers deceived a Coast Guard cutter into giving up its pursuit of the vessel, *Bear Cat.* Messages between the shore station to the ship that were decoded later read: "BEAR CAT: Am now 120 miles South South East Fire Island Lightship and still going. Advise." The shore station's reply: "Keep on going. Cutter not likely stay much longer."

Elizebeth reported that without timely solutions to the smugglers' messages, the Coast Guard vessel stopped trailing the *Bear Cat,* unaware that she was under orders to head out to sea far enough to convince the cutter commander that she would not return. "Having lost her picket the Black promptly returned to the rendezvous designated for two days previous and made contact."[63]

As further proof of the value of cryptanalysis in combating smuggling, Elizebeth mentioned the case of the Canadian-flagged *I'm Alone,* sunk by the Coast Guard in 1929, but still the subject of arbitration between the United States and Canada when the memo was written in 1930. "What is not known, even to the Canadian Government," she wrote, "is the existence of a file of messages in enciphered code, turned over to the American authorities by this office, which show beyond doubt that the owner of the IMALONE was an American." She declared that the "extremely embarrassing" arbitration case against the U.S. "will automatically collapse" when the secret messages proving American ownership of the vessel are presented as evidence.[64]

Finally, Elizebeth noted that the fuel costs of one cutter alone exceeded the total cost of her proposed upgraded cryptographic unit. Thus she concluded that increasing the unit's staff would "be the means of saving many thousands annually in fuel, not of one destroyer or patrol boat, but of every Coast Guard vessel engaged in the struggle against liquor smuggling." It was signed "E.S. Friedman, Cryptanalyst."[65]

The head of the intelligence section, Lieutenant Commander Gorman, believed that nearly all smuggling operations were directed by coded radio messages. Breaking those codes he stated would be such a handicap, that rum running could be cut in half. Thus, Gorman recommended that the appropriation for the upgraded unit be authorized in fiscal year 1931. The alternative, Gorman believed, would keep Mrs. Friedman in the Customs Agency and the Coast Guard would be left to "patrol the seas and operate precisely as if radio had never been heard of, spending hundreds of thousands of dollars in an effort to stumble across the information that is constantly on the air, i.e., the location and contact points of the rum runners."[66]

The arguments were persuasive. Elizebeth, who had been working unofficially with the Coast Guard as an employee of other agencies, was officially transferred to the Coast Guard as Cryptanalyst in Charge in June 1931. The average U.S. worker made $1,388 a year at that time[67]; Elizebeth received a salary of $3,800, $200 less than she had recommended, but still an increase from the $2,400 she had been making.[68] Some rum runner radio operators, however, were making $10,000 a year.[69]

She began hiring and training people for this beefed-up Coast Guard cryptanalytic unit located in a Treasury Department annex.[70] Elizebeth sought people who had passed the civil service examination and had training in the analytical sciences.[71] She wrote that "young people with the proper qualifications should be trained in this mental battle against the underworld of smuggling." She hired "girls" for the stenographer positions. Others with backgrounds in physics, chemistry or math were men; no women with the proper background could be found.

To a veteran cryptographer, the training may have seemed modest: "They were beginning courses in the solution of codes and ciphers without a knowledge of the keys or systems used," Elizebeth wrote. "They were simple, these preliminary lessons and the answers to the questions therein, were to be submitted to me in writing when finished." Yet after administering the course, she dismissed one applicant with a Ph.D. who received the highest mathematics score on the Civil Service exam, but performed poorly in cryptography. She concluded he had a poor understanding of English.[72] Two others that she hired in this group were still with the unit when it was subsumed by the Navy in World War II.[73] The War Department also trained some Coast Guard officers in cryptanalysis during this period,[74] including Leonard T. Jones, who would take over command of the unit from Elizebeth during the war.[75]

Just as this new unit was joining the battle against rum runners, another growing threat called for the cryptanalysts' expertise. Customs officials were finding that opium and other drugs were being smuggled with increasing frequency into the United States. In December 1930 a Bureau of Customs agent in Seattle appealed to the Treasury Department for help from a "Mr. Freeman" who, he wrote, was a civilian employee of the Army Signal Corps and recognized to be a "code expert." The agent enclosed copies of telegrams from a Chinese group "who, without question, are the largest smugglers of smoking opium on the Pacific Coast." He also enclosed some materials he had obtained that might help decode the messages.[76]

The matter that the Seattle agent intended to be forwarded to her husband, actually was referred to Mrs. Friedman. She responded that the agent needed to send even more messages from the Chinese organization "since the very nature of a code system requires considerable traffic to attempt a solution." She added, "With additional messages we shall be glad to do what we can in attempting solution."[77]

Elizebeth's official summary of three years of work breaking rum runners' codes also noted a great increase in requests to solve messages sent by narcotics and alien smuggling rings as well as crooks trying to evade income tax laws. She wrote that she had been called several times as an expert witness in court cases. "The past three years are thus shown to cover a range of work done for the Bureau of Customs, the Coast Guard, the Bureau of Narcotics, the Bureau of Internal Revenue, the Prohibition Bureau, and the Department of Justice."[78]

But even as other illicit ventures gained more prominence, the effort to reduce rum running was law enforcement's priority. The "all-source" intelligence promulgated by the Coast Guard helped reduce illegal seaborne liquor shipments by 60 percent, from 14,000,000 gallons in 1927 to 5,000,000 in 1928. The key factor in the reduction was the reading of the rum runners' codes—so effective, in fact, that to avoid using the radio and the Coast Guard's code breaking, some of them began dropping messages in bottles from airplanes with rendezvous information for the blacks to pick up at sea.[79]

"It is perhaps difficult for anyone who has never attempted to read secret correspondence, to understand just what are the processes involved," Elizebeth finished her summary, educating her superiors who had far less knowledge of cryptography. "This process, which takes so little time to describe, is in reality very laborious, and takes an infinitely longer time to transcribe, even by the correspondents thoroughly familiar with the modus operandi. Now to the non-expert all secret messages present the same appearance. But to the experienced eye a casual inspection will reveal many facts."[80]

This esoteric expertise began to shine a spotlight on Elizebeth Friedman as her work put her on public display in many locations around the country. Called as a witness in several rum running and drug smuggling trials, her star in the cryptography field started to outshine that of her husband, who labored largely in secret. In the next few years Elizebeth's work would be associated with such high-profile liquor and drug smuggling cases such as the *I'm Alone* sinking, the *Holmewood*, the Ezra Brothers, Consolidated Exporters and the Gordon Lim ring.

A decade after Elizebeth began breaking rum runners' codes, after Prohibition's demise, a *Reader's Digest* article described her as the "Key Woman of the T-Men." The author declared: "She is entrusted with more secrets of the crime world and of federal detection activities than any woman in history." As a result of Elizebeth's code breaking, the article continued, gang bosses had gone to prison and millions of dollars of smuggling enterprises had been interrupted.[81]

In some of those cases, federal agents deployed bodyguards to protect her. "After those smugglers got out of prison, some of them were in very, very mean moods," Elizebeth told a reporter years later.[82] "Daddy joked about her being taken for a ride because that's what those mobsters did in those days," the Friedmans' daughter, Barbara, recalls. "And it scared me to death, but also, she was gone quite a bit and I guess we all missed her."[83]

Her family may have laughed it off, yet "it was a very viable threat that they didn't take very seriously," according to Barbara Osteika, the historian for the Bureau of Alcohol, Tobacco, Firearms and Explosives. "Between 1920 and 1933 we lost 97 agents and that's the majority of our agents [killed in the line of duty]," according to Osteika. "So it was not a threat to be taken lightly."[84]

Elizebeth's unpublished memoirs gloss over the dangers she faced in this era. But they do cite incidents that show the public's ambivalence toward Prohibition, including bootleggers having access to the halls of Congress, police delivering liquor to speakeasies in broad daylight and a jury quenching their thirst from the evidence in a trial. "The country was a seething hotbed of irreverence and defiance for this unpopular law," she wrote. Yet her attitude must have been tempered by her law enforcement position. "Neither my husband nor I had ever been consumers of alcohol except an occasional glass of wine and therefore we were not among the people who during prohibition, insisted upon having their drink at all cost."[85]

At the height of Prohibition President Hoover decried that common citizens were condoning the law breaking. In his State of the Union message to Congress in December 1929, Hoover wrote, "If the law is upheld only by Government officials, then all law is at an end." The message continued: "the most serious issue before our people" was the "swift and even-handed administration of justice to all offenders, whether they be rich or poor."[86]

Nearly seven decades after the great social experiment ended, an article from the Center for Cryptologic History analyzed what Elizebeth's contributions meant to America when rum running was the greatest national security challenge: "Historians and sociologists are likely to argue for years about the wisdom of trying to enforce Prohibition.

This photograph of the Friedmans is undated, but is from the Prohibition era. Elizebeth wrote that she and William sometimes had wine, but were not among the people during Prohibition who had to have a drink "at all cost" (courtesy Chris Atchison).

What will not be in dispute is the fact that through a combination of teamwork, perseverance, and the prodigious use of cryptology, Elizebeth Friedman and an intrepid band of Coast Guard cryptanalysts were able to turn the tables on a worthy adversary at a crucial time."[87]

In addition, the seeds of the cryptanalysis unit planted by Elizebeth Friedman during Prohibition continued to bear fruit when the Coast Guard dealt with even greater national security threats in World War II.

=4=

Saving Face
for Uncle Sam

Dawn would soon be breaking over the Gulf of Mexico. The Coast Guard cutter *Wolcott* had been drifting through the night, west of what is now the Shell Keys National Wildlife Refuge on the coast of Louisiana. The skipper cut her engines so they wouldn't give away their position to any "blacks"—cargo vessels carrying illegal shipments of liquor—that were trying to rendezvous with small boats to run the illicit cargo ashore.

Just before six a.m. on March 20, 1929, the *Wolcott's* crew spotted a schooner nearby. They calculated the cutter's position: 29° 22 minutes latitude north, 92° 32 minutes longitude west, ten and a half miles from shore, waters suspected to be a haven for rum runners. The cutter's commander reported: "It was immediately apparent that this vessel, the same distance offshore ... was within the four league limit"—a prime target for interdiction and boarding. The 100-foot patrol boat started her engines and approached the suspect vessel, but the schooner got underway as well and headed south—out toward the open sea.[1]

As the schooner sailed into international waters, the Coast Guard was doing what it could to stop her. The *Wolcott's* skipper, Boatswain Frank Paul, reported, "As soon as it was observed that the sighted vessel was beginning to get underway, at about 6:10 a.m. I gave four blasts repeatedly on the whistle of the *Wolcott* as a signal to said schooner that she was being approached by a vessel of the United States and that we desired her to stop and submit to boarding."[2]

Soon the *Wolcott* came within hailing distance and recognized its quarry. The crew knew this vessel well: It was the *I'm Alone*. They had chased her in these waters without success just two nights before.[3] Yelling through a megaphone, Boatswain Paul demanded that the *I'm Alone* captain cut his engines and head into the wind so that he could be boarded. The Coast Guard's demand was ignored by the schooner's captain, John Randell.[4] The veteran Canadian mariner had endured much worse in his years at sea. As a lieutenant in the Royal Naval Reserve, Randell was decorated by Britain's King George V with a Distinguished Service Cross and by France with a Croix de Guerre for his service in the Great War.[5]

With Randell's refusal, the chase continued. Paul tried again to persuade the *I'm Alone* to submit to inspection. Once again, Randell did not comply. His reply to the Coast Guard: "You can shoot and sink [me] but be damned if you will board me." So Boatswain Paul ordered his crew to fire three blanks from a deck gun across the schooner's bow. Paul reported: "He failed to heave to, and I again demanded by megaphone that he stop. On this occasion, I understood him to reply, 'If you board me, I will shoot to kill.'"[6]

The *Wolcott* radioed the Coast Guard base at Pascagoula, Mississippi for help: "I'M ALONE FOUND TEN MILES FROM THE SHORE LINE REQUEST TWO PATROL BOATS OR A CUTTER TO HELP BOARD SAME FIRED ON RUM RUNNER BUT REFUSES TO STOP THEY THREATENED TO SHOOT TO KILL IF BOARDED ADVISE."[7]

Boatswain Paul organized a party to board the *I'm Alone*, but abandoned that plan when the crew observed Captain Randell strutting the deck with a firearm. Despite his belligerent appearance, the schooner's skipper invited the cutter commander to come aboard his vessel for a chat if he arrived alone and unarmed. Paul accepted and after motoring over in a small boat reported he was treated "courteously." Randell admitted that he was "carrying a load of liquor" and had no intention of going to Bermuda, the port which he had been cleared for when leaving Belize.

"He said further," according to Paul, "that he would never allow his vessel to be seized by the Coast Guard and that he would permit it to be sunk if necessary." After the hour-and-a-half conversation, Paul returned to the *Wolcott*.[8]

The chase and evasion continued into the afternoon, night and into the next day—and the day after that. Another 100-foot cutter,[9] the *Dexter,* was ordered from Pascagoula to join the pursuit as the building wind kept increasing the height of the waves. The cutter arrived at the scene of the confrontation—now about 200 miles offshore—on the morning of March 22nd. The commander of the *Dexter*, Boatswain A.W. Powell, arranged with the *Wolcott's* skipper that the *Dexter* "would make the necessary show of force to compel the *I'm Alone* to stop, and that the crew of the *Wolcott* would perform the boarding duty, if any."[10]

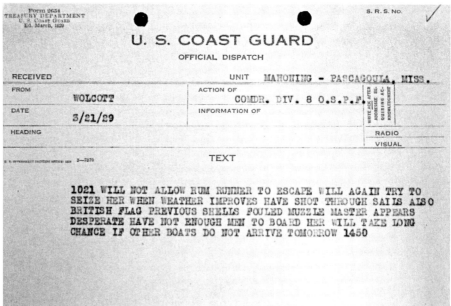

Top: The *I'm Alone* was already well known as an infamous rum runner when the Coast Guard sank the Canadian-flagged vessel in the Gulf of Mexico in 1929. There are several surveillance photographs of the *I'm Alone*, such as this one, in the official files (U.S. Coast Guard, National Archives, Washington, D.C.). *Bottom:* A Coast Guard radio dispatch shows the cutter *Wolcott* had already fired shots at the *I'm Alone* before another cutter sank the vessel a few days later (National Archives, Washington, D.C.).

Now the *Dexter's* commander hailed Randell and ordered him to submit to boarding. Again the effort failed. "At about 8:22 a.m., I directed three-inch gun fire at the *I'm Alone*," reported Powell, "instructing my gun crew to hit her in the rigging and on the main deck forward." That still didn't convince the *I'm Alone* to heave to. Powell ordered another volley to be fired at the suspected "black" as the *I'm Alone* crew huddled at the schooner's stern.[11] "Continuous gun fire was directed at her until approximately 8:58 a.m.," Powell's report continued. "At this time a three-inch shot hit the *I'm Alone* well below the waterline slightly forward the foremast, and tore a large hole in her side. The vessel quickly filled with water, went down by the head, and sank at 9:03 a.m."[12]

The cutter crews lowered dories into the rough seas to rescue the sailors from the Canadian-registered schooner. One of the *I'm Alone* crew drowned.

"I consider it a most cowardly action to blow my boats [sic] to pieces with a gale of wind blowing and a heavy sea running when any man but a strong swimmer would not be expected to live," Captain Randell told investigators when he and his crew were brought ashore in New Orleans two days later. The decorated war veteran complained about being held in leg irons and also denied making the statement that he would "shoot to kill" anyone attempting to board his ship. "I also wish to state that my men and I are shipwrecked seamen, taken out of the water 225 miles from the American coast, and as such claim the protection of our various consuls."[13]

Politicians and newspapers in Canada were merciless in their criticism of the incident. A conservative member of the House of Commons declared the sinking an "act of war."[14] The *Montreal Daily Star* published a cartoon depicting a menacing-looking U.S. Coast Guardsman "improving his technique" in "The *I'm Alone* Shooting Gallery."[15] Not only the Canadians were aggrieved; the British ambassador in Washington called on the State Department to investigate the matter.[16] Protestors in Paris stoned the American embassy and the consulate in Belize required police protection because of the incident.[17]

Soon "His Majesty's Government in Canada" filed a formal protest. It noted a 1924 treaty with the United States in which the U.S. agreed not to search and seize vessels more than "an hour's sailing distance from the shore unless initiated within territorial waters."[18]

The Coast Guard took pains to prove in its documentation that when the *I'm Alone* was first encountered that it was within U.S. waters. Logs of the cutter *Wolcott* indicated the longitude and latitude of the sightings[19]

The surviving crew of the *I'm Alone* claimed the protection of their consulates after their Canadian-flagged schooner was sunk by the U.S. Coast Guard. Captain John Randell is on the left in front. The British vice consul for New Orleans is the man in the hat in the rear (U.S. Coast Guard, National Archives, Washington, D.C.).

and memos revealed that at the start of the incident, the *Wolcott* requested that a tanker within sight of the other two vessels radio its position to the Coast Guard as well.[20] This would help justify the chase under the long-established doctrine of "hot pursuit."

Nevertheless, the Canadians argued that sinking the schooner two days after the chase commenced violated the treaty's provision against seizing ships more than an hour's sail from shore. Thus, the Canadian government sought "redress"[21] and nearly $400,000 compensation for the sinking of the *I'm Alone*.[22]

Getting the United States out of this international mess required cool-headed detective work. The break the detectives needed came from Elizebeth Friedman.

"In my office when we were requested to attempt to ascertain if we had any messages which might be tied in with the particular vessel the I'M ALONE, we found nothing which had so far as we could tell had any bearing on the case. Months went by and nothing turned up," Elizebeth wrote. "The Customs Agency Service, the Alcohol Tax Division and the Coast Guard, were chewing their pencils, racking their brains and getting nowhere."

Eight months after the sinking Elizebeth was ordered to Houston, Texas to attempt to solve a "trunk-full of messages subpoenaed from Western Union" that were evidence in another case. As she decrypted those messages, she discovered "a small number which were totally unrelated to the cases in Texas." As she worked on classifying those unrelated messages, she determined that they had been sent from Belize to recipients in New Orleans and New York. "The cable address used was CARNELHA which was easily determined to be a registered cable address for the Melhado Brothers, the foremost suppliers of liquor in the British Honduras area." That was the port from which the *I'm Alone* embarked on its last voyage.

On the receiving end, the cable addresses in New York were for either HARFORAN or MOCANA. "Since my husband was so well known in the world of communications companies," Elizebeth continued, "I asked him to ascertain, if possible, the identities of the New York cable addresses HARFORAN and MOCANA. He learned that both these addresses were used for one Joseph H. Foran, Hotel McAlpine, New York City." The second address, MOCANA, suggested that it had been intended for someone in Montreal.

On her return to Washington, Elizebeth made a side trip to New Orleans to meet with Edson Shamhart, the supervisor of the Customs

Photostat of a Western Union telegram with a coded message from Belize to Mocana in New York. Elizebeth Friedman's decryptions of a "trunk-full" of such messages helped federal investigators prove the *I'm Alone* was involved in rum running and was owned by U.S. gangsters (National Archives, Washington, D.C.).

office there. She presented the "unrelated" messages she had found in Houston and explained that she decoded them using a pocket edition of *Bentley's Complete Phrase Code*. She told Shamhart they also had a second layer of code from a specially-prepared supplement to *Bentley's*, using five-letter groups starting with W, Y or Z, that disguised the full meaning of the messages.[23]

An original message on a Western Union telegram form on January 30, 1929, was a jumble of letters: "MOCANA = NEWYORK (NY) = UGUCKMIOSD EPUJSAFAGS PEJYTUSENZ MITEPLPUJS REKRONY AZ POUDYYIOVB."

When Elizebeth partially decoded the message, it read: "Belize, January 30 1929. To MOCANA, New York. Referring to telegram of 29th, 8000 dollars additional required. Total amount 12000 dollars. Shall we pack in sacks (YIOVB)."

From a March 4th telegram from Belize, "MOCANA = NEWYORK (NY) = WYBABUCEGZ WYELMUCEFY LEVIRYIBUH LEVIRYICFE LOHOP-WYDOH AKBUZWYERS WYEMN," Elizebeth made this solution: "MOCANA, New York. WYBAB. Cannot supply. WYELM. Can supply 50. YIBUH, 50 YICFE, 500 WYDOH, also WYERS, WYEMN."[24]

She left the messages with Shamhart, suggesting that the five-letter words starting with W, Y and Z referred to brands of liquors. Ten days later, Elizebeth recounted that the Customs agent started matching her decryptions with other documents. "After a few minutes, Mr. Shamhart, with a shout, leaped out of his chair, he told me, when he observed that the dates in the twenty some messages I had left ... matched the sailing dates of the I'M ALONE."

As investigators pored over the decoded messages, plus documents they had received from the American consul in Belize, they began to build a case against the *I'm Alone*. A December 28, 1924, message had an order for 1700 YINOS and 300 YICKY. The *I'm Alone* cargo manifest for the same date showed it carried three lots of William Penn whiskey: the first lot with 200 cases, the second lot 1000 and the third lot 500 cases, for a total of 1700 cases. That accounted for YINOS; YICKY was another lot of 300 cases of malt liquor.

Elizebeth continued to work on the codes when she got back to Washington. She found additional meanings for some of the messages including that the five-letter groups of W, Y or Z meant not just brands of liquors, but people and places as well.[25]

"There was no question but what the messages I had isolated in Houston were messages to, from or for the I'M ALONE," Elizebeth concluded.

It also confirmed what the Coast Guard, Customs officers and the Bureau of Prohibition had suspected for years: the sole purpose of the *I'm Alone* was to make money as a rum runner.[26]

The Coast Guard had been tracking the *I'm Alone* since 1924. Records, listing her as a British schooner, indicate that she had made runs from the Bahamas, Cuba and Belize and was spotted several times near Cape Cod, Nantucket or Boston. The next to last entry was on March 12, 1929: "Cleared Belize for Bermuda with cargo of liquor." Eight days later, two days before she was sunk, the last entry indicated that the schooner was near Louisiana: "8 Miles N.W. Trinity Shoal, La."[27]

In fact, after being sunk, Captain Randell told interrogators that he had made two previous trips on the *I'm Alone* transporting liquor to the Trinity Shoals light buoy, one in November 1928 and the other in January 1929. Each time he was carrying a torn dollar bill given to him in Belize. He did not know the accomplices picking up his goods, so to make sure that the illicit cargo was delivered to the right person, the small boat operator offloading the liquor had to show the matching half of the dollar bill to Randell.[28]

Another piece of information turned up by the Coast Guard from sources in Boston indicated that when the *I'm Alone* was sunk, the cargo "consisted largely of narcotics, which was the principal reason for the desperate effort of the I'M ALONE to escape capture."[29] But Captain Randell told authorities that the only narcotics he had on board was "a small quantity of tincture of opium in my medicine chest which is authorized by all merchant service ships."[30]

The allegations of smuggling drugs were never proven. There was solid evidence, however, of the *I'm Alone's* rum running. Built using a "Boston fishing rig" design with enough speed to quickly bring a fresh catch of fish from the Grand Banks to market,[31] the *I'm Alone's* twin 100-horsepower engines could often outrun a patrol boat when the vessels crossed paths.[32]

An intelligence memo to the Coast Guard commandant the year before the *I'm Alone* went down also indicated the cutter *Agassiz* had difficulty following the suspected rum runner because she was towing three pieces of "old hawser[33] astern" to "discourage close contact between the vessels." That memo reported: "The I'M ALONE is a vessel that is very difficult to trail, her master being very adept in losing picketing vessels in a fog or blinding snow storm."[34]

The case was strong that the *I'm Alone* was engaged in rum running. What investigators still needed was evidence of something else they suspected, but could not prove: that the schooner was owned by U.S. mobsters—not Canadians.

One official document, from the U.S. Consulate in Yarmouth, Nova Scotia in April 1928, just a year before she was shot into her watery grave, reported "that the notorious liquor smuggling Schooner I'M ALONE has recently been sold to Robin, Jones and Whitman, Lunenburg, Nova Scotia. I am informed that the firm is engaged in the fishing business and that it is quite likely that the vessel is now permanently withdrawn from liquor smuggling."[35]

In his interrogation after being sunk, the *I'm Alone's* master, Captain Randell, told investigators that he was employed by the Eastern Seaboard Steamship Company of Lunenburg. He said he received his instructions from George Hearn, who was the company's general manager.[36]

Those statements increased the burden on American officials to prove that the schooner's owners were indeed U.S. citizens.

Agent Shamhart went to New York to track down the cable leads from Elizabeth's decryptions, but could find nothing on Joseph Foran at the McAlpine Hotel. A subpoena turned up an unlisted phone number for Foran in an apartment on 58th Street. Shamhart had an idea that Foran was actually Dan Hogan, who had been suspected of smuggling operations before. Shamhart took a U.S. Marshal and another agent to stake out the apartment, hoping to nab Hogan with just a description of the suspect.

After several hours two men drove up to the apartment building. Shamhart recognized one as Dan Hogan. Elizabeth recalled the encounter in her memoirs: "Unfortunately, Mr. Shamhart and his aids [sic] were not armed and the man they were after was armed, as well as an Italian cross-eyed bodyguard who accompanied him. The three federal men had no choice but to jump the two armed men, if (bullets, bluff) didn't work. Mr. Shamhart opened up the encounter by stepping forward and speaking to the two suspects saying, 'my men have you covered, you're under arrest Hogan.'"[37]

When booked, however, Hogan said they had arrested the wrong man: he said his real name was David Martin. Just prior to a hearing before a U.S. commissioner the next morning, a man with a briefcase approached the suspects asking, "Which of you is Dan Hogan?" The man identifying himself as Martin to authorities replied that he was Hogan.

Shamhart told the commissioner that he had no physical proof of the man's identification, but related what he had witnessed before the hearing. The commissioner ruled that Hogan/Martin should be held.

During that incarceration witnesses from Louisiana arrived in New

York and identified Martin as Hogan, known to them as the "Capone of the Bayous." After digging some more, authorities found another alias for Hogan, Daniel Halpern. He was a convict who headed a syndicate that did $15 million worth of smuggling each year. Agents were also interested in tracking down someone by the name of James Clark, whose car registration had been discovered in Hogan's New York apartment.[38]

Investigators in Louisiana also had been working other cases involving Hogan. While searching the swamps for evidence, Edson Shamhart and another agent were wounded by gunfire. Both were hospitalized, but recovered.[39]

A few months after the *I'm Alone* sinking, a grand jury issued an indictment for another smuggling case. It charged five people, including Daniel Halpern, alias Daniel Hogan, and G.J. Hearn of Montreal, the same man whom Captain Randell had named as issuing him instructions for the *I'm Alone's* smuggling operations.[40] One of those indicted, A.J. Delorsie, soon was talking to authorities from jail in Pensacola, Florida. Delorsie admitted he worked for Marvin J. "Big Jim" Clark, another liquor smuggler in Louisiana. That was the same Clark whose car registration was found in Hogan's New York apartment. Delorsie told an interrogator that on a trip to New Orleans, "Big Jim introduced Dan Hogan to me as his partner."[41]

With that, the *I'm Alone's* convoluted ownership—all seemingly by Canadians—began unraveling.

The vessel had been through a twisted title trail in its last few years. That made it difficult for investigators to pin down the true owners when she was sunk. In February 1925, the *I'm Alone* was in the hands of the Eugene Creaser Shipping Company of Lunenburg, Nova Scotia.[42] Three years later ownership transferred to Christian Iverson and his son, who then turned over a blank bill of sale to George Hearn. Hearn used the blank bill of sale to transfer the controlling interest of the schooner to Eastern Seaboard Steamship Agencies Limited on September 28, 1928. By the end of the year, that company was in liquidation and Hearn transferred the ship back to the Eugene Creaser Shipping Company, with Hearn in control.[43]

Facing a long stretch in prison on another smuggling conviction in 1932, Big Jim began spilling what he knew to agents in an effort to get leniency when he came up for sentencing. Clark told investigators that in the fall of 1928 Danny Hogan and a Frank Reitman invited him to join them in purchasing the *I'm Alone* for $20,000. Hogan and Clark each put down $5,000 for the venture; Reitman was in for $10,000. As the group's nautical expert, Big Jim was the one designated by his American partners to go to Nova Scotia in November 1928 to complete the deal. He negotiated the purchase price down to $18,000. Hearn received $500 for arranging the deal.[44]

On paper, the schooner still belonged to the Eugene Creaser Shipping Company. One of the former owners, however, told a U.S. investigator in Canada that Hearn was just a front; in reality he held the *I'm Alone* "in trust for the American parties."[45]

Clark declared his version of events in a sworn deposition for U.S. authorities. More details about the group's smuggling activities added credence to his tale. He told investigators, for example, that he commanded one of the small boats off the coast of Louisiana picking up liquor from the *I'm Alone* and had presented his half of a torn dollar bill to Captain Randell for identification. After making his deposition, Clark was released on bail while awaiting sentencing.[46]

A few months later Clark was shot to death in New Orleans. The killer was never caught; a smuggler associated with Big Jim, however, was strongly suspected of killing him for squealing to the authorities.[47]

The codes used by the *I'm Alone* would play still another role in unraveling the true ownership of the schooner.

One of the messages Elizebeth had decoded and given to Agent Shamhart indicated that the radioman on the schooner in its final months of operation was not very adept at using codes. "Cannot send or receive message. Operator no good," a December 6, 1928, message to MOCANA in New York said.[48] While investigating other cases in the Louisiana bayou, agents discovered a suitcase with a library book about wireless use. They surmised it belonged to the *I'm Alone's* radio operator. Clark told investigators that the smugglers got tired of struggling through the swamps with their liquor and other materials; the radio operator had abandoned the suitcase with the text. Agents tracked the book's New Jersey library card and got a statement from the radio operator who had checked it out, adding another testimonial against the *I'm Alone* and its owners.

"Thus it was that the evidence piled up slowly and painfully," Elizebeth wrote. "And finally the American investigators had what they felt, at least in the mass of it all put together, would prove their original suspicions which later had become a contention, but still disputed by the Canadian government, that the vessel I'M ALONE had been owned and operated entirely by Americans and was simply masking under Canadian registry and the British flag, but that the money invested was purely American."[49]

For her work, Elizebeth—though not explicitly named—received a pat on the back from her boss in a memo to the Coast Guard commandant. On December 28, 1929, Captain Charles Root summarized the investigation to date, with the indictments of Hogan/Halpern, Hearn and Delorsie. "I believe that we have at last found the owner of the I'M ALONE," wrote Root. He indicated that "intercepted cipher messages" provided clues, that when pieced together with "other facts which we had on file," pointed toward Halpern, an American, as the schooner's owner: "If we can prove this we have the Canadian Government in an awkward position."

Root concluded his memo with a reminder of the key role that cryptanalysis had played in solving the case: "I think that the results obtained in this case well illustrate the value of time and trouble which we have taken to break the enemy's communications."[50]

"The more you know, the more you see," Bureau of Alcohol, Tobacco, Firearms and Explosives historian, Barbara Osteika, said about Elizebeth's key role in the *I'm Alone* case. "She sees a reference to something. That's all source intelligence; she takes that and adds it to her puzzle that she's working on over here. No one else may have noticed that statement that was in there except for her because she's got this broad vision because she's working an entire link chart."[51]

Five years after making the breakthrough, however, Elizebeth Friedman still was not finished with the *I'm Alone.*

In 1934 the joint American-Canadian commission appointed to arbitrate the grievance over the sinking of the *I'm Alone* met to consider the United States' culpability. The commission convened its preliminary sessions in Ottawa. Elizebeth prepared an affidavit for the commission[52] and was called to testify at a hearing in Washington in December 1934.

"I was very much interested in this meeting," she recalled. "The two high Commissioners and all elements of the case excited my interest as I'd been told that I would be among the first witnesses to be called, and I was looking to the hearing to catch a personal glimpse of many of the principals in this now almost six year old dispute."[53]

The commissioners appointed to hear the case were Sir Lyman Poore Duff, the chief justice of Canada's Supreme Court, and an associate justice of the United States Supreme Court, Willis Van Devanter.[54] Counsel for both sides wore formal attire, befitting the occasion in what Elizebeth described as "the beautiful walnut paneled hearing room."[55]

Mrs. Friedman was examined by the U.S. counsel, Claude Pepper, a future U.S. senator and congressman from Florida.[56] He wondered about the process she used to decode the more than 20 messages that led to tracking down the culprits who operated—and more importantly, owned—the ill-fated schooner.

"They stood so apart from the rest that I appended a note to my copy of the messages which I handed Mister Shamhart saying that they differed from the rest of the correspondence, and had no connection with the cases then pending," Elizebeth testified.

"Will you tell the Commissioners just what you did in order to accomplish the solution of them?" Pepper asked.

"I recognized the code groups of the messages," she responded.

"Code groups?" Justice Van Devanter queried.

"There are two classes of secret message," Elizebeth answered. "One is cipher, and one is code. I recognized these at once as being in the class of codes. I recognized them, furthermore, as being groups which came from a certain very well known and commonly used commercial code book called *Bentley's Complete Phrase Code*.

"The messages did not yield plain language at once," she continued.

"I mean to say by that that the code group which you see here as 'Jeylv' did not have opposite the plain language meaning which I show in my affidavit, but the plain language meaning was found in every case five places removed in the code book. It is a very definite and easily checked system."

Pepper wanted clarification on how she was able to work through the book to determine the five-line separation process that broke the code.

"In checking the series of messages which I had, in every

Claude Pepper, shown here later as a United States senator from Florida, argued the U.S. case before the joint commission with Canada that arbitrated the *I'm Alone* case (Library of Congress).

case that method yielded plain language which made perfect sense," Elizebeth remarked. She added that the system of "encryptographing" was a form of enciphering "superimposed" upon a code. "It might be ten places removed in a different direction, it might be three places, it might be a hundred places removed, and that is a matter of experimentation, and by analysis it is discovered."

Justice Van Devanter suggested that cryptographers, instead of just displacing five lines to achieve a superenciphered message, often might "join five, six, seven, or some other lines." Then he asked whether Mrs. Friedman had "applied that knowledge" to see whether there was something that would explain the meaning of "these peculiar letters."

"Yes," Elizebeth replied. "This, of course, is a very simple form of encipherment. A number such as 1000, 2000, 3000, the number '987'

U.S. Supreme Court Justice Willis Van Devanter, shown here, along with Canada's Chief Justice Sir Lyman Poore Duff, judged the case in the bilateral commission investigating the *I'm Alone* incident. Justice Van Devanter questioned how Elizebeth Friedman determined that "code groups" proved the vessel was carrying liquor (Library of Congress).

might be used, to be added or subtracted from the original code group, and is still, if consistent throughout the use of the system ... and reduced to plain language, would be a proof that that was the system used."[57]

With that, Elizebeth Friedman's discourse on cryptography for the bilateral tribunal ended. But she remained at the hearing, fascinated by the cast of characters she had helped investigate, but had never seen. "Among those I was most interested to see, of course, were Dan Hogan himself ... and the master, Captain Randall [sic] of the sunken vessel, whose appearances before the public in Canada after the crew had been returned to Canada, whose statements to the press had been flamboyant and inflammatory."[58]

Hogan was under heavy guard in the courtroom, having been brought to the hearing from a federal penitentiary in Pennsylvania, where he was serving time for violating the National Prohibition Act. Since another potential witness had been murdered, Pepper presented the commission with an affidavit from the late Big Jim Clark that asserted the ownership of the *I'm Alone* was in American hands when she was sunk.[59]

As she watched the testimony and the interaction between attorneys for the two nations, Elizebeth recognized how her work had allowed the United States to build a convincing case for the commissioners. Her memoirs noted that the Canadian counsel, John Read, had admitted that the CARNELHA-MOCANA messages between Belize and New York that she had decoded "made a very clear picture of the operations of the vessel in the transfer of liquor in the smuggling operations which had clearly taken place; that these messages had definitely been shown to have a connection with Hogan and Clark."

In addition, investigators building upon Elizebeth's work provided information that allowed Pepper to examine George Hearn about the source of the money used to purchase the schooner. Hearn "admitted that the boat had been bought with American currency, being the cash dollars that Hearn had carried with him back to Canada from the United States in 1927." It was strong evidence that Hogan and Clark were the real owners of the *I'm Alone*, while Hearn was just their agent and messenger.[60]

With Big Jim Clark gunned down and two agents wounded while seeking evidence associated with these mobsters, an aura of danger hung over the hearing. As a key witness, a U.S. agent was assigned to protect Elizebeth inside and outside the courtroom. "I was given a word of caution by the Customs agents who had been so influential in carrying out the investigations. I was told by these men that both Hogan and Captain Randall [sic] were in what they termed as a mean frame of mind. I think they did not tell me in so many words but I got by implication their feeling that I should be a bit careful during this trial. This feeling was reinforced at the end of the case when I was told in so many words, that if ever in my battle against smugglers I would have needed a personal guard it would have been at the time of this incident."[61]

In the first week of January 1935, the joint commission issued its findings: that although the *I'm Alone* was a British ship of Canadian registry, she "was de facto owned, controlled and, at the critical times, managed and her movements directed and her cargo dealt with and disposed of by a group of persons acting in concert who were entirely or nearly so, citizens of the United States." Yet the findings indicated that the sinking was "not justified" and that the United States should apologize to Canada and pay $25,000 to His Majesty's Canadian Government.[62]

Elizebeth's decoded messages, revealing YINOS, YICKYS and other five-letter combinations stood for types of liquor, meant the Canadians could not dispute that the vessel was engaged in illegal rum running. Thus, the tribunal ruled that no compensation should be paid for the ship or cargo.

In addition, commissioners ruled that none of the crew was "a party to the illegal conspiracy to smuggle liquor into the United States." So they decided that the family of the sailor who drowned when the *I'm Alone* was sunk should receive $10,185. Commissioners also recommended compensation for the rest of the crew.[63] Captain Randell had testified that he could not get a job as a mariner after the sinking and had been working as a miner in Quebec and Newfoundland.[64] So, he was awarded $7,906. The commissioners said the other seven members of the crew should receive amounts ranging from $1250.50 to $965. Thus, the total monetary damages assessed against the United States came to $50,666.50.[65]

The U.S. secretary of state, as a result of the ruling, apologized to Canada for sinking the schooner.[66] Yet the compensation required was far less than the $386,803.13 that the Canadian government had sought.

So, four years after she had hinted in a memo to her superiors that the Canadian case would "automatically collapse" as a result of her breaking the rum runners' secrets,[67] Elizebeth's breakthrough, discovering connections from a trunk full of seemingly unrelated messages and then solving the codes in those messages—plus a lot of dogged detective work by various American agents—proved the *I'm Alone* was not Canadian-owned. As a result, the United States saved face in the international community and 336,000 taxpayer dollars—a princely sum in the Great Depression.

A few days after the joint commission's ruling, Elizebeth received a letter from the State Department's chief counsel in the case, William R. Vallance. He sent three copies of the commission's final report and stated his gratitude: "I want to take this occasion to express my deep appreciation of your unfailing cooperation and able assistance in bringing about the disallowance of all claims for damages for the vessel and the cargo. It is indeed a pleasure to work with an officer of your energy and resourcefulness."[68]

In an intelligence memo outlining the key role cryptanalysis had played in proving the *I'm Alone's* U.S. provenance, Coast Guard Commandant Frederick Billard had scrawled, "Most interesting and gratifying."[69]

Coast Guard Commandant Frederick C. Billard wrote that the role cryptanalysis played in exonerating the United States in the *I'm Alone* incident was "gratifying." In 1930, he also took Elizebeth Friedman's vision for an enhanced Coast Guard cryptanalytic unit to Congress to argue for funding (Library of Congress).

Elizebeth Friedman must have felt the same way.

═5═

A High Profile

As her children grew older and the cryptanalytical work became increasingly complicated and more hectic, Elizebeth Friedman found it more conducive to work at Coast Guard headquarters instead of at home, as she had when she first started breaking rum runner codes in 1925. So, after forming the expanded cryptanalysis section in 1931, with Elizebeth as Cryptanalyst in Charge, the head of the intelligence section requested an unlimited pass for her to enter the restricted-access annex to the Treasury Department. "The work of this unit requires frequent conferences and consultations with the Bureau of Customs, Bureau of Prohibition, Department of Justice and War Department," wrote Lieutenant Commander F.J. Gorman. "Frequent trips to Congressional and Public Libraries are made for reference books and data. The work is often of an emergent character and it is necessary ... to remain during the prescribed lunch hour, or after office hours."[1]

As the tempo of the work changed, the decade of the 30s also brought a load of high profile cases to Elizebeth's desk. In addition to testifying in the *I'm Alone* international tribunal, there were more rum running trials—and narcotics cases became more frequent as well. When the United States shook off Prohibition, dope smuggling gangs began to take precedence for the cryptanalytic unit. As she was called as a witness in highly publicized cases—for both liquor and drug offenses—Elizebeth Friedman's name started to circulate among newspapers and magazines nationwide. That became a mixed blessing for the woman who essentially labored in private, but found the public taking a great deal of interest in her arcane, secretive field.

When requests for interviews, information or appearances—which arrived from a wide variety of groups and people—first started coming in, Elizebeth dealt with them cheerfully. An early example was from an editor of her college sorority magazine, the *Arrow of Pi Beta Phi*. In a January 1930 letter Elizebeth apologized for not responding for two months to a request for information on an article about her: "I returned on November 10 from a month's absence in the South–where I deciphered, you may be interested to know, more than six hundred messages in twenty three different systems–and had not had a chance to get 'caught up' when on November 12 my housekeeper of seven years standing was taken ill. I have not yet found a satisfactory successor." She added that she had also undertaken graduate studies and was a "working member" of the board of the League of Women Voters. She signed, "Sincerely in Pi Beta Phi, Elizebeth Smith, '15 (Mrs. William Friedman)."[2]

Over the coming decade, the U.S. government would demand more of Elizebeth's time, not only managing the new cryptanalysis section, but traveling coast-to-coast to decipher messages collected by investigators or to testify as an expert before grand juries or in the smuggling trials of mobsters.[3] There is an iconic photo of her,[4] posing in a cloche hat, cloth overcoat with briefcase and purse in hand, standing near the front door of her Military Road home, poised for action in the battle against organized crime.

"Without Elizebeth, there was no one else to break out the intelligence that they needed, because really the first step is code breaking," according to Barbara Osteika, the historian for the Bureau of Alcohol, Tobacco, Firearms and Explosives. "She went out and visited agents in the field and would talk to them about their cases and about ... their informants and information they had picked up on their wiretaps, things that they had seen. She would actually physically go to these locations and she called it feet on the ground to see what they were seeing." As a result, it was Elizebeth who often started putting the intelligence together to steer investigators in the direction of their target.[5]

One of the cases that would take the most effort and time for her was Consolidated Exporters Company. By 1933, CONEXCO, as the group was known, controlled smuggling on both the west coast and Gulf of Mexico. It had become the largest and most powerful smuggling operation known to law enforcement.[6]

Elizebeth's involvement with investigating CONEXCO coincided with her start in reading rum runners' codes in 1925. At that time she recorded in a memo that Pacific Coast smugglers were divided between two groups, the Hobbs Brothers and Consolidated Exporters. The two negotiated to join forces in 1928.[7]

In 1931 CONEXCO's New Orleans headquarters was raided by Bureau of Prohibition agents.[8] Letters seized there as well as radio messages intercepted by the Coast Guard in Mobile were forwarded to the cryptanalysis section for decoding.[9] By 1932, the U.S. attorney in New Orleans was ready to go public with his case. Coast Guard officials received a subpoena for Elizebeth to appear before a grand jury. The Director of Prohibition informed her superiors: "This letter is only for the purpose of advising you that she will be needed, in order that you may have an opportunity to arrange for her to be away from her work in Washington for the time that she is needed in New Orleans."[10]

Never an agency to waste an opportunity in its war on smuggling, the Coast Guard sent Mrs. Friedman to help in other investigations along the Gulf while she was away from Washington. "At the conclusion of your duties before the Judge of the United States District Court at New Orleans Louisiana, in answer to a subpoena, and when released by the court or the United States Attorney, and while in route from New Orleans, La., to Washington, D.C., to resume your regular status," the commandant ordered, "you are directed to stop off at Mobile, Alabama, for a conference with the Intelligence Officer, U.S. Coast Guard, at that place." On that trip Elizebeth received a per diem travel allowance of $5.[11]

Elizebeth's testimony was crucial in gaining the indictment of 100 CONEXCO conspirators, including its ringleader, Bert Morrison. A Coast Guard memo outlines how Elizebeth's unit played a key role in linking the men to the smuggling operation. "There was only one way in which this could be done and that was through the radio messages in code and cipher originating in the office and illicit radio station of the Consolidated Exporters Company's agents in New Orleans, which show that the defendants actually directed the movements of the smuggling vessels."[12]

The memo credits Elizebeth and her unit with decoding "hundreds of radio messages" that the Coast Guard had intercepted between "blacks" and shore stations. "All of these messages were forwarded to Headquarters where they were deciphered, decoded and systematized by the Cryptanalysis Section."[13]

In May 1933, Elizebeth again received a subpoena to appear in New Orleans, this time at the trial of Bert Morrison and the other alleged conspirators of CONEXCO, including Al Capone's brother and others who had ties to the notorious Capone gang.[14] The trial was so important in the battle against rum runners, that the Department of Justice assigned the former Bureau of Prohibition director, Colonel Amos W.W. Woodcock, as a special assistant to the attorney general to prosecute the case.[15]

The government spent the unheard of sum of $500,000 to prepare its case against the 25 smugglers who eventually came to trial. The charge against Morrison was that he was the land agent for the operation, arranging liquor to be smuggled into the U.S. from Mexico and British Honduras. His co-defendants were charged with operating the boats that brought the cargo ashore.[16] A conspiracy conviction required prosecutors to tie together the smuggling vessels, illicit radio shore stations and the "bosses" who controlled the operations. To do that they needed CONEXCO's radio messages to be decrypted.[17] Thus, Elizebeth would be the key witness for the prosecution.

When Elizebeth was called to testify, however, defense attorneys raised an immediate objection. They argued that her testimony would be personal opinion, not based on science. Nevertheless, Judge Charles B. Kennamer permitted her to testify, ruling that Mrs. Friedman was a scientific expert.

Once her testimony began, reporters and editors sensationalized the event. One newspaper headlined her appearance for the prosecution: "CLASS IN CRYPTOLOGY."

Among the items she testified about was a message that declared the smugglers were "OUT OF OLD COLONEL IN PINTS." Another message that Elizebeth decoded ordered the liquor to be transferred from one ship to another on the high seas. After her initial examination by prosecutors, she was cross examined by attorneys for the defendants. Asked why certain "blanks" appeared in her translation of some of the code messages, Mrs. Friedman replied that, "I may be an expert on secret writing, but I am not an expert on names of liquors. Those blanks concerned cargoes of various types of liquor."

One defense attorney, Edwin H. Grace, questioned whether the cipher word for alcohol might just as well mean bananas or coconuts. Elizebeth replied that "once any particular cipher system is worked out, no doubt can be entertained as to any single word appearing in a sentence." She went on to proclaim that any other code expert would translate the messages "precisely as I have done."

"I recall very well the conduct of the class, as it was referred to in the foregoing news item," Elizebeth wrote in her unpublished memoirs. "The defense attornies [sic] had more or less naggingly continued questioning for sometime trying to trick me in one way or another and one of the things that they hit upon was to state that the names of liquors which I had used in the decipherment of the messages were not produced." Then she describes how reporters may have come up with the cryptology class theme. "I sought an opportunity here to silence the cross-examination in a decisive manner. I turned to the judge and said, 'Your honor, is there a blackboard available to the court?'"

The judge directed the marshal to bring in a blackboard.

> I was very quickly able to demonstrate the validity of the cipher method which had been used for the names of the liquors in many of the messages because that method was simple mono-alphabetic encipherment. For example OLD COLONEL has three el's and three o's. I put the words OLD COLONEL on the blackboard in caps and placed beneath the letters their cipher equivalents, thus the three o's were shown in each case to be the identical cipher letter and three el's likewise. E, the most frequently appearing letter in English and therefore is usually represented by the letter which appears most often in a frequency table of any mono-alphabetic cipher, was present here only once but there were other names of brands which of course contained one or more appearances of the letter E.

Elizebeth scanned her documents while testifying: "My eye was able to catch quickly brand names which contained more than one occurance [sic] of the letter E and also the word alcohol with el's and o's which, when put upon the blackboard, revealed the same cipher letters as had been used for the el's and o's of the OLD COLONEL."

Elizebeth summed up the results of her courtroom class: "By this time the defense attornies [sic] were nervously indicating that they had had enough of this black and white proof, that is, the blackboard proof and not black and white whiskey."[18]

Morrison and the other defendants were convicted and received the maximum sentence; their convictions and sentences were upheld on appeal. Later, when other members of the CONEXCO ring came to trial, Elizebeth's decoded messages also played a key role in their convictions.[19]

Elizebeth recalled that her testimony in the Morrison case, with text and photo coverage all around the country, "seemed to set the press on fire."[20]

The special prosecutor also was impressed by Mrs. Friedman's appearance in the Bert Morrison trial—so much so that he wrote a memo to the secretary of the Treasury, whose department managed the Coast Guard. "I am taking the liberty to bring to your attention the unusual service rendered by Mrs. Elizabeth [sic] Smith Friedman in the trial of the largest smuggling case which the Bureau of Prohibition made during the last two years," wrote Colonel Woodcock.

> Mrs. Friedman was summoned as an expert witness to testify as to the meaning of certain intercepted radio code messages. These messages were sent to and from Belize, Honduras, New Orleans, and ships at sea. Without their translations, I do not believe that this very important case could have been won.
> Mrs. Friedman made an unusual impression upon the jury. Her description of

the art of deciphering and decoding established in the minds of all her entire competency to testify. It would have been a misfortune of the first magnitude in the prosecution of this case not to have had a witness of Mrs. Friedman's qualifications and personality available.[21]

Woodcock's letter came at an opportune time for the Coast Guard Cryptanalysis Section. Less than two months before, the unit had received an efficiency rating of only 87 percent. That prompted Elizabeth's superior in the intelligence office, F.J. Gorman, to write the Coast Guard's chief clerk explaining the unique nature of the cryptanalysts' work. He argued that with only seven people in the unit, who deal "with material of an unknown nature," it "necessitates a considerably lower marking for the individual personnel of the section than would be necessary did the section consist of fifty, thirty, or even fifteen people."

The memo goes on to explain that some of the people in the section have done "exacting and meticulous" work and that "Mrs. Friedman's services are frequently requested by other bureaus and departments is in itself a testimonial to her professional capacity and experience."[22]

Thus, when Colonel Woodcock's letter praising Elizabeth's service in the Morrison/CONEXCO trial arrived a few weeks later, Commander Gorman jumped on the chance to extol her status as a "star witness" in the case. He also highlighted in his memo to the commandant, the unique niche the Coast Guard's cryptanalytic unit had filled in the struggle against smugglers. "It is an interesting commentary on this phase of law enforcement that the Coast Guard is the only agency of the Government connected with law enforcement which has such an extremely valuable section. The Department of Justice has no such section and in fact the only Department of the Government that does similar work is the Signal Corps of the War Department. The Navy, and its code building section, as one or two experts whose work is mainly directed toward the insuring of efficiency in Navy codes, but has no section which devotes its time to the deciphering and decoding of secret communications of all types."

Gorman closed his memo urging that the letter from Colonel Woodcock commending Mrs. Friedman's work be included in her personnel file. "The Bureau of Narcotics and the Bureau of Customs, Department of Justice, and other agencies of the Government, frequently send codes and ciphers to this office for solution, which was one of the aims when the unit was established—that of making the Coast Guard known as the law enforcement agency of the Government, in control of radio intelligence and cryptanalysis."[23]

In another case associated with the conspirators in the infamous *I'm*

Alone Canadian rum runner, a courtroom confrontation with a female defense attorney made an impression on Elizebeth. She described her as "a very buxom young woman, highly colored as to complextion [sic] with flashing black eyes and hair, and horror of horrors, shifting a wad of gum from one side of her mouth to the other as she addressed the Judge."

Elizebeth described this attorney, Sadie Bevalacqua, as having no more than a high school education, who associated with characters skirting the Prohibition laws in the Galveston area. At that time, there was no requirement for a lawyer to have studied the law in Texas, Elizebeth writes, but had to be approved by the board of Fire Examiners, which she noted were all men who were impressed by "Sadie's appearance and her vocal affluence."

As Elizebeth began testifying in a case against the Melhado brothers, whom Bevalacqua represented, the attorney objected that a decrypted message referring to "coconuts" could have been an innocuous reference to the fruit and not really liquor as the prosecution alleged. She requested the judge to require Elizebeth to explain her code breaking more fully.

"I thereupon, after the judges [sic] command, launched into an explanation of the terms code and cipher which I LOADED with as many technical terms as possible and made as complicated as possible and sat directly addressing Mrs. Bevalacqua hardly able to conceal my amusement as I saw her like a drowning sailor sinking underneath my barrage of polysyllabic phraseology. Sadie Bevalacqua struggled to her feet after about three minutes of my discourse and said, 'I object.' This statement on her part brought some laughter in the courtroom. For an attorney to object to the explanation which the attorney herself had demanded."

The judge overruled Bevalacqua's objection, saying, "You asked for this explanation, now you're going to listen to it." Despite that favorable ruling, the prosecution lost the case since they had failed to produce enough evidence to show the defendants were the ones using the aliases in Elizebeth's decrypted messages.[24]

Despite that setback, the Coast Guard seemed to be very proud of its cryptanalysts' accomplishments in a wide variety of liquor smuggling cases. Yet other agencies may have resented their prominent role in busting rum runners. Elizebeth noted in her memoirs, "As usual among government agencies, there was rivalry, many of the cases of those caught in this ramified game of rum smuggling were the source of jealousy and some suspicion among these operating agencies."[25]

That rivalry extended to branches within the Coast Guard as well.

In the fall of 1933 Customs agents and the Coast Guard combined to bust a British freighter carrying liquor that—in a clever ruse—had made it several miles up the Hudson River before being captured. This case made the headlines, too, but the New York Intelligence Office's effort to take credit for breaking the code[26] that busted the *Holmewood*,[27] raised Elizebeth Friedman's hackles.

Elizebeth began tracking intercepted radio codes regarding the *Holmewood* in November 1930. At that time she detected the ship and shore stations using a digraphic cipher. That is where two letters replace two different letters of the alphabet, instead of one letter standing for one other letter. In other words, instead of a "P" standing in for "T" and "X" substituting for "H," the digraphic cipher would use "PX" every time the letters "TH" would appear together in a message. "The purpose of such a cipher is to destroy the normal frequency since pairs of letters act in a very different manner from single letters in the mechanics of language," a memo regarding the *Holmewood* code breaking explained.

That memo—a year following the capture of the *Holmewood*—is unsigned, but must have been written by Elizebeth Friedman since it bears her writing style and is held in her collection of personal documents at the George Marshall Library. The Coast Guard's New York Intelligence Office had operated a subsidiary cryptanalysis unit since the late 1920s. The memo acknowledges New York's efforts to break the code, but assigns the major credit to headquarters in Washington, where Elizebeth's unit was located. "The cipher was broken here [Washington] and a skeleton digraphic table was sent to New York about January 15, 1931."[28]

Using the table provided by headquarters, the New York office was able to track some of the *Holmewood's* activities over the next few years. Yet the memo says an attempt in November 1932 by the New York office to solve a code related to the *Holmewood* group, ended up with a meaning for one word of the cipher that "proved to be wrong as did the meaning assumed for three code words."

About the same time, the memo's author notes, there had been a "radical change" in the *Holmewood* cipher "in an entirely different form from any digraphic cipher table which had heretofore been used. This possibly accounts, along with the scarcity of traffic, for the complete failure of the New York Intelligence Office to produce any solution." In early 1933, however, Elizebeth's office sent New York "the solution of the digraphic cipher which later proved to be so important at the time the HOMEWOOD [sic] was seized."[29]

In the fall of 1933, the *Holmewood* left Barbados with 25,000 cases of liquor on board. Investigators believed the alcohol would be stored in upstate New York until Prohibition was repealed "when it would have been sold at much higher prices than it would command at the present time."[30]

The *Holmewood* was tracked through radio interceptions to a point near Sandy Hook, New Jersey, just south of New York Harbor where the Hudson River ends its journey from upstate New York. An intercept in the New York office on October 2nd indicated that "some smuggling action was about to take place." The Coast Guard dispatched a cutter to find the *Holmewood*, but could not locate it, even though the decoded message had ordered the steamer to "Stand up the river toward Albany." The decrypted message also told the crew not to attract any attention and to come ashore in one of the life boats and then hide it "if possible."[31]

The reason the Coast Guard could not locate the suspect ship was that the vessel's crew had changed her name and flag. Instead of the British freighter *Holmewood*, she was now steaming up the Hudson disguised as the American vessel, the *Texas Ranger*, which also had been destined for the port of New York. The Coast Guard's New York office discovered the masquerade in time to board the vessel on October 5th at Haverstraw, New York, some 40 miles upriver from Manhattan.[32]

Re-flagging and repainting the Canadian-registered *Holmewood*, including the life boats and life rafts, as the U.S.–registered *Texas Ranger*, that the rum runners learned had been delayed at sea, was "the most audacious smuggling plot in the memory of customs men," according to *The New York Times*.[33]

Summarizing the seizure for the Coast Guard commandant, the chief intelligence officer, Commander F.J. Gorman, relied on the report prepared by his staff in New York. "Had it not been for the Coast Guard Intelligence Office at New York, which uncovered the plot and disseminated the information to Coast Guard and customs officers," Gorman theorized that the *Holmewood* would have successfully smuggled its cargo all the way to Albany.[34]

Elizebeth Friedman must have bristled for months over the issue before issuing her correction. The unsigned memo giving credit to headquarters—not New York—for solving the *Holmewood's* messages was issued exactly a year after Gorman's. "Only one message in code/cipher had any importance in the seizure of the HOLMWOOD [sic]," stated Elizebeth, "and of that message two cipher words only were important, namely 'toward Albany.'" Though noting that teamwork is required of all the units involved, she writes that the New York office was unable to decode any of the various *Holmewood* interceptions "until after the solution was sent out from Headquarters."[35]

It is not clear whether Elizebeth wrote this memo for official Coast Guard use or just for her own satisfaction. It is not addressed to any specific person. A copy is in her personal files, but does not appear in the official government archives.

Despite the internal squabble, the media did give Elizebeth Friedman credit for her role in the *Holmewood* seizure. A newspaper profile of her seven months later remarked that Elizebeth's work on the case had been a boon to Uncle Sam: "duty and taxes on the cargo amounted to just under one-half million dollars exclusive of the value of the vessel and its cargo of liquor, estimated at another half million dollars."[36] The same month, in an interview on NBC radio, Elizebeth credited the whole law enforcement team for the successful operation: "What happened is that the HOLME-WOOD, disguised as the TEXAS RANGER, beat the real TEXAS RANGER into port and was halfway up to Albany, the destination of the cargo of liquor, when the secret messages were deciphered by the combined efforts of the Customs and the Coast Guard and the ship and crew seized."[37]

The October 1933 *Holmewood* venture—aiming to stash liquor supplies in the U.S. until it became more profitable to sell when Prohibition ended—showed that rum runners were turning their attention to the future. Franklin Roosevelt had campaigned to end Prohibition in the 1932 presidential election. The ban on the manufacture, distribution and sale of alcohol expired in December 1933, just two months after the *Holmewood* seizure.[38]

After more than a dozen years of officially being dry, nearly everyone in America was ready for a *legal* drink. Contributing to the demise of Prohibition was the public's distaste for gang-related violence associated with it—the most infamous being the 1929 St. Valentine's Day massacre in Chicago. But in a depression-weary economy, the bottom line to enforce anti-liquor laws also became a burden. The government spent $300 million enforcing Prohibition laws,[39] but a 1933 Treasury Department report estimated the feds could earn $50 million in taxes a year by legalizing liquor. The report concluded that by repealing Prohibition, the government could make twice the amount that it was spending on the entire Coast Guard budget.[40]

Thus, when Prohibition was repealed, there was an immediate downsizing of the funds for all agencies dealing with its enforcement.[41] That is except for the Coast Guard Cryptanalysis Section, whose unique abilities would now focus on other law enforcement issues. A month after the *Holmewood* capture, a New York newspaper wrote about Elizebeth's exploits: "Now that the repeal of the 18th amendment is in sight, Mrs.

Friedman believes the narcotic and alien traffic will increase rapidly in scope. Eventually it will take the place now held in the underworld by the rum trade."[42]

"I'm afraid smuggling is here to stay. Prohibition taught the smugglers high-powered methods of organization," Elizebeth declared to a national radio audience after the nation was once again wet. "They are now turning what they learned in smuggling liquor also to account for other means of livelihood.... There is still much liquor smuggling going on for those who would evade the Government tariffs. But the ingenuity of the smuggler has also now been turned to narcotics, perfumes, jewelry, and even Pinto beans on the Texas border."[43]

Pinto beans, however, were far from the government's biggest concern.

Drug smuggling, already an issue in the early 1930s, became the Coast Guard Intelligence Division's biggest target by the mid–30s. By then the agency had formed an official alliance with not only the Bureau of Customs, but the Bureau of Narcotics.[44] Elizebeth gradually shifted from high-profile rum running cases to opium and other drug smuggling operations.

The narcotics bureau had been shadowing a west coast drug operation for years. Their break came when agents requested the Cryptanalysis Section's help to solve coded letters seized from the operation in San Francisco.[45] Elizebeth replied that her unit would need more information to help in the investigation of the Ezra Brothers ring that had connections to China. "The code material submitted is of such a nature that it can be solved only by the aid of collateral information. It is thought that there must be considerable information in possession of the Bureau of Customs which would aid me in solving this code."[46]

The Ezra Brothers, Judah and Isaac, were the sons of a wealthy Portuguese businessman in Shanghai, China, where the brothers grew up. After their father's death, however, they came to the west coast of the United States where they thought they could make a greater profit from their narcotics smuggling operation. Federal investigators in San Francisco got wise to the Ezras from looking into mail drops used by the brothers.[47]

After receiving more information, Elizebeth followed up with a solution to the Ezra Brothers' code. She reported that a letter from Shanghai that agents seized was intended for the Ezras in San Francisco, but in an attempt to throw off suspicion, was addressed to someone in London. It describes a shipment of 50 tung oil drums arriving on a Japanese ship, the *Asama Maru*.[48] The decoded letter designated the number and positions of drums with hidden narcotics. "WYRRA ARE 8 means 'You will find 8 drums containing your goods'– or words to that effect." Then Elizebeth's solution notes several numbered drums that contain narcotics, such as, WYFJO meaning drum number 56 or WYGGA specifying drum 60. The letter also contained code words for different types of narcotics: "WYRVO—smoking opium, WYSET—morphine*, WYSSA—cocaine*, WYSIV—heroin.* These two groups may be used in reverse order," she wrote.[49]

In the designated eight drums on board the ship, using the decoded letter to lead them, Customs investigators discovered 6500 ounces of opium worth $162,500 plus other types of narcotics.[50]

Agents arrested the Ezras, but that wasn't the end of the cryptanalytic investigation. The longer she worked on the Ezras' cables and letters, the more Elizebeth discovered about the mob's organization. From a double transposition based on a supplement to *Bentley's Complete Phrase Code*, she solved a list of code names for members of the organization and the ways the Ezras disguised their drug shipments: "YERAN, YEREP, and YERNA ... refer either to special containers such as milk tins with suspended compartments, or the like, or to some preparation such as beeswax, which in itself is capable of importation into the United States, but in which narcotics may be suspended when in liquid form."

Most of the drugs arrived in barrels of tung oil. "I wish to call attention to the fact that these meanings are the intent of the language arranged between the correspondents," Elizebeth explained in a summary of the Ezra code. "It could not be claimed that they are given in the exact wording of the correspondents. It is natural, for instance, to assume from the standpoint of Federal authorities that WYRRA means 'drums which contain narcotics' or 'drums containing hidden compartments.' These, however, are hardly expressions which the smugglers themselves would use. They would probably say 'drums to be watched for,' 'drums containing your goods,' or the like."[51]

A *Reader's Digest* article about Elizebeth a few years later claimed that her code breaking clinched the case against the Ezra Brothers.[52] In the *New York Times*, a writer declared, "Their activities had baffled for years all the Treasury operatives who had shadowed them in vain until Mrs. Friedman decoded the message which gave them the complete information required for conviction."[53]

Elizebeth herself noted that prosecutors used the evidence she had turned up about other members of the gang to pursue the investigation higher up the chain of command. But the seized narcotics and the cryptanalysis evidence were enough to convince the Ezras to plead guilty.[54] They each received a 12-year prison sentence and a $12,000 fine.[55]

A Universal Press Service article on the case remarked that a woman in the "de-coding Office of the Government at Washington, D.C.," whose name had been withheld by authorities was responsible for helping bring the Ezras to justice. "A woman succeeded in outwitting the Master minds of an International Narcotics smuggling ring, it was learned today. As a result, the activities headed by Juda and Izaac Ezra, stubbornly hidden by the brothers since their arrest, are now an open book to federal authorities."[56] A columnist for a Pacific coast newspaper wisecracked that the brothers would have 12 years in prison "to try to devise a code that a woman couldn't break."[57]

As more drug cases from Asia landed on her desk, Elizebeth, who had studied German, French and Spanish,[58] would have to become a semi-expert in Chinese in order to decipher codes originating from that country.

The Bureau of Customs sent the Cryptanalysis Section a message in Chinese enciphered code in February 1937. It was a typed copy prepared from a handwritten code letter confiscated from a Chinese man arrested earlier that month in Portland, Oregon. "A preliminary study of this message resulted in the development of the theory that it was a letter-encipherment of number groups which in turn were the code form of Chinese characters," Elizebeth reported. "The problem being attacked on the basis of this theory, the cipher key was solved and the letters of the message were converted into numeral groups. In turn, the groups were converted into the Chinese characters which comprised the plain language message."[59]

Elizebeth remarked in a summary of the case that she and her other cryptanalysts were working under pressure to solve this message for the Lew Kim Yuen case. The decryption process was hampered by the language differences: the Chinese version was five times longer than the English translation. The unit was working with a Chinese commercial dictionary to solve the code, yet each Chinese character in the code was represented by four-digit number groups. Once they had converted those, the cryptanalysts put the numbers into columns to aid in studying the message for translation.[60]

The cryptanalysts also consulted a professor in Washington who was fluent in Chinese who, in turn, brought in a native Chinese speaker to help. They had a problem, however, that the translators could not solve. Five letters in the typewritten copy had been omitted. So Elizebeth requested a "photostatic" copy of the original handwritten message. That resolved the problem.

"It was determined that the Chinese syllables, TAU FAI BAI YASEE, phonetic sounds for a foreign name in the beginning of the message, probably were meant to convey the name of the S/S TALTHYBIUS," Elizebeth wrote the chief intelligence officer. "At the same time information was obtained here through a reliable source that the name of KUOK GEN or, in another Chinese dialect, KWOK KUM, was the name of a member of the crew of the TALTHYBIUS, possibly the 1st Boatswain's Mate."[61]

After overcoming problems understanding the differences between Cantonese and other Chinese dialects, Elizebeth wrote that the decoded letter referred to "white goods" or "white stuff," which were commonly used terms for heroin or morphine. "You must not deliver the white stuff to the house of Chieh Tsu. White stuff difficult to get," read the translation of the coded letter.[62]

When the cryptanalysts solved enough of the puzzle on February 12th to discover that the SS *Talthybius* was due in Seattle on the 13th, Elizebeth's office notified Customs agents there by telegraph—just in time for them to board and inspect the ship.[63]

An assistant secretary of the Treasury department wrote the Coast Guard commandant to thank "Mrs. Friedman and her group" for the "splendid work" in the case. "The results accomplished are themselves the highest commendation of the excellence of this effort," wrote Harold N. Graves, "but I would like you to know that we all appreciate the fine job that Mrs. Friedman and her group did in this case."[64]

Another dope smuggling case involving Elizebeth stretched across an entire decade. In 1928 federal agents confiscated an historic amount of opium on a ship entering Honolulu from China. Members of the gang were indicted in the case, but were acquitted in a trial. Ten years later, however, in November 1938, a member of the group, Ching Chun Hee, attempted to bribe a Customs agent for $8,000 to board another ship in Honolulu and deliver "80 5-tael[65] tins" of opium. The agent notified his superiors of the plot; authorities seized the opium and arrested the conspirators.[66]

A Bureau of Narcotics news release on the case did not specifically name Elizebeth Friedman, but noted the Cryptanalysis Section's help in proving the opium came from suppliers in Hong Kong. "In this connection the co-operation of the cryptanalyst of the Coast Guard and decoding certain cable messages passing between Ching Chun Hee at Honolulu and Hong Kong was most valuable."[67]

Again, Elizebeth's superiors complimented her for work well done on the case. "It appears that in addition to your regular hours of duty you performed many hours of extra work," wrote Coast Guard Commandant R.R. Waesche. "I appreciate your untiring devotion to duty and thank you for your valuable contribution toward the success of the mission to which you were assigned."[68]

Elizebeth's success was continually highlighted by newspaper writers, who also found an interesting news angle in her gender. *The New York Times* headlined a profile of her, "Woman Wins Fame as Cryptanalyst," and described her this way: "Just over five feet in height, with a heart-shaped face and curly brown hair, in appearance she is far from the grim nemesis indicated by her record as a crime detector." Datelined in Washington the article continued: "No novel of international intrigue or high adventure on land and sea ever had a more distinguished heroine than this 'Ace' cryptanalyst of the American Coast Guard, who at 43 looks more like a college girl than a woman twenty-one years married, the mother of two children and the creator and possessor of a unique job in American history."[69]

By this time, however, Elizebeth was beginning to take a contrarian view of news reports about her work. She was growing weary in the late '30s of all the publicity—much of it authorized by the Treasury Department's public relations office. Her memoirs reveal that the most offensive stories, however, were ones that the PR people had not authorized. "Because they were written in a lurid manner or because they contained assertions and statements quite untrue, I wrote a letter recording in writing my protests to the Public Relations of the Treasury Department requesting that thereafter no one but no one from the world of the press or radio would be given permission to get so far as even an interview with me."

For the most part, she had "kindly memories" of women interviewers and feature writers. Male reporters, however, were another matter. She respected several male journalists who had written about her, but others, she confided, "I still feel a flash of irritation, after all these years." One, she recalled, but did not name in her memoirs, was "a thundering, blaspheming" writer who was "ill-bred" and "blunders into forbidden territories."

In her profession, where she acknowledged being "on more or less of an equality with men," she felt that the press was "intrigued" by the aspect that a woman could operate successfully in the fields of cryptography and cryptanalysis.

After testifying in New Orleans,

I appeared in press stories as "a pretty middle aged woman" (with photographs snapped of me as I stepped down from the witness chair one day and left the court chamber) and the same day in another part of the country I was described as "a pretty young woman in a frilly pick [sic] dress." I was still young enough at the time to be piqued by the earlier description and annoyed at the frivolous adjectives in the second.

One of the fictions which somewhere, somehow first appeared as a statement and then was perpetuated thereafter in a manner most annoying to me and which must have been extremely annoying to my husband, was the idiotic statement that I, this "wizard of codes and ciphers" had taught the science to my husband. Of all the unfounded statements made concerning me in the public press, this was the most confounding.

As a result of the increasingly annoying articles about her, Elizebeth supplied the Treasury Department's public relations officials "with the bare facts of my life and career" and instructed them to use the information in any way they "deemed essential." "But as far as I was concerned, I felt too uncomfortable not knowing from day to day what might be said about me in some far part of the world, for it had come to the point where unauthorized stores [sic] were appearing even in the European press."[70]

Despite Elizebeth's protestations, a woman cryptanalyst bringing international gangsters to justice remained a high-interest story for the press. The 1937 *New York Times* profile said of her, "Less spectacular, but no less important, are the many cases which never 'make' newspaper headlines and of which neither Mrs. Friedman nor any member of the Coast Guard can be induced to talk."[71]

As the globe marched closer to another world war, Elizebeth would grow even more reticent to discuss her work publicly.

≡6≡

Living with Flair
and Cheating Death

The mid to late 1930s were a very good—yet very troubling—time for Elizebeth Friedman. Both Elizebeth and William were at the top of their game in the field of cryptanalysis. While millions of Americans struggled to find jobs in the years following the Great Depression, the Friedmans remained gainfully employed, using their cryptanalytic skills in challenging work highly valued by the government.

Yet late in 1937 Elizebeth avoided death only by happenstance. That seemed to cause a great deal of introspection about the path she had chosen in life; the next year—1938—became a watershed for Elizebeth. She received an honorary doctorate degree. She won praise from both the Canadian government and her own superiors for bringing a notorious narcotics king to justice. She also questioned whether the limelight was shining too brightly on her work and whether she should even continue the seedy business of solving the codes of gangsters, smugglers and other ne'er-do-wells.

The Friedmans capped 1938 by hosting a progressive dinner party in November. It was far from a run-of-the-mill bash. They sent invitations telling their "detachments" of friends they would need to find their way from place-to-place for the party by solving various codes. The groups were not to exceed the authorized speed limits or follow other vehicles, not "peek at, pilfer, or purloin the solutions of the personnel of any other detachments or to knock down and trample upon the members of any other detachments who may arrive ahead of them at any one of the bivouac areas."

The guests had several cipher messages to solve to reach the final destination. The first detachment to solve the codes and arrive at the correct area would receive 25 points, the second 15 and the third 5 points.[1] The key for solving message number five was "Yes we have no bananas."[2]

Many of the participants were from the military and had a basic understanding of cryptography and what they needed to do to win the contest. At least one, however, was the wife of a junior Army officer who was out of her league. Yet she was the one who discovered the key to solving a coded menu for the party: "The first item was a series of dots done with a blue pen. The brains at the party worked over the number of dots in a group when it occurred to me it had to be 'blue points'—(oysters)—and it was! I had done my bit and from then on I was quiet."[3]

That event epitomized how the Friedmans lived—bon vivants in drab, dreary, undecadent, bureaucratic Washington. They did not make exorbitant salaries; Elizebeth was paid $3,800 in 1931[4]; she did not get a boost in pay until 1940 when it went to $4,000 per year.[5] The Friedmans worried about everyday financial situations such as house repairs and keeping a car running,[6] but since they remained employed throughout the worst of the troubled economic times, the Friedmans were able to afford things that most Americans would have considered exotic. Along with William and Elizebeth traveling to a couple of international communications conferences, the entire family made annual trips in the mid to late '30s to Barnegat Bay on the New Jersey shore for a summer vacation. While William played golf at the Army-Navy Club, Elizebeth created a garden with an aquamarine-colored flamingo pool in the back yard of their Military Road home. Daughter Barbara said that was Elizebeth's escape from work: "She had lots of roses and lots of iris in the front and the back and dahlias and things like that."[7]

As a career female employee of the federal government, Elizebeth also found herself invited to the White House on many occasions by First Ladies Lou Hoover and Eleanor Roosevelt. "Mrs. Roosevelt particularly never failed to include us in her winter tea parties and spring or summer garden parties, usually those for 'ladies only.'"[8]

Though the Friedmans did like a good party, they apparently eschewed alcohol when the government declared it illegal. Barbara recalls a green metal cabinet her parents kept in the kitchen that contained some wine, scotch and bourbon. But she was adamant that her parents only imbibed at home *after* Prohibition had ended, "never before. NEVER!" Barbara insisted.[9]

"My husband and I, during all those years of Prohibition, had had no particular strong conviction on one side or the other," Elizebeth wrote in her memoirs. "We were a bit disgusted with acquaintances, some of them even friends of ours who spent time at supper and dinner parties telling of how they created their bathtub gin and how much of it they consumed. During all of those years, whatever drinking we did, was on the two occasions when we were in Europe."[10]

The Friedmans made two trips to Europe for communications conferences. The first was in 1928 when Elizebeth was working only part-time for the Coast Guard. Elizebeth was able to free herself for the trip by arranging a Riverbank acquaintance and former U.S. Navy "yeomanette" to stay with her children. The woman "was devoted beyond description to our two children as, indeed, they were to her," Elizebeth wrote.[11]

When the SS *Leviathan* sailed from New York, William arranged a dinner on board to celebrate her birthday on August 26th. As they approached the disembarkation point in Cherbourg, there was a "*Diner d'Adieu*," in honor of several guests including "Major and Mrs. W.F. Friedman."[12]

For their second European conference in 1932, Elizebeth had to make special arrangements not only to take time off from work, but to send her children to Detroit to be cared for by her sister. William left for the conference in August.[13] When Elizebeth sailed to join him in early October, she wrote her six-year-old son a postcard from the *Ile de France*: "Darling John—This is the boat Mother's sailing on. I am on it now as I write this. Isn't it exciting to be in such a big city as Detroit?"[14]

That year's conference was held in Madrid. Elizebeth sent a six-page letter to her sister describing her awe of the elaborate setting and of meeting the president of Spain and his wife. "We filed into the gorgeous dining salon where 'tea' was served—and such a feast! Myriads of sandwiches, cakes, bourbons, wines, champagne, punch, tea, coffee. Quite a contrast to U.S. Presidents' receptions where one is offered not even a glass of water!" she wrote. The Friedmans returned on the same ship, the SS *Leviathan*, which took them to the 1928 conference. "The dining salon has been completely done over since we were passengers in 1928," Elizebeth's letter continued. "Instead of the vast, gaping hall that would be with the sparse passenger list of depression days, we now dine at small tables on a sort of balcony, with the orchestra and dance floor below."[15]

When the Friedmans returned to America in December 1932, Elizebeth wrote that they had missed "all of the hysteria, the incriminations, the bitterness, the ugliness of the Presidential campaign" that had ushered Franklin D. Roosevelt into the White House.[16] One of the policies the new

William and Elizebeth traveled on the *Ile de France* on one of their two trips to Europe for communications conferences. Elizebeth was in awe of a reception for the president of Spain, which she wrote served much better food and drink than presidential receptions in the United States. This postcard of one trip is in Elizebeth's files at the Marshall Library (photograph of document by the author; Elizebeth S. Friedman Collection, George C. Marshall Research Library).

president initiated was to end Prohibition. Yet Elizebeth reported that even with the repeal of the unpopular anti-alcohol laws, her office was still busy for at least three years "with the backlash of the Prohibition era." Many of the liquor smuggling cases on her desk were left unresolved.[17]

As Prohibition wound down, however, Elizebeth Friedman would find that narcotics cases would take up her time—and nearly her life.

In June 1937 the Coast Guard Intelligence Office received a request for assistance from the Canadian government to help decode messages "using an enciphering table comprised of letter equivalents used for the number of groups of the Chinese commercial dictionary."[18] With the Coast Guard Cryptanalytic Unit's success in solving coded Chinese messages in the Lew Kim Yuen case earlier that year, Elizebeth soon had urgent travel orders to travel by airplane "to assist the Royal Canadian Mounted Police (RCMP) in the prosecution of certain narcotic cases, and to testify as an expert, if necessary, relative to the deciphering of certain messages."[19] She would receive a per diem travel allowance of $5.[20]

With air travel still a unique way to cross the continent, Elizebeth was excited to head to the west coast flying in a DC-3 twin-engine aircraft.

She sent a postcard with a picture and a description of the airplane to her young son: "John, dear, this picture was made of a plane exactly like the one I fly to Salt Lake. I arrive there at 5 a.m. 7 your time and shall see the sunrise over the Great Salt Lake. Love, Mother."[21]

With just a few hours' notice, Elizebeth rushed home from Coast Guard headquarters to pack, give the housekeeper instructions, kiss her children goodbye and have William drive her to the airport in time for an afternoon flight instead of one scheduled at 10 p.m. "Something told me that I had to make that 4 o'clock plane; I don't know what it was. Why I was so, felt so impelled to do that, but I did."[22]

As a result, she arrived early enough for her Chicago connection to avoid a later United Airlines "Mainliner" flight that crashed in the Rocky Mountains east of Salt Lake City, killing all 19 people on board—the worst aviation accident in American history at the time.[23] Elizebeth called William at home to let him know that she was not on that ill-fated flight.[24] She also sent him a telegram the next day from Vancouver announcing that she had arrived there safely.[25] Yet when Billy heard the news of the crash on the radio, he telephoned the airline to confirm that she was safe. "I'm greatly relieved," he wrote in a letter to his wife that day. "What do you plan about returning? Will you take the chance again? I think you'd better not—the winter weather is here now and you've had the thrill of one trip across."[26]

For her part, Elizebeth told her family years later that it was fate that made her miss the doomed flight; it just was not her time to go.[27] "The reason I wasn't on it was because of this hunch that I had that I shouldn't wait until that 10 o'clock plane at night but should take the daylight one at four and do at least part of the journey in daylight."[28] When she arrived in Vancouver, Elizebeth dashed off a telegram to her family that makes no mention of her near calamity: "ENTIRE TRIP UNFORGETTABLE EXPERIENCE ADDRESS HOTEL VANCOUVER LOVE TO THREE = ELIZABETH [sic]."[29]

Elizebeth later turned more introspective. After arriving in Vancouver, when she received the air mail letter from her husband, it contained a newspaper clipping about the fatal airline crash. It noted that a "DC WOMAN ABOARD LOST PLANE." Friends had been calling William concerned that it was Elizebeth. She realized that by taking an earlier plane, another woman from Washington had taken her intended seat on the 10 p.m. flight. "The story was a considerable shock to me," Elizebeth wrote, "and I had for a few days thereafter a feeling of being resurrected."

With the unforgettable experience behind her, Elizebeth settled in to

Postcard that Elizebeth sent to her son while flying to Vancouver, British Columbia, to work on the Gordon Lim narcotics case. An early flight connection helped Elizebeth avoid a crash near Salt Lake City that killed everyone on board (photograph of document by the author; Elizebeth S. Friedman Collection, George C. Marshall Research Library).

work with Vancouver authorities on the challenging case against Gordon Lim, whom she describes as a university-educated, elegant Chinese gentleman millionaire who operated precious gem shops in both Vancouver and Victoria, British Columbia. Investigators in the province had been trying to link Lim to opium smuggling for years. They suspected that Lim's

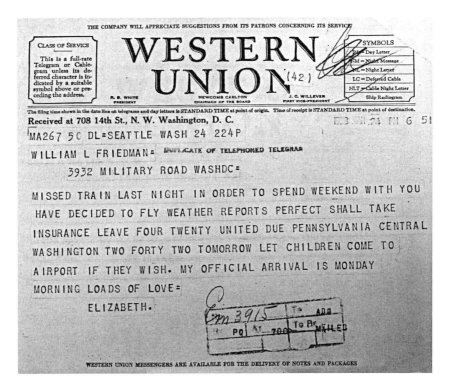

When she missed the United Airlines flight that crashed near Salt Lake City, William wanted Elizebeth to stop flying for work, but she refused to give it up, as this telegram indicates. She marveled at this new mode of transportation and found flying over magnificent landscapes comparable to viewing a Georgia O'Keefe painting (photograph of document by the author; Elizebeth S. Friedman Collection, George C. Marshall Research Library).

mob was also sending guns and ammunition out of North America and into China.

The RCMP had been following the ring ever since a serendipitous incident involving a cargo ship that was leaving the port of Windsor, British Columbia. The anchor of the ship had dragged up a very long, strong rope with a securely tied package wrapped in burlap. It contained several packets, each containing a five-tael tin of opium.

When investigators turned their attention to the Gordon Lim ring, the Coast Guard Cryptanalytic Unit received 17 messages to solve, all on Canadian Pacific Telegraph forms, and all assumed to be coded Chinese messages regarding shipments of narcotics. "Since Chinese characters cannot, it is obvious, be transmitted by telegraph or radio," Elizebeth wrote, "the original language must be converted into either numbers or letters for transmission." The cryptanalysts began looking at the five-letter groups searching for something in the messages that might represent Chinese characters in a dictionary or a commercial code book.

After poring over the messages, Elizebeth concluded that her staff was not facing a letter substitution system, but one that substituted numbers for the intended messages. After many attempts to work out a single number-substitution, Elizebeth came to this conclusion: "Alas! All messages were not in the same system of encipherment, as our analysis very shortly proved. In reality there were four different systems of encipherment in 17 messages."

This was one of the toughest ciphers that Elizebeth had come across in more than two decades of solving such riddles. "In the Gordon Lim messages each letter did not represent a single digit; on the contrary it appeared that each two letters represented two digits. In other words the Gordon Lim cipher method was biliteral that is, digraphic; there were 100 pairs of letters representing 100 two-digit numbers, instead of 10 letters representing 10 one-digit numbers."

Elizebeth instructed her cryptanalysts to prepare several digraphic tables, columns and horizontal lines of digits, as worksheets for each of the four groups of messages to compare to a Chinese commercial dictionary. As a result, they observed that each pair of letters contained at least one vowel. With further sleuthing of the worksheets they made more discoveries. Using frequency tables as their crutch, the cryptanalytic team made an unexpected discovery: "sequences of two to five letters in the top horizontal seemed to be alphabetical or in typewriter-key order. Some such fragments, such as KLIU ... HMNB, gave us a hint that perhaps someone had constructed the enciphering tables by simply tapping out segments of letters either in the same row or adjacent rows on the keyboard."

Trial and error produced some semblance of order in the messages, but no meaning. Dogged determination to break the messages eventually led the team to find that they could start replacing numbers with letters, which still needed to be deciphered. "I realized at this point that so small an amount of text in each category would be a severe obstacle to solution," Elizebeth described in a narrative of how she solved the Gordon Lim ciphers, "and that it was going to take an exceedingly long time to reduce them to Chinese text, thence English, if the task could ever be accomplished at all."

Elizebeth came to respect just how good Gordon Lim's cryptographers were at preparing their messages: they superimposed a cipher on a code that was extremely difficult to break because of the limited amount of messages sent in each system. "The staff seemed on the whole convinced that going further with this problem was an impossible feat without absolute information or additional material. It was indeed a questionable task, but there was something so intriguing about it that I could not let it go. I kept returning to it in odd moments and considering different ways of attack, and pondering what was needed for solution."

After puzzling over these for some time, Elizebeth decided the most feasible thing was to analyze the ciphers from both the beginning and the end where habitual greetings and farewells might have been inserted into the messages with some repetition. "I theorized that the Chinese with their rigid minds, their rigid language, and their rigid habits in doing business, would cause them to be very conventional and the way they expressed themselves in telegraphic communication. I had a feeling that they would end the messages in a conventional and habitual manner with phrases like 'reply immediately,' 'send money,' 'send goods at once,' or like inflexible expressions."

Elizebeth's knowledge of Chinese characters was limited; she could analyze only the simplest of the strokes. "Hence timidly, although tenuously, I selected three messages which for some intuitive reason I believe might end with the character for 'reply,' 'reply at once,' or even 'cable reply.'" Yet using this method, she determined from a Chinese dictionary that the numbers 6010 meant "reply." She worked her way back through the messages and found a few beginning with 7193. "This gave me a warm feeling: these could mean a request or order—CABLE REPLY," she wrote.

After many more hours of work, she found more four-digit numbers that seemed likely to represent words such as "send immediately" or "reply at once." Elizebeth was convinced she had made a "real dent in the problem," but needed to corroborate her findings. She wrote the Canadians seeking more information that might help determine the meanings of the coded words, people's names or the names of vessels. She also asked her superiors to provide a Chinese interpreter.

The interpreter, Dr. Julia Chen from the Library of Congress, soon confirmed Elizebeth's deduction that 7193 6010 meant "cable reply." The interpreter also opened the door to other discoveries such as suggesting that 0107 meant "thousand." Elizebeth countered that if 0107 substituted for "thousand," then then another number in the message, 0337, must mean "dollars." Yet another group of two four-letter groups made no sense to Dr. Chen because they were the meaningless phrases IK and CHEN. Elizebeth asked her to say the phrases out loud. When pronounced together they represented the name of a ship of the Blue Funnel Line.

Working with Dr. Chen and additional information from Canadian authorities, Elizebeth made more breakthroughs. One key message "convinced me beyond a doubt that all messages could be completely, or nearly so, solved with the aid of an interpreter who knew Cantonese thoroughly."

Breaking the Gordon Lim messages had taken more than four months—June to October. Elizebeth called the Royal Canadian Mounted Police to announce her breakthrough. She was flying to Vancouver within 24 hours.

Canadian police served a search warrant in May 1937 to obtain coded cable messages going back to 1934. The alleged conspirators, Gordon Lim and four accomplices, were to go to trial in October. That's when Canadian officials needed Elizebeth's help and testimony. Upon arriving in British Columbia, she began meeting with an RCMP Cantonese interpreter to fully decrypt and organize the messages obtained from the Lim ring.[30] Working with the Canadian authorities gave Elizebeth "a big idea or two" about the messages. With that collaboration, the decrypted messages "bloomed like flowers," she said.[31]

Work "progressed rapidly," Elizebeth told her superiors in a memo. Not only were they working on the messages sent to her in Washington four months earlier, "in addition there were several other messages brought to me for solution in Vancouver which were yet another system." She completed work by noon on Saturday, October 23rd.[32]

Yet when the case came before a judge, prosecutors asked for a delay so that investigators could gather more evidence in China and Hong Kong. So, after four days in Vancouver, Elizebeth's work there seemed to be finished.

Because of the recent air crash, Billy convinced his wife that she should return to Washington by train. As one who marveled at the wondrous western landscapes from the air, which were, Elizebeth wrote, like "Georgia O'Keefe paintings," with colors "ranging from the brightest of greens, the faded red of the barns, the contrasts ranging down in hue to pastel hues of green autumn yellows," she was reluctant to give up another chance of sightseeing from several thousand feet above the ground. As a consolation, her new Vancouver colleagues suggested that she make the return train trip through the Canadian Rockies, which she found more majestic than either the U.S. Rockies or the Swiss Alps: "The Canada range seemed so entrenched, so forever formidable, so majestically uncompromising."[33]

Once back in Washington, the accolades started pouring in for Elizebeth's work in the case. Unlike the incident over the sinking of the *I'm*

Alone several years before, when the U.S. and Canada squared off in an international tribunal, now the two countries had patched up their differences and welcomed the cross-border law enforcement cooperation.

In a letter to U.S. authorities, the RCMP assistant commissioner in Vancouver described Elizebeth's work: "During the ensuing week, with the assistance of our Official Chinese Interpreter, she was successful in breaking down and completely solving the coded cable grams, which are entered as exhibits in this case." R.L. Cadiz' letter continued: "I want to take this opportunity to again express our appreciation of the valuable assistance rendered this Force by Mrs. Friedman, yourself and your Department."[34]

Another letter arrived from the chief of the Narcotics Division in Ottawa, the Canadian capital. It advised Elizebeth's superiors that her services would still be required when the Lim case came up for trial in January: "The importance of this series of conspiracy charges may be gauged from the fact that the Honourable Gordon S. Wismer, Attorney General of British Columbia, is personally conducting the prosecution on our behalf."

C.H.L. Sharman further noted that every effort of the Canadians to decode the 40,900 cables found in their search warrant had been unsuccessful. Once the task had been turned over to the Coast Guard Cryptanalytic Unit, Sharman wrote that their solutions of the messages pointed to collateral clues that the investigators in Vancouver could pursue. "This is an outstanding instance of most generous and highly appreciated cooperation on the part of the officials of your country, and I would be most appreciative if you would be kind enough to advise the Chief of the Service in which Mrs. Friedman belongs, of our gratitude."[35]

The Coast Guard commandant also received a letter praising Elizebeth's work from the minister of Pensions and National Health in Canada: "The evidence thus made available is most valuable, and I would like to take this opportunity of expressing my sincere gratitude, not only to Mrs. Friedman for her most appreciated services, but also to you for so kindly making them available to us. Such cooperation from a neighbour country is indeed a welcome and invaluable asset in connection with our efforts to combat the illicit narcotic traffic."[36]

Commandant Waesche paid the compliment forward to Elizebeth: "I am pleased to note the excellent manner in which you represented the Coast Guard, and the fine impression your very helpful efforts have made on the Canadian officials."[37]

Having Elizebeth work on the Lim case was not merely a friendly gesture from one nation to another, however. The Coast Guard commandant justified the expense it took for Elizebeth to work on and travel for the Canadian case in a memo to the General Accounting Office. "It will be readily understood that it is essential that the Canadian and United States Customs authorities cooperate to the fullest extent, if the smuggling of contraband into the United States is to be prevented, and such cooperation has been carried on over a period of years." Admiral Waesche argued that since such short notice was given to the Coast Guard, "it was impossible for her to reach her destination by railroad travel" in time to testify in Lim's scheduled trial. So he requested that $30.79 for Elizebeth's "travel by commercial aircraft" for the October trip be allowed.[38]

On a less formal level, Elizebeth also kept up a correspondence with her Canadian colleagues. Some, such as RCMP Inspector G.W. Fish, she considered to be friends. "Personally I am more than delighted to have been able to accomplish results on what for so long appeared to be an impossible task," Elizebeth wrote Fish a few weeks after returning to Washington. "To have been of service to your Government is not only a privilege, but an honor. It is understood that there will be no objection to my coming to Vancouver in January, and I shall await information concerning the definite date of the trial. Please thank Mrs. Fish for her gracious note. I'm looking forward to seeing you both again."[39]

In January 1938 Elizebeth received orders to travel to Vancouver once again to testify in the Lim trial. "It is assumed the Canadian authorities will pay Mrs. Friedman's expenses from Seattle to Vancouver and return to Seattle, including her subsistence expenses during that period," noted the memo from the Bureau of Customs to the Coast Guard commandant.[40] Once again she was to receive $5 a day for expenses and "travel to Seattle is to be made either by commercial aircraft or railroads as the circumstances may necessitate."[41]

Now hooked on the speed, luxury and unrivaled views from aloft, Elizebeth chose to fly to Vancouver again, but because of bad weather, the airline routed her through Los Angeles, then San Francisco and up the coast through Portland and Seattle. She arrived in Vancouver the evening before the Lim conspiracy trial was set to begin on January 19th. She checked into the Hotel Vancouver using her married name, Mrs. William Friedman, instead of her given name because of what she described as "discomfortable attention," in other words, reporters seeking information about her involvement in the case.

Having experience testifying in a number of U.S. trials, Elizebeth expressed an interest in seeing how the Canadian system worked. With her growing aversion to attention from the press, she was especially intrigued by the law that prohibited publication of trial details until the verdict was announced.

Once the trial commenced, "I was excluded from the courtroom, until such time as I would be called to the witness stand," wrote Elizabeth. "I was kept informed as I waited in the judge's chambers about progress inside the courtroom and thus I learned that there was a prolonged struggle over the selection of the jury." The contest to choose the jury lasted for several days.

Finally Elizabeth was called to testify. "Dr. Leong [the RCMP Chinese interpreter] and I had prepared each message in a meticulous form which could be used as evidence and be entered as an exhibit. I read forth each message before it was turned over to the Crown Counsel to be placed with the other exhibits. I was not challenged and cross-examination was very slight."

As soon as she was finished testifying, Elizabeth found herself "importuned to grant interviews to two newspapers." Her friends in the RCMP advised Elizabeth that if she expected to have any peace, she should grant at least one interview. As long as the trial was underway, however, she was admonished to steer clear of discussing the case itself. After granting the interviews, the local newspapers did stories about an American "holidaying" in Vancouver and a "Secret Service operator" visiting the city, clearly obeying the law against publicizing the Lim trial while it was still in progress. "This was a pleasant change from the more or less sensational treatment I had received from the United States press in some cases in Federal courts," Elizabeth commented.

As the prosecution's case continued to unfold in court, a clearer picture emerged about how Lim was able to smuggle opium into Canada without being detected for so many years. The conspirators were able to place one of their men on freighters of the Blue Funnel Line and the Empress Lines. When they were ready to transport the narcotics from Hong Kong or China, the crew member would find a hollow stanchion on a specific deck, saw it apart and then stow the drugs inside attached to a heavy rope. The hollow post was then sealed. When the ship was about a mile off shore, the gang member would retrieve the stash of narcotics from the stanchion and toss it overboard— rope and all—to a confederate in the water. Then the smuggler would grab the rope in his teeth and swim ashore trailing the contraband behind him underwater.

When summarizing his case to the jury, Lim's attorney argued that the decrypted messages that referred to "goods" could just as well have referred to Gordon Lim's legitimate business in the gem trade. "However one message had been introduced which specifically used the word 'fook,' the Chinese word for smoking opium," Elizebeth's case narrative noted. "That message had ended with the name FONG DUCK:= Gordon Lim himself."

The jury convicted all of the conspirators in the trial. The judge sentenced them the next month.[42]

Another flurry of congratulatory messages greeted Elizebeth on her return to Washington. This time as well, there were a series of newspaper articles that highlighted her role in bringing the smugglers to justice. "Her job was to turn such messages as 'Uvooa masan aguso gukuu iuuia eiy' into 'Cable three thousand. Select fully the order list of Wat Sang,'" the *Washington Post* reported. "She declined for professional reasons to say how this was done, although she admitted the message was a code of Chinese words and that she did not know Chinese. After she solved the code a Chinese interpreter helped translate the message."[43]

The articles regarding the Lim case, thought Elizebeth, placed too much emphasis on her role and not enough on the other investigators. She felt compelled to write her friend in the RCMP to apologize: "My dear Inspector Fish, I have been utterly sick at heart this week over this dreadful burst of publicity upon my return to Washington. It was the farthest thing in the world from my mind to claim credit for winning the Gordon Lim case; interesting job that it was, I knew it was only one item in the whole case, and certainly not the decisive one. The mystery-lure of the words code or cipher, however, coupled with a woman's name always inflames the news reporters."

Elizebeth's letter declared that she had been "in hiding for three days and have answered no calls either at office or home." The Treasury Department's public relations policy was to grant interviews for closed criminal cases, she wrote, but neither she nor the Department had "claimed the credit for winning the Gordon Lim case." She told Fish that she also requested that the Public Relations office stop all further interviews on the case.

"I can only request that I be judged with a degree of charity," Elizebeth concluded. "Anyone who has had to deal with the American Press can appreciate the manner in which a very small thing, if it is deemed to have news value, often grows to gigantic and very unfair proportions."[44]

Elizebeth followed up with a three-page memo to the Coast Guard commandant. She claimed the press coverage had put her in an "unfair position," and that at no time had she claimed credit for winning the

Gordon Lim case. "Any one [sic] who has had to deal with the American Press can appreciate the manner in which a very small thing, if it is deemed to have news value, often grows to gigantic and very unfair proportions." The memo ended with a request: "If there is any action which you deem appropriate in order to correct the rumored attitude of Canadian officials as reported unofficially to me, I would greatly appreciate such action being taken."[45]

Later that month Elizebeth received a handwritten note from Inspector Fish. "Sorry you are fretting yourself over the idiosyncrasies of the Press. The gentlemen are the same all over possibly a little more rabid in your country." Fish's letter recognized her contributions to the Lim case: "The fact remains that without your able assistance, we could not have decoded the cable messages—and those same messages went a long way in convicting the five accused on the conspiracy charges."[46]

That, however, was not the end of the Gordon Lim case. An appeal overturned Lim's conviction on a count of possession of narcotics. In March Elizebeth flew once more to Vancouver for a retrial on that count. When Lim was hospitalized, however, the trial was postponed until April, so Elizebeth returned home again.[47] Elizebeth's own hospitalization for an unspecified medical condition kept her from heading to Vancouver a fourth time to testify when the narcotics possession case was retried in April. Nevertheless, the prosecution won a conviction without her.[48]

Elizebeth Friedman's early work on the Gordon Lim case coincided with an article about her in *Reader's Digest*, then the best-selling magazine in the country. After the article "Key Woman of the T-Men" appeared, Elizebeth began receiving mail seeking her help in decrypting personal messages, requesting her for speaking engagements, asking for her signature on a quilt and, of course, demanding more interviews.[49]

In reviewing a proposed article for *Good Housekeeping*, Elizebeth suggested that even though some of the copy wasn't "strictly in the forbidden class," it would be better to "leave unsaid." She requested that the magazine delay any article about her until after the "distasteful" publicity over the Gordon Lim case had died down. After receiving Elizebeth's comments, apparently *Good Housekeeping* never published the article.[50]

The drumbeat of articles about her unusual profession and her gender were beginning to take a toll on Elizebeth. "Hero worship has likewise never been something I have enjoyed when directed at me personally," she wrote in her memoirs. The period around the Vancouver narcotics case was particularly troubling to her: "Thereafter I found that my life was not my own."[51]

Yet along with Elizebeth's frustration over her growing fame, there was also joy. A few months after wrapping up her work in the Lim case, Elizebeth's alma mater, Hillsdale College, awarded her an honorary Doctor of Laws degree.[52] Following the award she sometimes used the distinction to sign her correspondence, "Dr. Elizebeth Friedman."

She also had the love and admiration of her husband. "CONGRATU-LATIONS, MY DARLING STOP DO YOU REMEMBER ME? IM THE MAN WHO THINKS YOURE GRAND," a telegram from William declared as Elize-beth received her degree. "IM PROUD AS I CAN BE OF YOUR RENOWN AND WELL EARNED CROWN OF HILLSDALE'S LLD STOP YES. IM THE CHUMP WHO PICKED A TRUMP IN LIFES SWEET LOTTERY YES, IM THE MAN WHO LOVES YOU STILL—YOUR DOTING HUSBAND, BILL."[53]

Although Elizebeth was becoming weary of her growing celebrity, William was anxious to show her off to friends. "I'm so glad you had such a nice time at Hillsdale and Detroit," he wrote in a letter while at Fort Monmouth, New Jersey less than a week after she returned from the degree-awarding ceremony. "It will be something to remember. I wish you could come here though. Everybody is dying to see you and I think you are the most famous woman in the Signal Corps, if not the whole army. They all want to see you in the flesh and talk with you."

After Elizebeth's frequent, far-flung travels, William must have been feeling needy: "It's been chilly enough so that we'd have wanted to double up in one of the twin beds. I want to be close to you and love you so much." Then he closed with, "And skeentillions of love to you, my sweetest. Billy."[54]

Despite her husband's devotion and pride in her work, publicity and fame were getting to Elizebeth. In addition, a decade of seeing the world through the messages of smugglers and gangsters had grown tiresome. Other things in life started to become more interesting. She was active in the League of Women Voters and served on committees that monitored the needs of and suggested reforms for the District of Columbia.[55] Besides chasing criminals, she had received a graduate degree in Archaeology,[56] perhaps looking for a career that veered away from the seamier side of life.

Being on the road, far away from her growing children, cheating death in an era when airline crashes were more common, also were taking their toll. Her unpublished memoirs reflect that concern: "I pack my bag and hug my children a goodbye which is to last for a week or a month or longer, I know not, and board a train with a prayer that the new fields to conquer will not be impossible of conquest."[57]

Recognizing that Elizebeth's work often required long hours that took her away from her family, the Coast Guard commandant sent her a letter of appreciation in the fall of 1938. Admiral Waesche did not refer to any specific case, yet he noted Elizebeth's extra hours of work and "untiring devotion to duty."[58]

Though her superiors admired her work, William remained Elizebeth's biggest cheerleader. "I have for some time noted—as I keep telling you so often—you are getting positively dashing in style, looks, personality," he wrote while she was in Vancouver in early 1938. "I think a life of mental toil—plus having to get up in the morning every day to face new and exciting problems—keeps one young. What if you had only bridge and bridge luncheons to look forward to? That, my dear, is one of the principal reasons why I have been reluctant to agree to your quitting office. We could get along on my own salary—but I fear you'd find life so dull you'd get like the other women I know—even though some of them do make a desperate effort to keep up a real interest in life."[59]

Something inside of Elizebeth accepted what William was prescribing. Despite her disenchantments, she did not abandon her pioneering path. She believed this notable quotation applied to her circumstances: "It's a great life if you don't weaken."[60]

Life, however, would take some unexpected turns over the next few years. As the world lunged toward another war, major changes in her family and job would further weaken Elizebeth's will to continue her groundbreaking career.

$=7=$

A Rocky Start
to the War

By the late 1930s Elizebeth Friedman's fight against rum runners was long over. Drug smuggling was still a major focus of her cryptanalytic unit. But with Asia already aflame with a conflict between Japan and China, and Europe on the verge of another conflict, the Coast Guard and its parent agency, the Treasury Department, started making the transition to a war footing. "From '38 through '41, my office was the eyes and ears for Henry Morgenthau, Jr., the Secretary of the Treasury, whose duties now in addition to domestic law enforcement, comprised also the enforcement of neutrality," Elizebeth's memoirs noted.[1]

The White House was especially concerned about the impact of Germans in neutral nations in South America. Presidential advisers expressed concern in 1938 that Brazil's government could be taken over by Nazi sympathizers. President Roosevelt himself worried that the U.S. could be attacked "on the Atlantic side in both the Northern and Southern Hemispheres."[2]

FDR's concern was being fed by Secretary Morgenthau, who sent a summary of Coast Guard decryptions directly to the president. On November 14, 1941, Morgenthau wrote: "My dear Mr. President: The Treasury Cryptanalytical Unit has just decoded the following messages sent by radio from German agents in South America to Germany on the dates indicated. The original coded messages were intercepted by Coast Guard monitors." Morgenthau's memo included two decrypted messages from CEL in South America to ALD in Germany; one was on October 5th and the other a day later. The messages outlined plans of the government of Portugal to re-establish itself in Brazil if Germany occupied Portugal.

In closing, Morgenthau spelled out to President Roosevelt the importance of the Coast Guard decryption: "someone inside the office of the President of Brazil is in the employ of the Nazis. I am informed that a particularly complicated code was used for the sending of this series of messages."[3]

By the time FDR received this message, Elizebeth's Coast Guard unit was already adept at decoding the messages of German agents in the Western Hemisphere. With a network of radio intercept stations "ideally placed" from the days of Prohibition,[4] months before the 1939 invasion of Poland by Germany, Coast Guard listening posts were monitoring communications from the ships of countries that either were already fighting in—or could be expected to join—the war. That was to forewarn the Treasury Department of any potential threats to the nation's neutrality and to help determine whether the department should freeze the accounts of belligerent nations.[5] With the expanded responsibilities to monitor not just smugglers, but "whatever type of ship might be crossing or in the

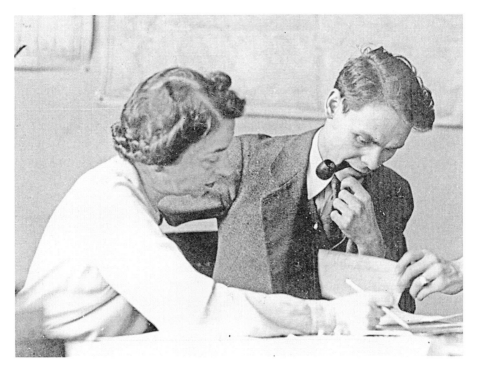

Elizebeth Friedman works on solving a code at the Coast Guard Cryptanalytic Unit in 1940 with Robert Gordon, one of the men she hired and trained (courtesy George C. Marshall Foundation, Lexington, Virginia).

water anywhere," Elizebeth said the radio intercepts increased into the thousands.[6] As a result, the Coast Guard "accidentally" began picking up and decoding clandestine radio traffic—German spies operating in the Western Hemisphere.[7]

With her eyes on the future—one that she feared could be filled with a conflict with other nations—Elizebeth took the animosity over publicizing her work to a new level. Now, besides being concerned about sensational stories about her code breaking, Elizebeth told her superiors they needed to make sure that America's potential enemies did not get a hint of what her unit truly was capable of achieving. Elizebeth might have known that the Navy was monitoring and reading some of the codes of Japanese fleet as early as 1930.[8] Certainly she was well aware of the damage that former cryptanalyst Herbert O. Yardley—a former dinner guest at the Friedmans' home[9]—had done with the publication of his book, *The American Black Chamber*, nearly a decade earlier, when the Japanese government changed its codes as a result of the revelations.[10]

The Coast Guard had been targeted by the Navy over publicity regarding its cryptanalytic unit beginning in 1934. A few months after the *I'm Alone* case was settled, just a week after a newspaper headline blared "MILLIONS ARE SAVED TO NATION BY DECODER OF SMUGGLERS," and mere days after Elizebeth had been interviewed nationwide on NBC radio about her work, a memo from an officer in Naval Operations went to the Coast Guard concerning "this question of undesirable publicity in connection with the cryptanalytical activities by Government agencies." The memo did not mention Elizebeth specifically, but there was no doubt that the Navy was concerned about publicity regarding her work. Coast Guard officials responded that they were "not entirely in sympathy" with the Navy position, but would "be glad to cooperate in this matter."[11]

The next Navy salvo at the Coast Guard Cryptanalytic Unit came from Joseph Wenger and took direct aim at the relationship between the code couple, William and Elizebeth Friedman. Wenger, who at the time headed the research section of the Navy's communications intelligence operation, and headed up its cryptanalysis operation at the start of the war,[12] had visited the Coast Guard unit and noticed I.B.M. tabulating equipment being used. Wenger noted in an August 16, 1937, memo that he revealed the Navy's use of the I.B.M. equipment "in confidence" to William Friedman. "The latter obviously passed it on to his wife who is head of the Coast Guard Cryptanalytical Unit," wrote Wenger. Tabulating equipment, the memo continued, "represents the greatest advance we have made in this field in recent years. It is in my opinion an important weapon of national defense which if revealed to foreign nations might deprive us of a great advantage in time of war."

Then the specter that disseminating the Coast Guard's code breaking abilities would aid potential enemies burst into full blossom: "In view of the extensive publicity given to the Coast Guard cryptanalytical activities I believe that immediate steps should be taken to inform responsible authorities of both the Army and Coast Guard that the Navy considers information pertaining to the application of machinery to cryptanalysis is a matter of national defense and should be withheld from disclosure under provision of the Espionage Act of 15 June 1917. It might also be well to take similar action with respect to the International Business Machine Company through their representative here in Washington."[13]

Wenger apparently didn't worry about cryptographic help flowing the opposite direction, that is from the Coast Guard to the Navy through William Friedman. William had visited the Coast Guard a year earlier and found an innovative use of the M-138 strip cipher device there. He persuaded a contractor to use leftover Bakelite parts to make one for him, "at no expense to the government," then showed it to Navy officers, including Wenger, for possible adoption by their department. "They agreed it had excellent cryptographic features, with great security," wrote William.[14]

With the Coast Guard's help to the Navy overlooked, forgotten, or swept under the rug, Wenger asked his superiors in his August 1937 memo to make sure that the Coast Guard would no longer benefit from information passed to the Army's chief cryptanalyst, William Friedman. "I have taken it upon myself to present the foregoing views to Friedman this morning and request that prompt action be taken to give this action official backing."[15]

Fifteen days after Wenger's blistering memo, Elizebeth spelled out how publicizing her work in the Lew Kim Yuen narcotics smuggling case could harm national security.

"I have suppressed actual acknowledgment that we solve messages in Oriental languages, because to practically everyone, 'Oriental languages' means Japanese and Chinese," Elizebeth counseled the Coast Guard commandant on August 31, 1937. "In view of the present situation in the Far East, I know definitely that to mention that we have ever solved a message in Japanese or Chinese will bring down upon the Coast Guard, the certain anathema of the Navy Department, and possibly of the State and War Departments. I have definite reasons for making these statements and shall be glad to make a full explanation verbally, if you so desire."[16]

That last part was something that Elizebeth obviously did not want to put in writing. Wenger's memo highlighted an ongoing ticklish family situation. William—the Army's top cryptanalyst—had already been dressed down by a superior officer for sharing information with his wife. That was something both the Friedmans adamantly denied[17] as they had a standing rule not to discuss secret matters at home.[18] "I was so completely taken not only aback, but also with surprise and by the vehemence of the Major-General's attack on me," William wrote well after the incident, "that I lost my tongue completely, and failed to ask for permission to sleep in the same room and/or bed with my wife."[19]

John Friedman, Elizebeth and Bill's son, wrote in an unpublished film script that at the time his father's Army team was working on breaking the Japanese diplomatic code, Bill began sleeping every night in a separate bed in a dressing room.[20]

Not being able to sleep together became a running joke in the family. The Friedmans' daughter, Barbara Atchison, pooh-poohed any professional rivalry between her parents. "Of course not!" Barbara declared. "Dad used to joke about how they were forced to sleep in separate bedrooms in case they talked about each other's work.... It was national security."[21]

Despite the levity over the situation, as war approached, seeing her duties switching from strictly law enforcement to protecting the wider national interest, Elizebeth took breaches of security very seriously. In consenting to an interview with *American Magazine*, she demanded that the subject be only about smuggling and that an "even stricter requirement" was that "my husband is a non-entity and unmentionable."[22]

Nevertheless, thorns from the press continued to prickle Elizebeth. An article headlined "The Woman All Spies in U.S. Fear," concluded: "the fame of Mrs. Friedman as a nemesis of plotters has gone around the world and secret agents will be extra careful to prevent giving her a chance to bare their handiwork."[23]

She sent a vitriolic memo to an assistant Treasury secretary after reading the 1939 article in the *Miami Herald* that mentioned the national security implications of her work. "It is a hodge-podge of plagiarism pulled from here, a bit from there, the whole misinterpreted and sensationalized to give color to the red-flag word SPIES—which was to snare to sell the article, of course. I had nothing whatever to do with the espionage trials, as you know."[24]

She may have had nothing to do with the specific espionage trials mentioned in the article, but one of the collateral benefits of Elizebeth's cryptanalytic unit now tracking and decoding radio messages from potential

Elizebeth was outraged by this 1939 syndicated newspaper article, which she thought sensationalized her work and compromised national security. The article is displayed on the wall memorializing her at the Elizebeth Smith Friedman Auditorium at the ATF headquarters in Washington, D.C. (photograph by the author).

enemy ships was also keeping tabs on potential spies. A few years before America entered the war, Coast Guard monitoring stations repeatedly intercepted traffic "from stations whose operating procedures and characteristics were in many respects similar to those so frequently heard on the air during the smuggling era. The solution of some of these messages revealed that the stations whose transmissions were being copied were engaged in espionage operations."[25]

"The years 1938 to December 1941 had been exciting, round-the-clock adventures, as we counter-spied into the minds and activities of the agents attempting to spy into those of the United States," Elizebeth wrote after the war.[26]

Thus, well aware of tipping the United States' advantageous—albeit highly secret—hand to what one day could be an enemy, Elizebeth's memo concerning the *Miami Herald* sought some remedy: "I am angry enough over the matter to lobby for a law making it libel to the press even to use the name of a government employee without written consent of that person and the department wherein employed." She concluded that America's free press doctrine would likely preclude such action: "Forgive the sputtering, but that's the way I feel about it, just now."[27]

Indeed, five years later at the height of World War II, a secret Army-Navy report seeking legislation to criminalize the unauthorized disclosure of communications intelligence activities noted the examples of pre-war disclosures that Elizebeth had cited to her superiors. "In 1934 and again in 1937, newspaper stories discussed the activities of several American cryptanalysts whose existence had been disclosed when called upon to testify in court as government witnesses, or when discussed in civil service newspaper columns. Public attention was thus drawn to the Army's, Navy's, and Coast Guard's cryptanalytical units," said the June 1944 report that was not declassified until 2007.[28]

As for Elizebeth's specific concerns about the *Miami Herald* article, the response from Assistant Treasury Secretary Charles Schwartz a few days later was sympathetic, but offered little to assuage Elizebeth's anger: "We felt that there was no practical purpose to be served in keeping alive public attention centered upon counter-espionage identified with the Coast Guard." He suggested that the best recourse was to ask the White House to require that "all personalities engaged in current United States counter-espionage activities be freed of attention for the present."[29]

That may have done the trick. Elizebeth did not register any complaints about press coverage after that date.

Yet Elizebeth remained unsatisfied. Even after her husband urged her to stick to her cryptanalysis career fearing she would "find life so dull,"[30] Elizebeth continued to be restless about her work, seeming to long for something more uplifting. She had completed a master's degree in archaeology at American University in Washington in 1930.[31] "Mother and dad had been interested in the Mayan hieroglyphics forever, ever since we were children," their daughter, Barbara, recalled.[32]

That passion came forth in one of Elizebeth's personnel documents. When she filled out a routine Civil Service form in June 1940, asking whether she had "any preference for types of positions other than that you now hold," Elizebeth responded, "Research in archaeology, particular reference to ancient languages, or Mayan hieroglyphics." Not only that, but she would have been willing to take a 40 percent pay cut to switch careers—from her current $4,000 a year to $2,400.[33]

She also had communicated with a professor from the University of Texas who sought help in deciphering a 150-year-old document containing Spanish, music symbols, pictures and a bit of Greek and German as well. In agreeing to try to solve the mysterious document, instead of being paid, Elizebeth responded, "I would prefer not to make a financial charge, but to have scholastic recognition for the accomplishment."[34]

Elizebeth was able to indulge her career-changing dream the same month as making her Civil Service statement. She took a multi-week driving trip to Mexico with her daughter, Barbara, and sister, Edna Diniens, in June 1940. The vacation included excursions to explore Mayan ruins in Oaxaca and Aztec temples near Mexico City,[35] certainly of great interest to someone who had studied archaeology in depth and who maintained a curiosity about Mayan hieroglyphics as Elizebeth had.

William and Elizebeth kept up a steady correspondence during the trip.

On June 4th William wrote that nothing unusual had happened at home, "except it is a lot quieter. John said to me on Sunday afternoon: 'Say, Dad, isn't the house nice and quiet without all the telephones constantly in use by Barbara and Mother?'"[36]

From Mexico later that week: "Dearest, I have had enough mountain driving to do me the rest of my life," Elizebeth wrote on Hotel Virrey de Mendoza stationary from Morelia, Michoacán. "I'd give a lot to be able to stop right this minute, settle in M. C. [Mexico City] until time to start home, then fly home."[37]

The Mexico vacation coincided with troubling news from the war that was raging in Europe. While they were enjoying the ancient sites,

Elizebeth and her companions were keeping an eye on the evacuation of British troops at Dunkirk. Elizebeth admitted in her letter to Billy, "I read only the headlines, and shrink from those."[38]

William wondered in one of his letters, "Say, what kind of blitzkrieg is that daughter of ours conducting in Mexico?" He was reacting to letters pouring in from a young male admirer of Barbara's who had been the female trio's guide in one city. William kept his wife abreast on the mundane matters of running the household, living on $2 a day while she was away. But he was also paying closer attention to the news than his wife: "the world scene looks mighty bad now and I'm afraid that we are in for a storm the end of which none can now foresee," William offered. Then in an intriguing finish, he remarked that he was wrapping up writing a paper that evening: "I wish I could write about forbidden subjects. What a story could be told."[39]

That story may have been about William's Army cryptanalysis team making breakthroughs on creating a machine to decrypt the Japanese diplomatic cipher system known as Purple. "It required almost two years of concentrated effort to break down this system and it was indeed fortunate that this had been accomplished by September 1940," William wrote in "A Brief History of U.S. Cryptologic Operations 1917–1929," classified "Secret" in 1942 and not declassified until 2008.[40]

William's superiors accused him of discussing the highly secret work on Purple with his wife. "To the end she said that the day they cracked Purple he never said a word to her about it, he never mentioned it," said Virginia Military Institute history professor Colonel Rose Mary Sheldon. "He just came home like it was any other day, said 'What's for dinner, honey?' and they sat down and had a meal."[41]

Elizebeth reiterated to an NSA oral historian in 1976 that William never discussed any of his secret duties with her.[42] Although she denies discussing their secret work at home—even at the critical juncture of breaking Purple—Elizebeth must have had some inkling of the important work William was doing. The Friedmans' son, John, wrote that his parents talked in "generalities" about their work and the ongoing conflicts in Asia and Europe led Elizebeth to "guess that he [William] has been given some special extra responsibilities."[43] The couple, by this time married for more than two decades, were also adept at reading each other without words. Elizebeth told a historian that "many times there was a certain grim look" on William's mouth. "Any expression on my face he certainly could read, and he might be, ah, very cognizant of what I thought about something," she said.[44]

The one exception Elizebeth noted in her memoirs about the prohibition on discussing their government secrets was the day General Mauborgne told William that, because work on the Japanese ciphers was not going well, he should drop everything else to "take care of it." "It's the only time that my William ever mentioned to me anything," about the Japanese code, she later admitted.[45]

Thus, whether through words, body language or action, Elizebeth must have recognized the toll that working on this secret project was taking on her husband, recalling that he would be up until two or three in the morning. "Sometimes I awaken and find him down in the kitchen making a Dagwood sandwich in the middle of the night."[46]

About the time of the Purple breakthrough there was a difference in William's demeanor. Barbara, who was still living at her parents' home, said one night her father came down to make a Dagwood around midnight. Quoting a guest of the Friedmans whose name she did not remember, Barbara said, "He knew that he had done something important because he seemed so elated, so triumphant." Her father hadn't given up any secret information, but showed "that it was a great relief, that it was a great joy almost."[47]

Less than four months later that joy would turn into a crisis for the Friedman family.

On January 4, 1941, William was admitted to the Army's Walter Reed Hospital. After the strain and "overwork" of shepherding the creation of the Purple deciphering machine, he had collapsed from extreme nervous fatigue. Elizebeth traveled each day to Walter Reed during William's 11-week stay in the psychiatric ward. She spent a large part of the day with her husband, but also consulted with his doctors.

William returned to active duty as a full colonel in April, but was honorably discharged less than a month later "by reason of physical disqualification." William continued in his post as a civilian, but protested his dismissal as an Army officer; his appeal of the discharge was turned down.[48] William's commission was not restored until 1946, after a review of the case by the Army's adjutant-general.[49]

So, on top of her fear of press leaks, fantasy of leaving the Coast Guard and creating a different career for herself, now Elizebeth faced another quandary: would her husband's important work cause a relapse that would put him back in the hospital?

With what she considered the Army's mistreatment of her husband, busting him to a civilian, is it any wonder then, just a month before the United States entered the war, that Elizebeth, when faced with a major decision about what her role in the war should be, asked to remain in a non-military post, rather than be transferred to the Navy?

There was a rivalry—as well as distinct differences in missions—between the Coast Guard and Navy that kept the maritime agencies from merging in peacetime. A 1933 proposal to combine the two was shot down because it would not result in any reduction of duplication or federal expenditures. "The morale of the Coast Guard would be destroyed by transfer to the Navy Department," one memo concluded.[50]

Yet there was no question that the Coast Guard would be absorbed by the Navy when the U.S. entered the war. The Secretaries of the Treasury and Navy signed a policy declaration in September 1936 that merged the Coast Guard's communications "as part of the Navy organization in time of war." That included assigning secret or confidential classifications to Coast Guard cryptographic publications.[51] A study a year later concluded that Navy and Coast Guard intelligence personnel needed to cooperate and have an "exchange of technical information and in making plans for war."[52]

Heading into the war, the Navy had an acute shortage of communications personnel. The communications security section, OP-20-G, which housed Navy cryptanalysts, found it had an especially high need for more trained code breakers.[53] The five-member Coast Guard Cryptanalytic Unit would help ease the Navy's manpower shortage in that specialty.

Presidential Executive Order 8929 transferred the entire Coast Guard to the Navy on November 1, 1941.[54] But Elizebeth Friedman dragged her heels in making the transition; her career was anchored in the Treasury Department. A few days after the official transfer, at a staff meeting with Treasury Secretary Morgenthau, his assistant, Herbert Gaston, reported Mrs. Friedman's recalcitrance. "She is very discontented about the prospect of having to work for the Navy. She doesn't want to work for the Navy." Gaston outlined Elizebeth's work history, starting with Customs, then being borrowed by the Coast Guard where she created the cryptanalytic unit, "perhaps ... as good as there is in the Government, as you know."

Gaston said that all of Elizebeth's civilian employees wanted to remain with the Treasury Department as well. "What she is very rebellious and gloomy about is the prospect of working with the Navy and the question is would you want to ask Secretary Knox [secretary of the Navy] for permission to transfer that unit over to the Treasury."

Secretary Morgenthau was reluctant to grant Elizebeth's request. "I want Mrs. Friedman to write me a letter, 'My dear Mr. Morgenthau, I would like to stay in the Treasury for the following reasons,'" the secretary told his assistant, "and then based on that letter, we will write a letter to Secretary Knox. I just don't want it to appear that I am taking the initiative."

Another assistant reminded the group that the nation was on the precipice of war and that "if she was best in the Government she belongs, at a time like this, in the War and Navy [departments]." Assistant Secretary Gaston replied, "I think if the Navy wants the outfit we would be in a weak position to try to hold them."

The final word on the subject came from Secretary Morgenthau: "The woman wants to stay. We could use her. The chances are nine out of ten the Navy thinks they are so good they don't need her, but if Frank Knox says, 'Yes, we want her,' I won't argue any more than when Stark [chief of Naval Operations] called up and said, 'I need the Coast Guard today,' I said, 'You say you need it, and I say you have it,' just like that. So if he comes back and says, 'I want Mrs. Friedman.' But why shouldn't I give her a chance to stay? It will be just as a matter of kindness, that is all."[55]

Elizebeth's memoirs are silent about her discontent with being transferred to the Navy.

Nothing in the official or her personal records indicates that she ever submitted a letter to Secretary Morgenthau requesting that she remain with Treasury.

However, Treasury Secretary Morgenthau did request that the Cryptanalytic Unit remain with his department rather than be transferred with the Coast Guard. Navy Secretary Knox countered with a letter on December 3rd authorizing the Treasury Department to keep half of the cryptanalysts, but the rest would be transferred to the Navy.[56]

As a result of that letter, just a day before the Pearl Harbor attack, Elizebeth was called to the commandant's office to participate in a telephone negotiation among Coast Guard, Treasury and Navy officials. An agreement was reached that the Coast Guard cryptanalytic section that Elizebeth created in 1931 would remain whole and not be split up, but its five members would be transferred en masse to the Navy. Yet the Coast Guard unit would continue to perform cryptographic services for the Treasury Department if requested.[57]

Perhaps Elizebeth declined to submit a request to remain with Treasury, because by that time, November 1941, she was already spending long hours working for various federal agencies that needed her to prepare for the coming war. She often was away from home at dinner time, so

Elizebeth arranged for a local restaurant to bring a meal every night to her 15-year-old son, John.[58]

Elizebeth's job description listed her as performing "difficult and responsible work requiring considerable cryptanalytic training," as well as training and instructing others in cryptanalytic work.[59] Beyond breaking codes, her job also required cryptography—that is creating codes and ciphers to be used in communications—for about 40 percent of her work.[60]

Thus she became a utility player for agencies that, in the months preceding the war, needed to develop their own cryptographic services or train people in cryptanalytic science. In December 1940 the FBI had created its own code breaking section, mainly to keep tabs on German spies in the U.S. As the unit continued to grow over the next several months, the FBI requested that Elizebeth give its neophyte unit additional cryptanalysis training, perhaps to expand its efforts to break German and Japanese diplomatic codes.[61] Elizebeth gave the FBI's cryptanalytic branch chief, W.G.B. Blackburn, an intensive training program that took nearly two months.[62]

About the same time, June 1941, Treasury Secretary Morgenthau, authorized his staff and other employees to cooperate with the head of the newly created Office of Coordinator of Information (COI), Colonel "Wild Bill" Donovan.[63] Morgenthau followed up with a memo stating that the president had authorized all agencies to give defense information and assistance to Colonel Donovan.[64]

So at the same time that she put out the feeler to halt her transfer to the Navy, Elizebeth received a major assignment to create "an independent code room and message center"[65] for Donovan, whose Coordinator of Information unit would soon become the Office of Strategic Services (OSS), the forerunner of the Central Intelligence Agency. Any overseas communication from the COI was going through the cryptographic services of the State Department. Colonel Donovan wanted his own separate cryptographic devices and codes to communicate with embassies and agents in the field.[66]

Elizebeth had already shown a talent for procuring such devices as well as creating the Treasury Department's cryptographic systems.[67] In an NSA lecture many years later, William Friedman credited his wife with increasing the Coast Guard's "cryptosecurity" in the 1930s by obtaining an innovative strip cipher system that he had trouble getting for the Army. It was called the M-138-A, the same Coast Guard instrument that William had shown to Navy officers in 1936; it had an aluminum base to hold cardboard strips of alphabets to create cipher messages. "It may be of interest to you to learn," said William, "that after I had given up in my attempts to find a firm that would or could make such aluminum grooved devices in quantity, Mrs. Friedman, by womanly wiles and cajolery on behalf of her own group in the Coast Guard, succeeded in inducing or enticing one firm to make them for her." Besides being the Coast Guard's cryptographic device, Strip Cipher Device, Type M-138-A was used from 1935 to about 1942 by the Army, the Navy and the Marine Corps as well as the Treasury and State Departments. Even after finding more secure systems early in World War II, the armed services continued using the M-138-A as a backup.[68]

So, with an already established relationship between Secretary Morgenthau and Colonel Donovan and Elizebeth's expertise in training cryptographers and procuring cryptographic devices, she seemed to be the perfect choice to fill the code making needs of the COI. As a result, Elizebeth received temporary orders to fulfill the demands of Colonel Donovan. Starting in mid–November, coordinating with one of Donovan's chief aides, Marine Captain Jimmy Roosevelt,[69] the president's son, Elizebeth and her team worked at night and on weekends assembling supplies and equipment from their own stores to stock the new COI cryptographic facility. She also began evaluating potential employees to use the newly created cipher system.[70]

Within three weeks of Elizebeth starting this new assignment, a reluctant America was shocked into entering the war. The Japanese bombing of Pearl Harbor on December 7th seemed to surprise even William Friedman, who had been leading the Army Signal Corps team using the Purple machine to decode Japanese diplomatic messages. Those messages—code named "Magic"—hinted strongly at the empire's intent to attack somewhere, but not necessarily Hawaii. On that fateful Sunday, cryptanalysts in the U.S. War Department actually decoded the final section of a 14-part message Japan was sending to the State Department, reading Japan's intention to break relations with the United States, before code clerks in the Japanese embassy officials decoded it and presented it to the secretary of state.[71]

The Friedmans' daughter, Barbara, was attending a performance of the New York Philharmonic Orchestra that afternoon. "And they broke in at three o'clock to say the Japanese had bombed Pearl Harbor and that was when I got on the phone and I called mother and dad. And I said, 'I heard this.' Dad said, practically sobbing, 'It's true, it's true. They knew, they knew, but they knew.'"[72] Elizebeth's memoirs never addressed her husband's enigmatic reaction regarding the attack. She wrote that after working until noon on Saturday, William was called back into work Sunday. She pieced together information about William's team breaking Purple only by following the Congressional hearings about the attack five years later.[73]

On Monday, December 8th, the pre-war preparations in the Coordinator of Information headquarters resumed with urgency now that America had joined the worldwide conflict. Then the tug-of-war over Elizebeth Friedman's highly valued skills escalated.

The day after the Pearl Harbor bombing, Colonel Donovan sent the War Department a request for two lessons in cryptography to be sent "by safe hand."[74] Donovan's assistant, W.A. Kimbel, reported that "Mrs. Friedman of Treasury," along with others, were proceeding in establishing the COI's cable and code section: "Basic principles have been established. Certain personnel are already under consideration and the proposed organization should be made effective at an early date."[75]

But apparently things were not proceeding quickly enough for Colonel Donovan. Now the COI wanted Elizebeth to work there fulltime. "Conversations had been had with Secretary Morgenthau and Mr. Gaston concerning transfer of Mrs. Freedman [sic] to this office pending return of Lt. Jones [Leonard Jones of the Coast Guard[76]]," reported another Kimbel memo. "An official request from Colonel Donovan to Secretary Morgenthau is now in order to complete this matter. Mrs. Freedman [sic] is urgently needed."[77]

Donovan followed up with a letter to Secretary Morgenthau, requesting that Elizebeth be assigned to him until Lieutenant Jones returned from duty in England. "I make this request only because of the urgent need for her services pending the establishment of our permanent code section," wrote Donovan.[78]

A staff meeting of the Treasury secretary the next day sealed Elizebeth's fate for the rest of the war. Assistant Secretary Gaston told Morgenthau that despite having a need for her services within Treasury, moving Elizebeth from the Coast Guard and Navy had not been achieved. "She has not come over here because they all agreed and Mrs. Friedman agreed herself that to split the unit would be bad, that it would interrupt their work and it would take her a long time to build an organization where she could function effectively."

Morgenthau seemed to be exasperated and gave in: "Will you write a letter for my signature to Donovan that Mrs. Friedman is in the Coast Guard and he should take it up with the Secretary of the Navy? All right?"[79]

Four days later a letter from the assistant secretary of the Navy to the chief of the civilian personnel section of the Coast Guard gave notice that Elizebeth was to be "detailed to the Office of the Coordinator of Information until further notice."[80]

She continued her feverish work to create a workable cryptographic system for Donovan. Working nights and weekends Elizebeth and her staff created versions of double transposition and strip ciphers for the COI to use exclusively. After setting up the system, her team also spent time encoding and decoding the COI's first encrypted messages.[81] They labored to install communications links between Washington and the COI office in London. And just as she had used her "womanly wiles" to obtain the sophisticated M-138-A for the Coast Guard several years earlier, now Elizebeth used her years of contacts in the cryptographic community to pull off a coup. She obtained two Hagelin cipher machines for the COI that had been scheduled to be delivered to other federal agencies.[82]

Elizebeth had established the COI cryptographic system by Christmas Eve. "For the information and guidance of those concerned, the cable section, which shall be referred to as a message center, has been established in the basement of the administration building," a memorandum to Colonel Donovan declared. "Its purpose is to send and receive coded messages from agents and offices in other parts of the world."[83]

Though she was still working on some additional "aids and materials," Elizebeth wrote a confidential three-page memo to Colonel Donovan on December 29th. It outlined the work that took several weeks to achieve.

> I together with my staff at Coast Guard Headquarters and assisted by Lieutenant Jones, prepared a large volume of material and supplies which was necessary in the preliminary setting-up of cryptographic communication with your London office. As a consequence of the delay in the arrival from abroad of the cipher machines intended for your organization, it was necessary to make some provision for carrying on communications in the meantime by this method. This was arranged by the joint efforts of Lieutenant Jones and myself, by borrowing of machines from two other sources, none being available for purchase in this country.
>
> Through the generous authorization by the Commandant of the Coast Guard, I have had transferred the cryptographic devices and material necessary for equipping the cryptographic section of your message center, as well as your representatives going out into the field. This includes cipher devices of special manufacture which would be impossible to procure by purchase at any time, and which would be impossible to have manufactured under present conditions without the passing of many months, if not years.

Elizebeth complained, however, even with her vast experience and "capacity for judging and aptitude or flair for this type of work," the selection of cryptographic personnel had been taken away from her—assigned to others in the COI.

She also made three recommendations to Colonel Donovan. The first was that field agents be "thoroughly drilled in the systems of communication provided for them." She suggested that the training should be for a few hours each day for at least five days. The second recommendation was for "a general indoctrination in the discussion of and handling of classified informational matter" throughout the organization. Acknowledging that this "indoctrination is a long and difficult process," she thought that a special manual should be issued for COI personnel.

"Finally," Elizebeth—ever mindful of maintaining secrecy—wrote in the memo, "I should like to recommend that a specially prepared oath be taken by all persons in your organization, including Civil Service employees and all others without distinction. I prepared a special oath applicable to the message center, and all persons employed therein so far have executed this oath. An oath suitable for the general personnel could be devised and prepared by the Personnel Office, and executed in each case as the person reports for duty."[84]

The next day Colonel Donovan started acting on Elizebeth's recommendations, sending a request for cryptographic training literature to the Army Signal Corps.[85] Over the next several weeks he sent more memos to enact Mrs. Friedman's recommendations on training[86] and security[87] for the new COI communications section.

A history of the OSS noted that the new message center developed and organized by Elizebeth was "as completely segregated as possible to meet the requirements of cryptographic security." In an indication of how well Elizebeth and her team had accomplished the tasks assigned, "The Message Center was the only communications function set up adequately during COI," according to the agency's history written six years later.[88]

As she wrapped up her work for "Wild Bill" Donovan, America was three weeks into the second world war of Elizebeth's lifetime. Secrecy oaths and loyalty to the government were paramount in her mind. For years the Coast Guard had conducted investigations of potential civilian employees "to root out any potential liabilities from its intelligence network."[89] The secrecy oath she proposed for COI officers reflected a method to address Elizebeth's longstanding concern that information leaking out about cryptanalytic secrets would harm national security. Just six months before, Elizebeth herself had been required by law to sign an affidavit stating that she did not advocate the overthrow of the government nor was a member of a political party that did advocate its overthrow by force or violence.[90]

Even though she resisted being transferred to the Navy, Elizebeth's sense of duty and patriotism may have kept her from protesting too strongly. Her common sense—plus some hunch about her husband's important work in the Army—must have told her that she could do more for America's war effort as a cryptanalyst in the Navy than if she had remained with Treasury.

When 1941 ended, the die was cast—her doubts were left behind; Elizebeth Friedman was in the Navy now. As the United States entered its second month of World War II, she was in command[91] of Coast Guard Unit 387—soon to be called OP-20-GU by the Navy—whose mission was to intercept and decode the messages of enemy spies in the Western Hemisphere.

=8=

"The spy stuff!"

As America's war machine geared up early in 1942, Elizebeth Friedman's band of Coast Guard cryptanalysts, that had already been monitoring and decrypting the radio messages of German spies in the Western Hemisphere for several months, was positioned to have a great impact on the war effort.

Late in 1941 the United States ambassador to Brazil reported a large number of Axis-controlled clandestine radio transmitters were sending messages about South Atlantic shipping that could harm the nation's defense.[1] The Coast Guard had stationed radiomen in Brazil to intercept those messages. One of them, Glen Boles, told an oral historian that German agents sent their encrypted messages in "a tiny signal underneath bigger signals," but the Coast Guardsmen were able to intercept all of the land and sea messages being sent back to Germany.[2]

Those messages from Brazil went to Elizebeth's group, which deciphered them. Following the ambassador's warning, the information was then passed to President Roosevelt, who had the FBI dispatch an agent to Rio de Janeiro to investigate.[3] The Coast Guard also passed along its knowledge of how to solve the ciphers used to transmit messages from Brazil to Germany to U.S. Army code breakers.[4]

Axis agents in South America were feeding information back to Hamburg, one of the principal sending and receiving stations for the Abwehr, the German intelligence agency.[5] Some agents were tasked with finding information about American companies that handled uranium ore, an indication of Germany's desire to keep abreast of the United States' atomic bomb prospects.[6] Others sought intelligence on the Panama Canal[7] or U.S. aircraft being ferried through Brazil to help British forces in Africa.[8]

One of the primary aims of the German Naval High Command,

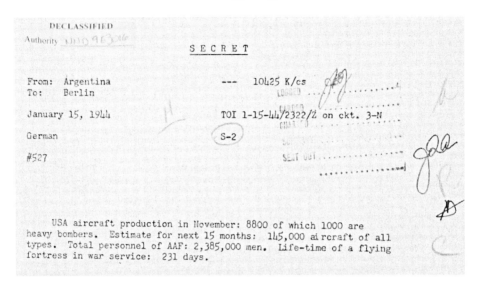

SECRET

From: Argentina
To: Berlin

January 15, 1944

German

#527

--- 10425 K/cs

TOI 1-15-44/2322/Z on ckt. 3-N

S-2

USA aircraft production in November: 8800 of which 1000 are heavy bombers. Estimate for next 15 months: 145,000 aircraft of all types. Total personnel of AAF: 2,385,000 men. Life-time of a flying fortress in war service: 231 days.

A Coast Guard Unit 387 decryption of a German agent message in Argentina shows Berlin was interested in tracking aircraft production in the United States early in 1944 (National Archives, College Park, Maryland).

however, was to obtain detailed information on the routes of Allied convoys and individual ships in North and South American waters so that U-boats could track and sink them. As a result, the Abwehr prioritized Atlantic ports in Latin America as "rewarding locations for clandestine observation posts."[9] There was no doubt that German spies were aiding the Reich's war machine. "Not only did they forward a quantity of basic economic data useful to Nazi analysis," reported the Office of Naval Intelligence, "but the shipping information supplied resulted in the loss to submarines of British and Allied ships."[10]

In a nation that, prior to Pearl Harbor, was ill equipped for a global conflict, America nearly lost the Battle of the Atlantic in the first few months of World War II. As devastating as the December 7th Japanese attack was, the losses to German submarines—1027 ships sunk in 1942 alone[11]—had a greater impact on the U.S. and her allies.[12] In June of that year, Navy Commander in Chief, Admiral Ernest King noted that "the losses by submarines off our Atlantic seaboard and in the Caribbean now threaten our entire war effort." King reported to Army Chief of Staff George Marshall that the Navy had been unprepared for the German U-boats attacking convoys carrying supplies vital in the effort to defeat the Nazis: "I am fearful that another month or two of this will so cripple our means of transport that we will be unable to bring sufficient men and planes to bear against the enemy in critical theaters to exercise a determining influence on the war."[13]

Thus the Allies had an urgent need to combat German submarines in any way they could. As the war progressed, agencies in both the United States and Great Britain would attempt to decrypt secret German naval messages that used the highly respected Enigma cipher machine. The Germans believed that early three-rotor Enigmas used for communicating with submarines, with a theoretical possibility of each rotor generating 10^{114} ciphers, was unbreakable. With a web of internal wiring and a variable plugboard the Germans called a "stecker" to modify the output, the Germans changed the cryptographic key for the device every day. The machine destroyed the standard cryptanalytic technique of alphabet frequency counts because any infrequently used letter could appear just as often as one that was far more common in normal communications.[14] Using just three rotors the Enigma had more than one million possible settings. When the stecker was added, the combination increased to about 200 million variations.[15]

In February 1942 the Germans improved the Enigmas used on their U-boats by adding a fourth rotor that extended the cipher generating capabilities of the machine even further.[16]

Coast Guard Unit 387, the cryptanalytic team that Elizebeth headed at the start of 1942, did not work directly on German naval codes. Yet with the submarines' slaughter off America's shores, the Allies were searching for any method to end the crisis, including the Coast Guard's specialty, breaking clandestine radio messages of German spies feeding information from their Atlantic watch posts.

"All the countries of the world were trying to develop something that nobody else could read and make sense out of," Elizebeth dictated to her memoirs long after the war. "They were all playing with machines and the Germans for years before the war had been using a machine called the enigma [sic]. It was a very complicated machine with a lot of different parts and the machines would be built with one arrangement of parts to be used between Germany and Chile and another arrangement of parts to be used between diplomatic offices in Germany and Mexico."[17]

One of the Allies' goals during the war was to figure out how to break the various Enigma machines used by the German Army, Navy, air forces, and yes—their spies. Until the day of her death 35 years after World War II, Elizebeth remained mostly mum about her secret work from those years. Yet her memoirs hinted at a pride in being part of the thousands who had been tasked with detecting and decrypting information that the enemy wanted kept secret: "They even had a less superior enigma [sic] machine that was used by Germany and her confidential agents—her spies, and that's what I did! The spy stuff!"[18]

Elizebeth may have been proud of her war work, which included the Coast Guard breaking some of the vaunted Enigma ciphers.[19] But from the limited information available about her during those years, it seems she also must have had many frustrations as well.

One of Elizebeth's biggest irritations had to have been losing command of the Coast Guard cryptanalytic unit that she had created more than a decade earlier, nurtured through numerous rum running and drug smuggling cases and managed to put on a war footing as threats from Axis powers loomed. But, with the Navy overseeing the Coast Guard now, she was fully engaged in the military, where there were a couple of institutional biases working against her.

One was the Navy tradition that officers should not report to civilians.[20] Another prevented women from being in charge of men. Elizebeth wasn't the only female to face such discrimination. Agnes Driscoll, a long-time code breaker for the Navy, also faced the same issue. In an oral history of a Naval intelligence officer after the war, the National Security Agency (NSA) interviewer asked: "How come they didn't commission Mrs. Driscoll?" The answer seemed obvious to the male officer: "She's a woman." The interviewer's response, "That's right,"[21] indicated how routine gender bias was.

Still another prejudice working against Elizebeth was that she was married to William Friedman, a man with a distinctly Jewish heritage. One of England's top cryptanalysts outlined his thoughts about a number of issues the two countries faced as they joined forces in early 1942. "The dislike of Jews prevalent in the U.S. Navy is a factor to be considered," wrote Lieutenant Colonel John Tiltman,[22] "as nearly all the leading Army cryptographers are Jews."[23]

So it was in this atmosphere that in the spring or summer of 1942 that the Coast Guard appointed a male officer with less experience in cryptanalysis than Elizebeth to head the operation. While a Coast Guard lieutenant in the 1930s, Leonard Jones had trained with William Friedman.[24] Jones had assisted Elizebeth in December 1941 while she created a message and cryptography center for the Coordinator of Information (COI), Wild Bill Donovan.[25] Now, midway through 1942, and elevated to the rank of Lieutenant Commander, the Coast Guard named Jones to oversee Unit 387. An analysis of Unit 387's accomplishments written by a Coast Guard captain in 1998 reports that Jones oversaw the high-frequency radio monitoring stations, while Elizebeth "spearheaded" the "technical cryptanalysis effort."[26]

The exact date that Leonard Jones began leading the crew is unclear. Memos at the COI show that he was still working there until early April 1942[27]; the first document indicating Lieutenant Commander Jones[28] was in charge of Unit 387 shows up in August of that year,[29] but he may have taken command in mid–May.[30] Whenever the transition did occur, Elizebeth would remain Jones' deputy commander for the remainder of the war,[31] though she considered herself to be "just one of the workers" in the group.[32]

The 329-page *History of Coast Guard Unit 387*, stamped TOP SECRET ULTRA,[33] extensively details the methods that the 23-member Jones/Friedman team[34] used to break both hand-made and Enigma ciphers on the Green and Red clandestine circuits in South America, but it says nothing about the individuals who worked in the outfit. Afterwards Elizebeth herself refused to venture into her war work in public, referring to it only as "that vast dome of silence from which I can never emerge."[35] She also told an NSA historian prior to an interview in 1976 that the information she provided about the war "should be held in confidence and not included in histories or articles." Regarding the wartime secrets that Elizebeth did not want published, the historian, Robert Louis Benson, wrote that in the full transcript, "this information is underlined in red." As the result of a Freedom of Information request, the NSA was unable to find that transcript, but did locate and release a six-page summary 39 years after the interview.[36]

Elizebeth's war-time story is inextricably intertwined with that of her Coast Guard section. To get a clue of what Elizebeth Friedman did in the Second World War's cryptanalysis sanctuaries, one has to extrapolate from the Unit 387 history, then fill in the holes with a few, once-secret documents that can be found in the archives of the United States, England and Canada, plus oral histories of Elizebeth and other Friedman papers that the NSA declassified in 2015—70 years after the war's end.

One of the most intriguing of those documents is an April 15, 1942, memo to Elizebeth from the Coast Guard commandant for "temporary duty; orders; travel." The memo does not spell out what the travel orders are for, referring to another memo, "see file ET 14."[37] No follow-up ET 14 file for the travel orders have been found. Other documents show that ET stands for the Treasury Department and ET 14 signifies the Coast Guard. Another administrative code on the memo is "531," which a 1936 Coast Guard manual explains is a reference to mileage or transportation.[38]

Elizebeth's April 1942 travel order coincides with a major meeting that took place among the cryptanalytical czars from England, Canada and the United States. The meeting was called in Washington April 1st to the 17th to coordinate the cryptanalysis activities among the allies for the duration of the war. In what had been described as "a chaotic state of Allied intelligence gathering," the allied nations agreed to work jointly on enemy cryptanalytic problems and divide the effort because the "challenges were greater than could be met by the resources of a single nation."[39]

Elizebeth fit right into the group. As the head of the Coast Guard unit, she already had been coordinating with British and Canadian cryptanalysts. She told her 1976 NSA interviewer that she "probably" had contact with British COMINT (communications intelligence) "prior to Pearl Harbor."[40]

In March 1942 she received a letter from the Canadian Examination Unit, that country's secret cryptanalysis agency. The letter was written by Oliver Strachey, whom the British Government Code & Cypher School (GC&CS) had named to head the Ottawa operation, replacing the discredited Herbert Yardley. Strachey was so instrumental in the United Kingdom's effort to break Abwehr ciphers that the decryptions coming from his group were code named ISOS, for Intelligence Service Oliver Strachey.[41]

With his success already proven against the Germans, Strachey offered his arcane expertise in working on Abwehr hand ciphers. His March letter to Elizebeth explained how to break a "comb," which was a grid system that blacked out some spaces in the vertical columns with messages written horizontally[42]:

> Dear Mrs. Friedman:
>
> Here is the little volume I promised you. Keys change every month, a multiple of 30 pages apart: e.g. 1st October was page 251, 2nd 252, 3rd 253 etc. 1st November was page 311, etc.
> The key is formed in the usual way from the first 26 letters on the page.
> The comb is derived from the same 26 letters counting A as 1, B as 2, etc., so that if the key begins HERTOWN etc. the comb will have its first line 8 letters long, the 2nd 5 long and so on.
> Read down the odd columns and up the even.
> In January 1942 the page was 21 (a different series of thirties from 1942).
> Yours very sincerely, OLIVER STRACHEY, Examination Unit[43]

So, with an established relationship with Canadian and British code breakers, and Lieutenant Commander Jones not yet in charge of Coast Guard cryptanalysts, Elizebeth participated in the three-nation exchange of ideas to defeat the Axis powers' cryptographic abilities. Her participation is revealed in a report on the Washington meeting filed in Great Britain's archives. In the April 8th minutes of Committee B, which dealt with the "Method of obtaining W/T [wireless transmission] intelligence from intercepted W/T traffic, including D/F [direction finding] bearings," there is a list of the committee members. Present are seven members from the U.S. Navy, three from the U.S. Army, four from the U.S. Coast Guard, four from Canada plus six British representatives. Friedman is the name at the top of the Coast Guard delegation, but—in another indication of the era's gender bias—someone, apparently assuming no woman would have served on the otherwise all-male committee, has struck out the "s" in "Mrs.," leaving the name "Mr. Friedman." There is still a faint "s" detectable under the whiteout.[44]

At that meeting, chaired by Navy Commander Joseph Wenger, participants noted that the U.S. effort to analyze German transmissions was

BRIEF OF MINUTES

COMMITTEE B

METHOD OF OBTAINING W/T INTELLIGENCE FROM INTERCEPTED
W/T TRAFFIC, INCLUDING D/F BEARINGS

COMDR. J. N. WENGER, CHAIRMAN

1430 April 8, 1942

Present:
U.S. Navy	U.S. Army	U.S. Coast Guard
Comdr. Wenger	Maj.Schukraft	Mr. Friedman
Comdr. Redman	Capt.Brown	Lt.Comdr. Polio
Lt.Comdr.Welker	Lieut.Rowlett	Lt.Comdr.Peterson
Lt.Comdr.Parke		Mr. Bishop
Lt.Comdr.Scott		
Lt.Comdr.Daisley		
Lieut. Fravel		

Canadian	British
Capt. Drake	Capt. Sandwith
Comdr.de Marbois	Sq.Ldr. Morgan
Lieut. Foster	Capt. Maidment
Lieut. Hope	Major Haigh
	Lieut. Bartram
	Mr.Stutton

This page listing attendees at a U.S., British and Canadian meeting on cryptanalysis in April 1942 illustrates the subtle discrimination Elizebeth faced as a woman in a field dominated by men. Note the white out over the "s" in "Mr. Friedman." Beneath the white out, one can still see a faint "s" (National Archives of the U.K.).

"more or less at the beginning stages due to the small amount of traffic available." The group discussed problems in identifying signals, frequencies and training of personnel. A British representative remarked that the Allied traffic analysts "must be steeped in the enemy's wireless organization. They must think like a German; they must know the German procedure; they must know the mentality of the man who is controlling their communications."[45]

When the chairman noted that they had not yet heard from the Coast Guard, Lieutenant Commander Peterson said, "I don't believe we have anything to offer that has not already been covered." Wenger replied, "Of course, the Coast Guard is working in a special field of their own, but nevertheless they have some of these problems to contend with."[46] That special field, of course, was clandestine—or intercepting and decrypting the messages of spies. The final report of the three-nation conference concluded that the Allies needed a better system for coordinating, correlating and decrypting military and diplomatic systems "the same as is now being done with clandestine radio traffic,"[47] suggesting that the organization led by Elizebeth was a model for others attempting similar work.

More than seven decades after that meeting a Coast Guard admiral revealed an even closer collaboration between Unit 387 and the British. Speaking at a 2014 ceremony naming the Bureau of Alcohol, Tobacco, Firearms and Explosives auditorium for Elizebeth, Rear Adm. Christopher Tomney said Jones and Elizebeth "traveled to England for cryptographic exchanges." No documents verifying such a trip for Elizebeth can be found in the archives, but Tomney highlighted the team's accomplishments: "Under the leadership of Commander Jones and Mrs. Friedman, Coast Guard Unit 387 went on to intercept over 10,000 encrypted clandestine messages from 65 different German clandestine circuits. And of that total, more than 8,500 of those signals were actually cracked."[48]

Another agency that Coast Guard cryptanalysts dealt with was the FBI. As early as May 1940, FBI Director J. Edgar Hoover concluded that the "best way to control Nazi espionage in the United States was to wipe out the spy nests in Latin America."[49] With the pre-war Coast Guard already intercepting and decrypting the clandestine messages from German agents in South America, Elizebeth's operation began receiving frequent requests from the FBI for solutions to those intercepted messages. "At the outset Coast Guard relations with the FBI were cordial," Jones wrote in a 1944 report. "As the situation developed however it became increasingly evident that while the FBI was demanding everything the Coast Guard had, it was at the same time withholding information which would have been extremely useful to the Coast Guard. This led to a deterioration of the initially friendly relations."[50]

The rivalry and differing priorities of the U.S. agencies involved in secret cryptanalysis created a bureaucratic jungle of red tape and animosity among the players. Those involved included the Army, Navy, Coast Guard, FBI, Office of Strategic Services (OSS) as well as the Federal Communications Commission (FCC). A few months before America entered the war, when the FBI refused to share the COMINT that it received from the Coast Guard with other agencies, the Treasury Department ordered the Coast Guard to distribute its decryptions to the State Department, Army and Navy as well.[51]

One of the circuits that the Coast Guard monitored in 1941 was designated "VVV TEST-AOR." In July of that year, when the FBI arrested 33 members of a German espionage ring in the United States, Coast Guard officials learned that part of VVV TEST-AOR was an FBI-controlled radio station that had been retransmitting signals from Mexico through a Long Island station to the Abwehr in Hamburg. Coast Guard intelligence officials determined that the information the FBI was feeding to Hamburg seemed to be "of demonstrable value to German U-boat operations."[52]

Even the British, whose cryptanalytic efforts were centralized in the GC&CS, took note of the Americans' bureaucracy issues. Following the April 1942 Washington conference, a British memo on the coordination of intelligence in the Western Hemisphere considered the "absurdity" of the United States' decentralized system: "Within the Services there is, it is true, some rivalry between Naval Intelligence and Army Signals. But this is nothing like as serious as the complete lack of sympathy between both of these and the F.B.I. The result has been much unnecessary duplication of effort, and a mutual secretiveness which has inevitably ended by confusing both policy and action."[53]

The memo gave an example of the difficulty in cutting through American red tape, explaining that the Coast Guard's chief responsibility for intercepting clandestine messages, led to "paradoxical results" and made it difficult for the unit to help in other areas. "If the Coastguards suspect that an intercept is Japanese, they have reluctantly to recommend that it be passed to the F.C.C. The F.C.C, in order to identify it, are obliged to consult the Army and Navy. The Army and Navy are at least able to say that it is, or is not, of a type familiar to them, and accordingly is, or is not, to be treated as illicit. Fortunately, our relations with both Army and Navy are now such that this cumbersome procedure can be dispensed with."[54]

In an effort to rid itself of the "cumbersome procedure," Unit 387 instituted a plan to register all unidentified signals, which the British noted had "already proved its value." The Coast Guard shared its files in a weekly Friday conference with the British Radio Security Service (RSS), which the British deemed "highly successful."[55] The FBI, however, "took exception" to those weekly exchanges, according to Jones' 1944 Coast Guard memo, because it violated the FBI's own arrangement with the RSS. After that there was no weekly Coast Guard/RSS exchange "to the detriment and dissatisfaction of both parties."[56]

The British noted that the "roots strike deep" in the troublesome relationship between the FBI and the U.S. military services' cryptanalytic operations. If the British received information from the FBI, they could not inform either the Army's or Navy's military intelligence officials. Likewise, if they received intelligence from the U.S. military services, the British could not give that to the FBI. The British memo made this conclusion about the U.S. rivalries: "On the other hand, contact with the Coastguards is essential, as, although a smaller organization than the F.C.C., they are extremely efficient."[57]

It's hard to determine if Elizebeth had a hand in setting up the weekly exchanges and improving communications among the British and American agencies since the British memo lacks a specific date. But it is likely that she did have some input because there is a reference to the "recent Washington conference,"[58] which took place before Jones became commander of Unit 387. After Jones took command, he became the official liaison with other agencies.[59]

In an effort to consolidate and better manage the cryptanalytic operation among the various U.S. agencies, the Army and Navy worked out an agreement in mid–1942. The Army would handle diplomatic and enemy military decryptions, the Navy was tasked with enemy naval cryptanalysis.[60]

The FBI wanted to continue working on Western Hemisphere clandestine traffic. Thus the Navy had discussions with the FBI to pick up a greater workload in that area, because, as a Navy intelligence officer intriguingly wrote, "we wanted to use the Coast Guard for other projects." That officer did not spell out what those other projects might be, yet concluded that the FBI "admittedly could not undertake the whole effort when offered to them, despite the fact the cryptanalytic organization was ten times the size of the Coast Guard."[61] So, to avoid duplication of effort between the FBI and Coast Guard, the June 1942 agreement designated that the Coast Guard would handle both Western Hemisphere and other international clandestine decryptions, while the FBI was relegated to domestic criminal, voice broadcasts and "Cover Text Communications." The OSS was cut out of cryptanalysis operations altogether.[62]

Unit 387 commander Jones wrote that the clandestine allocation was "logical since the Coast Guard, a part of the Navy, was already doing the work and had acquired considerable experience in the field and had a force of monitors with several years of practice locating and copying clandestine transmissions." President Roosevelt later approved the code breaking arrangement.[63]

The June 1942 Naval intelligence memo suggesting that there might be other projects for the Coast Guard prophesied another frustration for Elizebeth, one that put her in conflict with her new boss, Lieutenant Commander Jones, over what Unit 387's wartime mission should be.

Early in the war Argentina, Brazil and Chile were hotbeds of Axis spy operations, but the Abwehr ran agents in several South American countries.[64] The agents used hand-keyed radios about the size of a suitcase. They kept their messages to Germany brief, only about 50 to 100 letters to avoid detection. Generally, it took about a minute to transmit those short messages.[65]

The Coast Guard was listening to those short messages, some of them encrypted with the Enigma machine. The Unit 387 history shows the Coast Guard solved the traffic "passing between Hamburg, Berlin and Mexico," determining that they were based on a commercial code, the Rudolph Mosse Code that used both transposition and substitution to hide the meaning of the messages.

Unit cryptanalysts also identified the names of two German agents, MAX and GLENN, locating a dictionary that was used as the key for the messages. "With the alphabet recovered and the vocabulary divided into alphabetic blocks," the group's history recalled, "whole words were identified. Messages containing ship names afforded most opportunities for identifications, since in this type of message words were used involving arrival and departure dates, types of cargo loaded and discharged, etc."[66]

Before they were excluded from clandestine code breaking, FBI cryptanalysts had been unable to break many of the early Abwehr agent codes.[67] The Coast Guard, however, was so good at its job in the early months of the war, that Jones' summary of the unit's work during that period reported: "Solutions of additional systems and discovery of new circuits eventually led to the fairly complete reading of an extensive clandestine net spread over Mexico, Chile, and Brazil."[68]

In March 1942, authorities in Brazil used some of those decrypted messages to start rounding up German spies in the country.[69] With much of its Brazilian operation shut down, the Abwehr concentrated on Argentina, which was heavily populated with pro–Nazi German settlers. With Argentina now believed to be "a center of world espionage,"[70] the Abwehr relied on its agents there to maintain communications with the Fatherland.[71] But, with the arrest of its Brazilian agents, the Germans were aware that the Americans were reading their clandestine messages and completely changed their cryptography systems.[72]

Throughout that period, Elizebeth was keeping in contact officially, as well as informally, with some of her British counterparts. Numerous letters between William Friedman and British GC&CS representatives end with "best wishes to Mrs. Friedman,"[73] or similar sentiments. Other letters from British officers mention dining at the Friedmans.[74]

One British visitor to the Friedmans' Military Road home was particularly noteworthy. Navy Captain Edward Hastings arrived the afternoon of December 7th, after hearing about the Japanese attack in Hawaii. The summary of the NSA interview with Elizebeth recounts the episode: "He sat down and proceeded to 'laugh and laugh' about the Pearl Harbor attack. Mrs. Friedman was shocked and offended and never understood his behavior on this occasion."[75] At this point in time, Elizebeth was unaware of her husband's Army Signals Intelligence Service breaking and reading the Japanese diplomatic cipher named Purple. Hastings, who served on the British Joint Intelligence Committee,[76] was likely well aware of Purple, and realized the irony of the Allies receiving strong hints about an imminent strike by Japan, but not reacting in time to do anything about it. Or he might have been laughing because America could no longer remain an isolationist nation, officially thrust into the war on the side of the British. Despite Hasting's enigmatic behavior, he and Elizebeth became "close personal friends," and the Friedmans even stayed at the Hastings home during a trip to England in the 1950s.[77]

During her husband's various trips to Great Britain to meet with officials at Bletchley Park or other locations, Elizebeth and William kept up a steady correspondence. On May 13, 1943, Elizebeth wrote, "This has been a very good day, for it brought two messages from you." She noted that the official "V-mail" letters seemed to arrive even more quickly than air mail. "I'm so glad things are going better and that you feel you are 'doing good.'" Then she squeezed in at the bottom of the page: "All my love E."[78]

On his end, William's diary of that 1943 trip showed that he tried to send roses to Elizebeth for their 26th wedding anniversary through a mutual British friend. "I'll try to get special word to Elizebeth thru Maid-ment but am somewhat embarrassed to ask favor," he wrote.[79] Maidment was British Captain Kenneth Maidment, whom Elizebeth had served with on "Committee B" during the Washington conference in April 1942. She responded to William on May 31st, "Hope my late letters, by special method, have been getting through. And thanks so much for all yours; and the messages. Since Capt. M. phoned your anniversary message long distance, think it would be nice if you could bring Mrs. Maidment some-thing." She ended: "Always and forever yours Elsbeth."[80]

William's journal records his thoughts on his wife's response to her anniversary surprise: "She [sic] ecstatic about the roses which on 21st but saying nothing re the number, which I suspect was 2 dozen, not exactly 26."[81]

Because of the Friedmans' warm relations with their British crypto-graphic counterparts, it is no surprise that one of Elizebeth's frustrations surfaces in a British document and not one from the U.S. archives.

A "Most Secret" British memo in June 1942 said that the only "illicit" wireless link "known to be working between South America and Germany" was one from "Valpariso [sic]" to Hamburg.[82] In November a U.S. docu-ment listed four stations in the Eastern Hemisphere "are the only German clandestine radio circuits which can be heard, with the facilities available to the Navy and Coast Guard, well enough for decryption and translation purposes."[83]

Elizebeth's involvement in the situation shows up in a December 24, 1942, British memo titled "Clandestine." In it Major G. G. Stevens wrote: "1. At the request of Mrs. Friedman I went this afternoon with Maidment to the Coast Guard to discuss their 'future.' 2. They are in the position that their South American stuff is dying on them and they want something to do."[84]

Germany did not send its Latin American agents Enigmas until December 1942. Agents also lacked proper training in using hand ciphers, which resulted in intelligence being sent back to Hamburg with "weak" cryptography.[85]

Elizebeth told the NSA historian that nearly all German clandestine codes and ciphers during this pre–Enigma era had been "easily broken."[86] Because the Coast Guard's code breaking efforts against South American Abwehr agents had been so successful, Elizebeth seemed determined to find a new mission to keep Unit 387 occupied. Stevens told Elizebeth there might be some ways the Coast Guard could launch into new territory, including bringing "their brains to hear [sic] alongside ours on outstanding

econd Copy sent
2 Page .

MOST SECRET

W. 116

Washington,
December 24, 1942.

D.D.(S)

From: Major G.G. Stevens.

CLANDESTINE

At the request of Mrs. Friedman I went this afternoon with Maidment to the Coast Guard to discuss their "future".

They are in the position that their South American stuff is dying on them and they want something to do. They asked if I had any views.

A declassified document in the British Archives demonstrates that Elizebeth Friedman thought her Coast Guard Unit could be doing more to help the war effort. She believed that the work decoding German agent messages in South America was "dying on them" (National Archives of the U.K.).

problems." Stevens noted that the Coast Guard was "very willing" to do anything to help. "In this, I think, they are considerably influenced by the desire to keep their identity. Failing anything for them to do they would probably be absorbed into Op-20-G," which was the Navy Communications Security Section[87] that oversaw Unit 387.

Major Stevens also sought advice from an unspecified superior, "to know whether you would consider it a good thing for one of them to pay a visit to B.P [Bletchley Park] apropos. For this one would like to see Mrs. Friedman go, but probably at this end it would be considered more suitable to send Lieutenant-Commander Jones, the official head of the section."[88]

Unit 387's mission apparently became an ongoing issue between Jones and his subordinate. Even though she no longer commanded the section, Elizebeth had strong feelings about the direction it was taking. "Mrs. Friedman was not that impressed with the importance of the clandestine problem or at least the nature of the intelligence material," remarked the 1976 NSA interview summary. "She believed that the C/A [cryptanalysis] and cryptographic talents of the unit could have been better used on more important projects. She believed the problem was worked to the point of overkill." Then the interview summary hit the key point: "She believes that Commander Jones had too narrow a view of USCG Comint operations and that his outlook was influenced by excessive concern as to what was best for him professionally. She and Jones frequently debated the proper mission of the unit."[89]

Jones dismissed Elizebeth's opinion about the importance of breaking clandestine traffic as he spelled out his view of the Coast Guard's mission: "It is the opinion of the writer that clandestine traffic should be ranked as of equal importance with diplomatic traffic, which it in many cases resembles and in some instances seems to supplant." Jones cited instances of cracking clandestine codes that allowed the Allies to determine what information the enemy lacked, which was highly useful to war planners. "It is believed therefore that the reading of this traffic is of substantial importance to our national interests. If a large part of it is of no direct and immediate interest to the Navy and useful from the standpoint of Naval operations, it is none the less of importance to our government and should be processed."[90]

Jones apparently won the argument since the Coast Guard continued working on clandestine codes until the end of the war.

Early in 1943 the Coast Guard was transferred to a new facility and Unit 387 received a new name. Because of the rapid expansion of personnel, the space problem at the Navy Department had become "acute." The Navy decided to move OP-20-G to the Mount Vernon Seminary in northwest Washington at the corner of Massachusetts and Nebraska Avenues.[91] Located in one of the District of Columbia's most attractive areas and an architecturally restricted neighborhood, the city's planning commission asked the Navy to explain the seizure of the school. The Navy responded that it was vital to the war effort and that it was immune to zoning regulations—not to mention that the seizure of the property should not be publicized because of the secret nature of the new facility.[92]

Thus the Navy, in March 1943, moved Unit 387 from Coast Guard Headquarters to the new Naval Communications Annex. To cement its ties to the Navy intelligence operation, the Coast Guard unit was renamed OP-20-GU.[93] Instead of one of the stately seminary buildings, however, the Coast Guard now occupied the second floor of a wooden structure.[94] Elizebeth described it as a "grubby, ramshackle temporary building with its flat roof and thin walls in which the temperatures had risen in those three war summers to many degrees above 100; on one occasion the thermometer registered 114, but there is a war on, remember, so there was no early closing of offices."[95]

At his first OP-20-G staff meeting a few days after the move, Jones explained to other officers what his unit's duties were and how they fit into the overall operation. "The unit is small, at present consisting of twelve individuals, but it is to be expanded to twenty within the near future. Frequencies schedules and other characteristics of Clandestine stations are listed and are watched very closely by this section." Lieutenant Commander Jones said his people were delighted with their new quarters and "were very anxious to be of use to the other sections in the Naval Communications Annex."[96]

It was in these new quarters that the Coast Guard had its greatest successes in cracking the Enigma.

Prior to moving to the Naval Communications Annex, the Coast Guard used a commercial Enigma obtained before 1940 to help them solve a good number of the Abwehr's ciphers. An NSA history described the accomplishment: "Coast Guard cryptanalysts developed a technique for stripping off the effect of the reflector and then of successive wheels, resulting in a complete solution of the machine with all wirings."[97]

Now, in its new facility, OP-20-GU had access to Bombes,[98] a giant, computer-like device that the Americans adapted from the British, to simulate Enigma rotors.[99] They also called on other sections of OP-20-G to use machines such as the Hypo and M-8 to try to solve cryptanalytic problems.[100] That gave the Coast Guard more sophisticated means to attack the German clandestine Enigmas.

Starting in October 1942 the Allies began intercepting messages from Europe to South America with a volume of "impressive proportions." The Coast Guard found a variety of systems employed in the Berlin to Argentina transmissions, but a German mistake in the double transposition, in which they repeated a few messages previously intercepted "without change in preambles or cipher text" gave U.S. cryptanalysts an edge because it "provided a classic example of the cumulative effect of an apparently innocuous blunder." The Unit 387 history recalls that "no success was had in attempts to solve messages in the system until a message transmitted on 16 March, 1943, was solved by the British and the keys furnished this office."[101]

The Coast Guard used the lessons it had learned in solving the commercial Enigma to help break another circuit between Berlin and Argentina. Once again, the British GC&CS supplied some help in solving this cryptomachine. The decryptions on this circuit, from a station designated TQI2, used what came to be called the Green Enigma.[102]

Then in November 1943 a new Abwehr circuit started appearing which also used the Enigma. This was dubbed Red. The Germans helped the Coast Guard solve this circuit as well since the Nazis sent messages on the Red circuit in the same key for another cryptographic machine called Kryha that the Coast Guard already had solved.[103] The Unit 387 history gives the section a good deal of credit for the accomplishment: "Although the wiring recovered in this solution later proved to be known wiring, this recovery of wiring assumed to be unknown was achieved without prior knowledge of any solution or technique for the recovery of Enigma wiring and is believed to be the first enstance [sic] of Enigma wiring recovery in the United States."[104] Unit 387, or OP-20-GU, apparently became the go-to American agency on the Enigma, even sending a 74-page wiring diagram for the "E-MACHINE" to Army cryptanalysts.[105]

This is the solution of one of the initial messages on the Red Enigma: "The trunk transmitter with accessories and Enigma arrived via RED. Thank you very much. From our message number 150 we shall encipher with the new Enigma. We shall give the old device to GREEN. Please acknowledge by return message with new Enigma. LUNA."[106]

LUNA was one of the operations the Coast Guard had been tracking. Others included INCA and JOLLE, an Abwehr code name for a transportation operation[107] which had plans for an apparent submarine landing of German agents in Argentina.[108]

The U.S. National Archives has hundreds of declassified Coast Guard spy decryptions. Americans dubbed COMINT they gathered from decrypting high-level German ciphers ULTRA.[109] This is from operation JOLLE stamped in bright purple, TOP SECRET ULTRA:

TOP SECRET

From: Berlin	JXA 13670 K/cs
To: Argentine	
August 2, 1943	TOI 8–3–43/1932/Z
German	S-4
#982–984	
INCA 162	

Preparations for sending-over of O.P. BOETTLER [Boettger?] via JOLLE to DREY-FUSS are almost finished. Because, in spite of repeated exhortations we are still lakcing [sic] data on place of landing, which should be determined by you, BLUE shall, if no report in this respect reaches us by August 4 ... [6 letters garbled] ... determination of the landing place, by which you must be guided. Provide stocks [money] for the coming O.P. [BOETTGER].

Serial CG3–1540

TOP SECRET[110]

Another ULTRA decryption revealed the Germans' desire to obtain U.S. weapons secrets:

From: Berlin	S2FK 10139 K/cs
To: Argentina	
August 10, 1944	TOI 8–10–44/2152/Z on ckt. 3-N
German	S-5
#986	GHEXK CLRFC
INCA 661	

Try with all means to find out the state of USA research in the field of rocket propulsion weapons as well as projectiles. In case of success, report all details.

German Clandestine	CG Decryption
	CG Translation (VB)
Serial CG4–5344	CG Typed 8–14–44[111]

Elizebeth said the greatest single effort of the Coast Guard cryptanalysts was against a four-letter group on a system used by German agents. Without a full transcript of her NSA interview, it is unclear which system she was referring to, but it took one and a half years to break it. When her unit made that breakthrough, however, she said there had been "much celebration."[112]

An NSA history four decades after World War II indicated that starting in 1940, Coast Guard cryptanalysts had successes against the German Enigma used by the Abwehr on five different circuits: the Commercial machine, the Green machine, the Red machine, The Berlin-Madrid machine and the stecker, or plug board, on the Hamburg-Bordeaux machine.[113]

Breaking those clandestine ciphers helped the Allies nullify many of the Abwehr's efforts in the Western Hemisphere. They gained details about a German-backed attempted revolution in Bolivia in December 1943 as well another one in Chile.[114] In a post-war summary of how cryptanalysis aided the Allies, William Friedman cited the case of secret agent Osmar Hellmuth, the Argentine consul to Barcelona, who was a German collaborator. British officials learned through Coast Guard decryptions which ship Hellmuth was using to sail to Spain. They arrested him when the ship stopped in the British colony, Trinidad. That ended Hellmuth's true mission: to travel to Germany to reassure the Fuehrer[115] that Argentina would not sever relations with Germany.[116]

Unit 387's clandestine decryptions also played a role in avoiding an invasion of the island of Martinique.[117] Allied forces used the information to persuade a Vichy French naval commander to immobilize his warships in exchange for a promise not to bomb or invade the Vichy-controlled islands in the Caribbean region.[118]

KOP SECRET-ULTRA

From: Argentine   ISY 11130 K/cs
To: Berlin

September 28, 1943   TOI 9-28-43/2120/Z

German   S-2

#585-586-587-588

BOSS 43.

Reports on the USA military economy will be treated chiefly, as their procurement is extremely difficult. It is out of the question to send ROSSO over. Lack of money caused postponement (abandonment?) of the plan. We expect early arrival of 300; in the meantime, as a makeshift we pay with pesos. Paying and receiving "Reichsmarks" is the occasional task.* Securing of the amount in case of break (of relations) is guaranteed. Current expenses of the present organization are 10,000 monthly, including contributions "T", official car, airplane, station, officer, messengers. We did not try to approach "QBCLBUR(O)" (pol. bureau?) because inquiries sound bad. CHILE-contact (man?) reports unreliable and refuses connection. KUNZE in Brazil is free; his shift to Argentina was made impossible by change of government. Ambassador ESCOBAR eliminated (as) RAWSON's successor and is not trustworthy because he is a USA man. We shall continue our efforts. Organization has independent agents (who work on their own), in part Argentineans; more were engaged; assignment areas were specified.

                                          VIERECK

*Translation of this sentence is doubtful.   .

Serial CG3-2021

                        TOP SECRET

Many of the Coast Guard Unit 387 decryptions of German Abwehr clandestine radio transmissions are marked TOP SECRET ULTRA, which was a designation for enemy codes and ciphers broken by the Allies. It was the highest level of secrecy for the United States in World War II (National Archives, College Park, Maryland).

Elizebeth's memoirs also mention that famed Argentine first lady Eva Peron was a German agent,[119] something most likely learned through clandestine decryptions.

At the end of the war scholars and historians debated how useful breaking German spy communications had been to the Allies' victory. A 50th anniversary summation of the overall cryptanalysis effort concluded, "The ability to read the enemy's messages shortened the war by perhaps as much as two years and saved tens of thousands of Allied lives."[120] Yet an NSA history of the German clandestine activities, opined that the time and expense spent to gain intelligence on the spies had little impact: "It appears that most of the intelligence passed to Germany was of little significance. Station AOR, run by the FBI, probably passed more useful, valid intelligence to the Germans than all the rest of the German nets put together, and according to the Coast Guard, was responsible for the sinking of several Allied ships. But this was a minor contribution to the Battle of the Atlantic."[121]

But in 1942 the Allies did not know exactly what would change their fortunes when they were so desperate to find a way to turn the tide against German U-boats. They sought any method to help them, including monitoring the shipping information sent by Abwehr spies to Hamburg. In fact, a post-war OP-20-G memo said that allowing the Coast Guard to focus on clandestine cryptanalysis left the Navy free "to devote all of its efforts to Naval work, which then required its undivided attention."[122]

No member of Coast Guard Unit 387 could go back to sea because of the risk that their capture might reveal the Allies' code breaking secrets.[123] Even far-flung radio operators such as Coast Guard Radioman First Class Glen Boles, who intercepted Abwehr signals in Brazil, were told to keep quiet about their operations: "Here's this place down in the jungle and everybody's, 'Shhh, don't tell anybody,'" he told an historian.[124]

As a result, every member of Unit 387 remained silent about the section's secrets in the years after the war.[125] Being part of the collective effort of thousands in the United States, Great Britain and Canada who succeeded in the struggle to understand the Axis nations' intentions through cryptanalysis allows Coast Guard Unit 387 members to share in the glory of the Allies' World War II victory. "The solutions of PURPLE and ENIGMA were intellectual accomplishments of the first brilliance," wrote NSA historian David Hatch. "Both were team efforts and the members of these teams ought to be listed among the important contributors to victory in World War II."[126]

Enigma machine used by German military units as well as spies to send and receive encrypted messages. The Germans thought their cipher machine was unbreakable. The Unit 387 history credits Elizebeth Friedman's Coast Guard section with the first Enigma wiring solution in the United States (National Security Agency).

In September 1944, by now promoted to Commander, Leonard Jones summarized what the Coast Guard had accomplished in the area of clandestine cryptanalysis. Citing several examples of information gained by intercepting and analyzing spy messages, he believed the information obtained in this manner gave planners a clearer path to prosecute the war: "In a high percentage of cases the existence of Clandestine stations has been more of an Allied advantage than a source of danger."[127]

Jones also indicated that by that time in the war, he was coming around to Elizebeth's way of thinking: Coast Guard cryptanalysts would need a new mission for continued relevance in the war effort. He believed that after Germany was defeated Japan might take over its clandestine networks. "Should this prove to be the case, it may be expected that the information will be transmitted to Japan from some such center as Madrid via regular diplomatic channels," wrote Jones. "It seems highly improbable however that the network of stations feeding information into the Madrid center would be operated by Japs. It could possibly be operated along its present lines by the same personnel in which case solution of the traffic on subordinate links would provide excellent clues for the solution of Jap Naval Attaché systems which indeed, has already found to be the case."[128]

Whether it was an addition or change to its mission or something they had been doing all along, there is some indication that the Coast Guard did bring its code breaking skills to bear on messages sent by the Japanese.[129] The Coast Guard supplied translations from intercepted Japanese messages to the Army's Military Intelligence Service,[130] but apparently only for merchant vessels and weather stations.[131]

Elizebeth may have paved the way for modifying the mission when she mentioned to her British counterparts that the Coast Guard's clandestine mission was "dying."

Debating her section's mission and coordinating with the British and Canadians fell within the purview of Elizebeth's job description. A 1943 Civil Service Commission form described Elizebeth's Senior Cryptanalyst duties: "subject only to general direction as to administrative policy with the widest latitude for the exercise of judgment, initiative and finality of decision and the application of thorough professional knowledge and experience." It noted that as the civilian head of the Cryptanalytic Section of the Coast Guard, she "assists and shares in the broadest phases of the overall administration, direction and control ... for independently handling the most important and highly specialized work of the Section." The Civil Service form said she also had to keep up-to-date with the science of cryptanalysis.[132]

Even though she considered herself "just one of the workers," Elizebeth completed a series of Navy training conferences required for supervisors.[133] Thus, her duties included managerial functions for "maintaining close contact with and keeping currently advised on the latest developments in the field of crypt analysis for the purpose of utilizing and making available such progressive developments to the Coast Guard and in this connection to study, devise and initiate new or revised procedures and methods for the more efficient and expedient operation of the Section."[134]

That seemed to give Elizebeth wide latitude in carrying out what she perceived to be her wartime responsibilities.

If her superior, Commander Jones, objected to Elizebeth's opinions about the unit's mission, he could have done so repeatedly. Over the course of the war, Jones evaluated her work three times. In March 1943 he gave her an excellent rating with 15 pluses for outstanding work and eight check marks for adequate performance.[135] A year later, Jones gave Elizebeth another excellent review with 15 pluses for outstanding work and in another 14 categories, checkmarks for an adequate rating.[136] In the final months of the war, the efficiency rating was a near-clone of the two previous years, overall excellent, with 15 pluses and 14 checks for adequate work. This time her evaluation was also reviewed by G. Van Graves, who agreed with the overall excellent rating.[137]

For his work leading Coast Guard cryptanalysts in their notable successes, Commander Leonard T. Jones received the Legion of Merit for "exceptionally meritorious conduct in the performance of outstanding services to the Government of the United States," as well as the World War II Victory Medal, National Defense Service Medal, American Campaign Medal, Navy Unit Commendation Ribbon and the Order of British Empire.[138]

By all measures, Elizebeth also gave "outstanding services to the Government" during the Second World War. The Friedmans' daughter, Barbara, said both of her parents worked six days a week, nine to ten hours each day. "They were gone long before I came down to have breakfast," she said.[139]

Even though Elizebeth at first commanded and then remained second-in-command of Unit 387 and OP-20-GU,[140] as a civilian, she did not receive any medals or commendations. All she got was a pay check, which rose from $4,200 a year at the start of the war[141] to $5,390 by July 1945.[142]

At the end of the conflict, the government, to which she had provided such valuable service for two decades, no longer had a need for a civilian with her specific skills. As a result, in the post-war downsizing, she lost her job and the Coast Guard lost the cryptanalytic unit she had founded.

=9=

The Doll Woman

In 1942, as Elizebeth Friedman and her Coast Guard unit were tackling the ciphers of German spies in the Western Hemisphere, a Japanese spy in the U.S. had slipped under the radar of American authorities. To help bring the spy to justice, Elizebeth would be called on to decode the spy's seemingly innocuous messages to Japanese contacts in South America:

> January 27, 1942
> My Most Gracious Friend
>
> Please forgive my delay in writing to thank you for your kindness in sending my family the beautiful Christmas gifts. The girls were especially pleased.
> I have been so very busy these days, this is the first time I have been over to Seattle for weeks. I came over today to meet my son who is here from Portland on business and to get my little granddaughters [sic] doll repaired. I must tell you this amusing story, the wife of an important business associate gave her an old German bisque Doll dressed in a Hulu [sic] Grass skirt. It is a cheap horrid thing I do Not like it and wish we did not have to have it about. Well I broke this awful doll last month now the person who gave the doll is coming to visit us very soon. I walked all over Seattle to get someone to repair it, no one at home could or would try the task. Now I expect all the damages to be repaired by the first week in February. In the meanwhile I hope and pray the Important gentlemen's [sic] wife will not come to visit us untill [sic] after that date.
> I do hope you can read my typing, I am trying to learn to type so I can be able to type records for the Red Cross.
> Please accept love and rememberances [sic] sent to you form [sic] Elizabeth.
>
> Sincerely
> (Signature) Maud Bowman[1]

More than two years later the U.S. attorney in New York asked for Elizebeth's help in decoding this and other correspondence from the spy who came to be known in the press as the Doll Woman. This is what Elizebeth understood the January 27, 1942, letter to mean:

This is a somewhat belated rejoicing over the victory at Pearl Harbor. The Japanese Navy is to be much congratulated on their good work. We, their friends here, are elated over it.
(Please recognize your authorized correspondent. I am in Seattle and have the following to report).
There is a battleship here, damaged at Pearl Harbor, being repaired. It is one of the older battleships; but is considered of sufficient value to be worthy of repair. It is expected that repairs will be completed by the first week in February. I wish that the Japanese could make a visit to the Navy Yard here and destroy it completely before that time.
(I hope the reference to my poor typing, like the paragraph above referring to family, will convince you that I am your authorized correspondent for this type of information).
(Another signal of authentication is personal greetings from "Elizabeth").[2]

The supposed author of the letter, Maud Bowman, was not a spy. The name was just a foil, a former customer of the real Doll Woman who owned a high-end doll store in New York City[3] that became a cover for writing double entendre messages about exotic dolls to her Japanese contacts. Before she came under the scrutiny of the FBI and the U.S. attorney, Velvalee Dickinson would write four more suspicious letters about dolls. Federal Bureau of Investigation cryptographers made an "interpretation" of the hidden meaning of Dickinson's letters,[4] but to nail the case against the Doll Woman, the U.S. attorney turned to Elizebeth Friedman.

* * *

Velvalee Blucher Dickinson was born in Sacramento, California, in 1893.[5] She graduated from high school in 1911, then attended junior college and the University of California at Berkeley.[6] The young Miss Blucher transferred to Stanford University where she earned a B.A. degree in 1918, but an FBI investigative file shows that she did not receive the degree until 1938 because she failed to return several Russian books to the university until that year. Starting in 1923 she worked at a bank in San Francisco.[7] Then in 1928 Velvalee started working for the man who would become her third husband, Lee Dickinson[8]; he owned a produce brokerage firm until the company went broke in 1937.[9] Up until that time Velvalee "handled all of the Japanese accounts in Imperial Valley and was very friendly with many Japanese." The couple also entertained many Japanese in their home.[10] "Educated, vivacious and shrewd, Velvalee danced and talked her way through endless social functions," gushed a later profile of Mrs. Dickinson.[11]

FBI investigators discovered that Velvalee joined the Japan-America Society from 1931 to 1935. A source in the Society told the Bureau "Mrs. Dickinson was very friendly with the members of the Japanese Consulate in San Francisco." After a year's lapse, she was reinstated in 1936 when her dues were paid by an attaché at the consulate.

When Lee Dickinson's business failed, the couple moved to Madison Avenue in New York, just a block from Central Park. At first Velvalee worked as a doll saleswoman at Bloomingdale's. Then in 1938, she opened her own doll store— initially at 714 Madison Avenue, then moving to 718 Madison Avenue in 1941.[12] The store carried foreign, regional and antique dolls for wealthy collectors and hobbyists.[13]

Her connections to the Japanese did not end, however, when the Doll Woman moved east.

Once in New York, she visited both the Nippon Club and the Japan Institute.[14] Witnesses also said that they had seen Mrs. Dickinson in the

Velvalee Dickinson was known as the "Doll Woman" for sending letters in an open code talking about various dolls to describe U.S. warships. Elizabeth Friedman's work on the case helped convince Mrs. Dickinson to make a plea deal with the U.S. attorney in New York (FBI).

lobby of the Fairmont Hotel in San Francisco in August 1941 talking to the Japanese General Consul from New York.[15]

Then, less than two weeks before the Pearl Harbor attack, on November 26, 1941, the Japanese naval attaché from Washington, D.C., Ichiro Yokoyama, walked into Mrs. Dickinson's doll store on Madison Avenue to see Velvalee and her husband who had been ailing from a heart condition. They were no strangers. Three or four years before moving to New York, Mrs. Dickinson had met the naval officer on a Japanese battleship visiting San Francisco.[16]

Mrs. Dickinson said that she was in the shop when Yokoyama called from a pay phone to announce his visit. "We were sitting in the shop and I noticed out the window ... he walked by up and down the street." She explained that the attaché wanted to make sure that he wasn't being followed. "He ... walked up and down the street a couple of times before he approached the store."[17]

He had been to the store two days before, but now Yokoyama came with $25,000 in hundred dollar bills. Along with the money, he presented a code to be used to transmit information to the Japanese government. To avoid the suspicion of censorship authorities in the United States, Yokoyama instructed Dickinson to use her customers' return addresses when sending messages to Japanese contacts in South America.[18]

Mrs. Dickinson recalled Yokoyama telling her she could pay off her business obligations for the store and move to California. "He said, 'Now I have some money, you can pay off your debts.' I had just leased my shop there and I had borrowed capital, I never had counted on such assistance, I never expected it."[19]

With the serendipitous cash to finance their travels, a few months later, after the United States had declared war against Japan, Mr. and Mrs. Dickinson returned to the West Coast. They stayed at the Earl Hotel in Seattle beginning January 27, 1942; from February 4th to the 8th they registered at the Hotel Stewart in San Francisco. Both cities had active defense establishments with vital national security interests to protect. The couple returned to Seattle, to the Hotel Roosevelt in early May. Later that month they stayed at Hotel Oakland, across the bay from San Francisco.[20]

Five letters—ostensibly from Mrs. Dickinson's customers—resulted from the trip west. The first letter was from Maud Bowman on January 27th. Next was a letter from Sara Gellert on February 1st. That was followed by a missive on February 22nd from Mary Wallace. Sara Gellert was the apparent author of another letter on May 20th. The last letter was sent June 2nd with the signature and address of Freda Maytag.[21]

All of the messages were addressed to Señora Inez Lopez de Molinali in Buenos Aires, Argentina. Her husband was a former foreign affairs official in Argentina who had pro–Fascist leanings.[22]

The letters never made it to their intended destination. British Imperial Censorship authorities in Trinidad intercepted and examined the February 1st mailing from Sara Gellert. "Because of the suspicious language content which referred to peculiar activities in connection with dolls, the letter was immediately referred to the FBI Laboratory in Washington, D.C." One by one the other four letters came back to the United States to the ostensible authors' legitimate addresses—all of them returned as undeliverable in Argentina. The women to whom the letters were returned knew they hadn't written them and had no idea why their names and addresses were used. Each contacted the authorities and turned over the curious correspondence. The five letters underwent a document and cryptographic examination in the Bureau's lab.[23]

The FBI soon gave the Doll Woman espionage investigation its own code name: the Velvet case. Agents in charge made sure they apprised Director J. Edgar Hoover of their progress.[24]

The crime lab did its usual diligent job. Experts determined that signatures on the five letters were forgeries "prepared by tracing or copying from original signatures in the possession of the forger."[25] They matched the type faces of typewriters at hotels in Seattle and San Francisco to the suspect letters. They found that the Maud Bowman letter was prepared on a typewriter from the Earl Hotel in Seattle where the Dickinsons had stayed. One of the Sara Gellert letters had been written on an Underwood typewriter available to guests at the Hotel Stewart. The Dickinsons also had stayed at that San Francisco hotel. Another typewriter, a Royal, was used at the Hotel Roosevelt to write the second Gellert letter; this was

Velvalee Dickinson's doll store on Madison Avenue in New York was visited by a Japanese naval attaché less than two weeks before the Pearl Harbor attack. FBI investigators said the Doll Woman had previously met the attaché on a Japanese battleship visiting San Francisco (FBI).

another Seattle hotel which the Dickinsons had visited. Finally, Freda May-tag's dispatch was written with a typewriter at the Hotel Oakland where Lee and Velvalee Dickinson had been guests from May 29th to June 3rd.[26]

It took several months for the FBI to trace the source of the letters to Velvalee Dickinson. Yet several days after staking out the doll shop and the vaults of the Bank of New York a block from her store, agents were ready to move on January 21, 1944.[27]

They arrested the 50-year-old Doll Woman on charges of violating the censorship code.

"The woman is scarcely five feet tall and weighs perhaps 100 pounds," the *New York Times* reported.[28] "Battling furiously, the mousy little woman kicked, scratched and yelled at the top of her lungs," was the *World-Telegram*'s account of the arrest. "Finally she gave up and let herself be led by two men from a bank vault in Midtown Manhattan."[29]

The "G-Men" discovered between $15,000 and $18,000 in Mrs. Dickinson's safe deposit box.[30] They suspected much of the money came from the Yokohama Specie Bank, a branch of a Japanese bank[31] that was a member of the Japan-America Society, the same organization that Velvalee Dickinson had been a member of several years earlier.[32] Yet the FBI was unable to "definitely trace this money from the Yokohama Specie Bank directly to the person who apparently paid it to Dickinson."[33]

On February 11th a grand jury in New York indicted Velvalee Dickinson on a wartime censorship violation for sending one of the letters "on or about the 1st day of March, 1942." The indictment charged that she attempted to "use a code and device for the purpose of concealing from the Office of Censorship the intended meaning of the communication by mail passing between the United States and Argentina."[34]

The forensics on the typewriters was damning evidence against Velvalee Dickinson. Yet with the inability to directly link Mrs. Dickinson's confiscated cash to a payoff from the Japanese attaché, plus the handwriting experts' uncertainty about who traced the signatures onto the suspicious letters,[35] the U.S. attorney didn't feel he was on solid ground to prosecute the Doll Woman for espionage. The prosecution needed more solid cryptographic evidence than the scant information provided by the FBI.

* * *

An FBI memo credited Technical Laboratory employee, C. A. Appel, of making an "interpretation" of the first Doll Woman letter to start the investigation. "Mr. Appel immediately concluded that this letter was in code and that the word 'doll' referred to 'warship.'"[36] Yet this was an "open code," one without a complex system to protect the messages.[37] The vague nature of the code could be interpreted in multiple ways and made it difficult to pin down the letter's meaning. "It has been impossible to definitely determine the exact accuracy of Appel's interpretation," the memo concluded.[38]

When the FBI presented its case to the U.S. attorney's office, the information seemed sufficient to prosecute a censorship violation. But there was not enough evidence of the "national defense character" to "sustain filing a complaint against Dickinson for violation of the Espionage Statutes."[39]

To make an espionage case stick, the U.S. attorney realized he would need more expertise. On March 9th he requested help from the Navy Department. With the service's own interest in keeping the Navy's sophisticated cryptanalysis operations a secret, the chief of Naval Operations consented to lend their expert, Elizebeth Friedman, to the case with conditions. The stipulation was that any code breaking done in the Velvalee Dickinson case would not be attributed to the Navy. "Relative to your possible request of Mrs. Elizabeth S. Friedman for her personal review and interpretation of the above-mentioned letters," read the letter responding to the U.S. attorney, "the Navy Department will interpose no objection to Mrs. Friedman affording you this cooperation subject only to her consent and convenience and to the same provisions attached to the transmissions of the enclosure."[40] That meant she could help investigate, but not testify in a trial where publicity about the government's code breaking abilities could harm the war effort.

That is how Elizebeth became FBI Confidential Informant T4 in the Velvet case.[41]

Since it was the U.S. attorney's office—and not the Bureau—that had initiated the request for outside cryptographic help, the prosecutor sought to assuage any hurt professional feelings. Assistant U.S. Attorney Edward Wallace advised FBI agent L. Vernon Ewing, "that Confidential Informant T4 had been recommended to him as a cryptographer with an excellent reputation and as an individual who might possibly open up a new avenue of thought from an interpretative standpoint in regard to the five questioned letters in this case." Wallace recommended that Mrs. Friedman be allowed to examine the five letters without any other background on the case and "would merely have the informant's results furnished to the [FBI] Laboratory for its consideration and evaluation in connection with the cryptographic analysis of the questioned letters."[42]

In mid–March Elizebeth received a packet of information from the U.S. attorney's office with photo copies of the five Doll Woman letters and some background to help evaluate them. That included Velvalee Dickinson's educational history plus information that the ostensible signatures on the letters were those of Mrs. Dickinson's doll customers. "She [Dickinson] became acquainted with various personal details of their family lives, some of which appear in the various letters," wrote U.S. Attorney James B.M. McNally. His letter also included information about the typewriters Dickinson had used to prepare the notes as well as the dates the Dickinsons had stayed in the cities where they were written.[43]

After reviewing the Doll Woman's letters, Elizebeth realized that she needed more information on the circumstances of the case if she were to make any progress on cracking their open code. Even an FBI evaluation noted that the preliminary analysis of the letters by Confidential Informant T4 "had been necessarily restricted and impaired because of a lack of knowledge of the complete facts developed as a result of the investigation of VELVALEE DICKINSON."[44]

About a week after receiving the Doll Woman letters, Elizebeth wrote the U.S. attorney with four questions. "There are so many queries and possible connections with the collateral information in these letters, that it seems rather hopeless to attempt to discuss them by mail," stated her letter of March 29th. "It is suggested that I be given free and complete access to all information on the case, either by coming to New York or by some investigator in the case bringing the material to me here." The questions Elizebeth sought the answers to were whether the letters took the same route to South America, whether a person named Martinez lived at a suspect address in Buenos Aires, had Mrs. Dickinson ever been known by a name other than Velvalee and when did Mrs. Dickinson "begin to show signs of an increase in her financial status?"[45]

The questions seemed substantial enough to bring Elizebeth to New York. As a result of a request from the Department of Justice, she received orders from the Coast Guard to travel by train and work in New York from April 4th to April 10th.[46]

Before she made the trip, however, she made a stab at decoding the letters with the information she had already been given. In a working memo to herself, Elizebeth created an outline of three "general classes of cover-language" used in the letters:

> One, ACTUAL CODE-LANGUAGE, conveying information about ships, damage, repairs, anti-invasion preparations, etc.; Two, ALIBI-LANGUAGE, that is, the words, phrases, and sentences used to cover up the identity of Velvalee Dickinson

and merge it with the identity of the person whose name is signed to each letter; Three, AUTHENTICATING SIGNALS. Having adopted the device of [2], which seems not to have been arranged and agreed upon in whatever previous understanding was made, the writer feels that she must make frequent use of the "SIGNALS" which seemingly were a matter of record and agreement.

She concluded that the references to bad typing and learning typing would fit into both classes two and three.

In the final paragraph of her working document, Elizebeth noted the amateurish nature of the material in the letters: "This information is in almost every case, rather indefinite, and, in my opinion, is characteristic of the type of information a layman, who knew little of types and classes of ships, would be able to pick up. These could be collected by means of her own observation, from conversation with cab drivers who carried about personnel from the ships, or by hanging about in places where the conversation of crew members who were ship yard workmen could be overheard."[47]

By April 1st she was confident enough to write the U.S. attorney a four-page letter with her findings. "I am setting forth here some queries and statements which may be accepted for what they are worth, mindful of your statement on the telephone that you hope to obtain 'leads,' and that you understand that the 'code' in the letters is the intangible type of method not susceptible to scientific proof."

Even without being able to subject the steganographic letters to statistical cryptanalysis and lacking investigative details, Elizebeth's initial memo lived up to the prosecutor's hope that her review would "open up a new avenue of thought from an interpretative standpoint" as well as suggesting possible new "leads" for investigators.

First, Elizebeth questioned whether the incorrect address in Buenos Aires was intentional. She wrote that it was "inconceivable" that the address the letters were being sent to "should be recorded wrongly five distinct times." She suggested a "Confederate" friendly to "Axis associates" might have been at the address to forward the letters to their proper destination. She also wondered whether the addressee in the letters really was the intended target. With more than two years of working on the Germans' clandestine ciphers in South America, Elizebeth had considerable expertise in the matter. "Common practice among undercover agents," she wrote, "is to change the feminine to masculine and vice versa, and I have a more or less distinct feeling that 'Señora Inez' is really meant to be 'Martinez.'"

Elizebeth also suggested that the Doll Woman's contact in the U.S.

who gave her the information for South America might actually have been someone from China, because the letters were addressed to the name Molinali instead of Molinari. "It is a well-known fact that the Japanese have frequently employed Chinese agents. The Chinese cannot pronounce the letter r and almost invariably use the letter l instead, whereas the Japanese have difficulty with the letter l and are wont to speak r instead." With the prospect of a Chinese agent working for Japan in the U.S., Elizebeth questioned if "all leads to Dickinson's contact on the West Coast been exhausted."

After speculating on potential leads for investigators, Elizebeth made extensive comments on the Doll Woman letters themselves: "It is obvious that even a casual examination of these letters indicates their suspicious nature." She wrote that there must have been "a prearranged 'code,' however limited in extent." The different nationalities of dolls mentioned in the letters were references to ships of different nations. Knowing which ships were in port at the time the letters were written, she added, would provide circumstantial evidence to break the code.

Then, one at a time, she dissected the meaning of each letter.

In the January 27, 1942, Maud Bowman letter, Elizebeth determined that "My family" could mean either the Japanese fleet or a group of agents. The term "Christmas gifts" was information which assisted in the attack on Pearl Harbor or remuneration for previous information. The word "Girls" referred to Japanese naval officers or other agents in the group. The phrase "visit of important gentleman's wife" was an "invitation to the Japanese navy to bomb the harbor" and finally, the name "Elizabeth" was a signal that the letter was authentic or might also mean another agent.

Elizebeth interpreted a few of the same words in the Sara Gellert letter on February 1, 1942, as she had in the first letter. New code words came into play, however. "Three English dolls" were three English warships of three different classes such as a battleship, cruiser and destroyer. A "doll hospital" was a reference to a dry dock that was busy with repairs. The name "Catherine" in this letter again was a signal that the letter was authentic.

In letter three, on February 22nd from Mary Wallace, Elizebeth added several new words to the Doll Woman code book. "Nephew in hospital" was a warship in for repairs or new construction. A "tumor on the brain" meant some added structural feature to a ship's bridge or conning tower. An "old fisherman" was a minesweeper, an "old woman" a warship with a superstructure and "little boy" was a small warship: a destroyer, torpedo boat or auxiliary warship.

This long letter also included the terms "Mr. Shaw"—a reference to the destroyer, the USS *Shaw*. A reference to "back to work" meant that repairs on the *Shaw* were nearly finished. The term "family" was other vessels of the American fleet in port. The letter's referral to "trip for mother for business" was an indication that Mrs. Dickinson was "conscientiously traveling about with the attempt to collect information." The misspelling of the Kentucky city as "Louville," was "an obvious reference to the U.S.S. *Louisville*," and a likely confession that the agent was unable to obtain information about the ship.

In the May 20, 1942, Sara Gellert letter, "rock garden" was a reference to ammunition factories. "No longer in shops" meant that ships that had been in port had returned to sea. Another reference to a "Siamese dancer" doll that had been "torn in the middle" referred to an aircraft carrier that had been torpedoed amidships. A "mate for the Siam dancer" conveyed that a ship was being converted to an aircraft carrier. Catherine being married indicated that an agent had withdrawn from activities or had been arrested. "French dolls" meant that some foreign ships were in the same shipyard as the carrier described above.

When Elizebeth decoded the final letter, it seemed to indicate that the Doll Woman was getting frustrated at not being able to find all the information that she wanted. It was the letter from Freda Maytag. References to "shopping," a "walk through Chinatown without success" and "make a purchase at Gump's without success" all indicated that the writer was looking for information or was unable to contact another agent.

Other references in this June 2nd mailing were to a "Chinese family of dolls," which was the construction of, or the outfitting of seven warships. "Five English dolls" were foreign ships—probably English—two of them at anchor in the harbor and the other three at the docks. The reference to the "Saratoga Trunk" was Velvalee Dickinson's desire for the Japanese Navy to sink the USS *Saratoga*, along with her promise "to send the information which will enable them to do so."

Finally, Elizebeth wrote the U.S. attorney, the Doll Woman must have had accomplices to carry out such a mission for the enemy. "A few paragraphs of these letters suggests [sic] to me that Dickinson <u>received</u> information which she then turned over to her contact in the U.S. for transmittal by some means for the use of the Japanese Navy."[48]

A few days later Elizebeth made the train trip to collaborate with prosecutors in New York. "During the period extending from April 5th to April 8th, 1944, Confidential Informant T4 conducted a cryptographic analysis of the five questioned letters," FBI agent Ewing reported. "As a result of this examination, the interpretation given to the letters by Confidential Informant T4 was furnished to the writer on April 8, 1944 by Assistant United States Attorney Edward C. Wallace. Mr. Wallace furnished these interpretations in order that they might be made available to the F.B.I. Laboratory in connection with the additional examination of these letters."[49]

Then the FBI report has Elizabeth's verbatim decoding. With more background provided by investigators, Confidential Informant T4 now added detail, letter-by-letter, that her initial analysis to U.S. Attorney on April 1st had lacked. The February 1st letter had information about submarine nets and anti-barrage balloons in the harbor. The February 22nd letter mentioned a ship that was "damaged beyond repair."

The May 20th letter, along with the information about an aircraft carrier that had been torpedoed amidships added: "Alongside it is another ship being converted into an aircraft carrier. It is somewhat smaller than the regular carrier, but otherwise appears exactly the same." With the information of ship repairs progressing, this letter with the updated decoding added, "In the same ship yard as the aircraft carriers, two capital ships are almost ready to leave, complete repairs having been made." With her additional investigative data from this trip to New York, Elizabeth added this note at the bottom: "2 battleships, the *Nevada* and the *Pennsylvania* were both in Puget Sound Navy Yard for battle damage repairs in May of 1942."

The extra details in the June 2nd letter were that the seven battleships in San Francisco came in for alterations. "These are not major repairs, such as from battle damage, but are additions of a lesser degree of costliness, such as would make them combatworthy." An additional investigative note at the end of this decoded letter showed that in May 1942, San Francisco had seven battleships in for alterations or minor repairs. "All came in on the same day—for seven battleships all to arrive on the same day would be a sufficiently unusual occurrence that it would be certainly observed."[50]

Within days of receiving the decoding of the letters, prosecutors had grand jurors review the new evidence provided by Confidential Informant T4. Elizabeth's involvement gave prosecutors the ammunition to raise the ante against the Doll Woman from a censorship violation to a full-blown spy case.

When Velvalee Dickinson was arraigned on the grand jury's new espionage charges on May 5th, the *New York Daily News* reported: "Death looked across a Federal Court room at the Doll Woman of Madison Ave. yesterday as she was arraigned on an indictment charging her with being a spy for the Imperial Japanese Government. As far as is known here, she is the first American woman to be so accused since the outbreak of World War II." Then the article quoted the U.S. attorney: "Yesterday, after court, McNally said the code used by the Doll Woman finally had been broken, but he would not reveal the contents of the letters."[51]

The two-count espionage indictment gave prosecutors extra leverage against Dickinson—a possible death penalty if she were to be convicted on the charges.[52] Now that the Doll Woman's coded letters "finally had been broken" by Elizebeth Friedman, all the U.S. attorney's cards were on the table.

Velvalee Dickinson also had an ace up her sleeve that she would soon play against the government.

* * *

With the new indictment against her, authorities continued to hold Velvalee Dickinson in jail. She had been unable to raise the $25,000 bond since her arrest in January.[53] She was alone in defending herself. The court had appointed an attorney to represent her, but her husband, Lee, had died of his heart condition more than a year before.

That was Velvalee Dickinson's ace: she planned to use Lee's death to her advantage.

A judge set her trial for July 31st.[54] Facing death if convicted of espionage, and with a preponderance of evidence against her—including the convincing letters decoded by Elizebeth Friedman—the Doll Woman found it prudent to take a plea deal. Yet the U.S. attorney also found it practical to settle for a plea to a lesser charge as well. Dickinson's lawyer signaled that he would throw a good deal of doubt into the prosecution's espionage case by naming not Velvalee, but her husband, as the real spy in the Doll Woman case.

Mrs. Dickinson's attorney, Maurice Shaine, made an agreement with the prosecutor on July 28th. If she pleaded guilty to the censorship violation, the U.S. attorney would dismiss the espionage indictments, but Mrs. Dickinson would have "to furnish information in her possession concerning Japanese intelligence activities."[55]

Velvalee nervously twisted her black-gloved hands during the hearing. Yet a *New York Times* reporter noted that she seemed more relaxed and "resigned to her predicament" than she had been in previous proceedings. "Gone was the tense, defiant manner in which she had demanded 'Who are all these people?' When she found Federal Bureau of Investigation men and reporters present at her first arraignment."[56]

After the hearing U.S. Attorney McNally for the first time laid out the evidence, including the decoded letters, for reporters covering the Doll Woman case. He admitted if he had gone to trial on the espionage charges the defense might have sown enough reasonable doubt for a jury to acquit Mrs. Dickinson: "The proof against the defendant was highly circumstantial in nature. In the absence of her confederates now in Japan, in my judgment the defense to be offered by the defendant was to have been that the letters were written by her husband, Lee, who died March 29, 1943."[57]

The judge ordered a probation report and set the Doll Woman's sentencing for August 14th.[58]

FBI agents quickly scheduled an interrogation with Mrs. Dickinson. The investigators wanted to find out as much as possible about the codes used by the Doll Woman and whether she had received information from any accomplices—as Elizebeth Friedman had suggested in her analysis. But Velvalee kept spinning the tale of her husband as the spy master, angling to convince prosecutors that she deserved a reduced sentence.

In a series of interviews Mrs. Dickinson told FBI agents that when the Japanese attaché, Yokoyama, came to her doll store in November 1941, he was actually looking for her husband.[59] When asked how she had so much money in her safe deposit box when arrested, she claimed that the cash came from her doll business profits. It was there to help take care of her husband who had been in ill-health for several years. The FBI report on the interrogation, however, notes her inconsistency: "When it was pointed out to her that her income tax return for 1942 showed a net loss of $1,600, she hysterically stated that she had found this money hidden in her husband's bed at the time of his death."[60]

The interview transcript on the subject shows Velvalee's volatility under FBI questioning.

Q   Only a few moments after his death, weren't you tearing his mattress apart or something. Does that sound to you like the act of someone who is—
A   Stop it! Stop it! Stop it! I knew he had money left in there. Why should I have somebody come in and find that money that I knew he had put away.[61]

A report on the matter concluded, "She said she did not know where her husband had obtained this money and refused to discuss the matter any further."[62]

In another interview, Mrs. Dickinson heaped even more blame on her late husband. She said the Japanese had given him two packages, one with money and the other with the South American contact information.[63] At first Mrs. Dickinson said the Japanese told Lee they wanted the couple to move back to the West Coast. When she objected because of wanting to continue with her business in New York, Lee told her that she should visit the West Coast alone once a month to observe Allied aircraft carriers, battleships and "things of general interest." Those observations were to be in repayment for the money they had received from the Japanese.[64] However, she had no idea how much money had been paid until she tried to estimate the amount later from what was in the safe deposit box.[65]

Velvalee said she and her husband had "terrific arguments" over using her customers' names, but did concede that she prepared the letters at her "husband's request" on the various hotel typewriters.[66]

The agents didn't believe her. An FBI memo concluded: "it should be pointed out that Mr. Dickinson did not know the Naval Attaché but Velvalee was very friendly with him. Furthermore, that the doctor's examination of Mr. Dickinson at the time of the alleged payment to him showed that Mr. Dickinson was not only physically disabled but also that his mental faculties were impaired. It is believed that all available evidence should be used so that there is no doubt in anyone's mind reading this interesting case write up that Velvalee and not her husband was the spy."[67]

The interrogations of Velvalee Dickinson, however, did prove that Elizebeth Friedman's decoding of the Doll Woman letters were highly accurate. She admitted the names of dolls reflected in the letters referred to either carriers or battleships. Where the letter indicated a dislike of a certain doll, this was a reference to a ship damaged and undergoing repairs. There were some variations from Elizebeth's interpretation of the vague open code. Dolls with the names of countries from the Eastern hemisphere indicated carriers and those from the Western hemisphere referred to battleships—something that Elizebeth did not detect. Mrs. Dickinson destroyed the code book she used to write the letters immediately after her husband's death.[68]

As for Elizebeth's suggestion that Mrs. Dickinson must have had an accomplice to obtain all the information gathered for the letters, agents established that the Doll Woman did have some help. She contended that the information concerning ships in Seattle was gathered through "casual discussion with shipyard workers" as well as from an insurance broker in the area who was fond of fishing and a keen observer of the harbor's activities.[69] When the FBI agents interviewed the insurance broker, however, they determined he was just a dupe who "was not aware that the Dickinsons were working for the Japanese and merely revealed his information during social conversations."[70]

When Velvalee Dickinson came up for sentencing, she was dressed in black and weeping, begging for leniency from the judge. She denied being a Japanese agent and instead put the onus on her late husband. She was unaware, she said, of the meaning of the letters she had typed. U.S. Attorney James. B.M. McNally refuted Mrs. Dickinson's claim about her husband, "He can't defend his good name, but I can. There is evidence in existence which proves beyond peradventure of doubt that Velvalee was a hired Japanese spy. When the Japanese hired her, they were hiring an old friend. It was Velvalee, and not Lee Dickinson, who admits forging her customers' names to these letters. I charge that at least ten days before Pearl Harbor she had definite information that the Japanese were planning to go to war with this country."[71]

Federal Judge Shackelford Miller, Jr., sentenced the Doll Woman to the maximum for the censorship violation: ten years in prison and a $10,000 fine.[72] "Some people do not realize that our nation is engaged in a life-and-death struggle. Any help given to the enemy means the death of American boys who are fighting for our national security," said Judge Miller in imposing the sentence. "The indictment to which you have pleaded guilty is a serious matter; it borders close to treason. You were fortunate that the Government did not have you tried on espionage charges."[73]

Court records show that Mrs. Dickinson's fine was paid in March 1946, but it does not indicate by whom.[74] Then in 1951, three years shy of serving her full sentence, the Doll Woman was released from prison.[75] She contacted government officials to see if any of the funds confiscated from her were available, but they had all gone to pay fines or taxes.[76]

Over the years various people contacted the FBI about information concerning Velvalee Dickinson, but in 1972, Bureau officials confided that her "whereabouts have been unknown" since 1955 when she attempted to recover her confiscated cash.[77]

* * *

The FBI likewise lost track of Elizebeth Friedman's key role in bringing the Doll Woman to justice. Just a few months after the conviction, the FBI sought to highlight its investigation in the highly-publicized incident. "It is felt that exhibits available in connection with this case would make an extremely interesting and valuable display which might well be placed in the Director's Reception Room," a memo on the Velvet case suggested in September 1944. "It is recommended that ... an appropriate display be prepared as soon as possible."[78]

Ever mindful of boosting the public image of the FBI, its director, J.

Edgar Hoover, signed off on the idea a few weeks later.[79] Another memo from Hoover to the FBI's New York office sought photos of Velvalee Dickinson, "her possessions, her apartment and her doll shop suitable for publication."[80]

It is understandable that the FBI would want to promote a case where its agents played a significant role in protecting national security. To this day the Bureau's website devotes considerable space to the Doll Woman case. Yet that website incorrectly credits FBI Laboratory cryptographers—not Confidential Informant T4, Elizebeth Friedman—for solving the codes in the Doll Woman's letters.[81]

Elizebeth never wrote about the Doll Woman in her memoirs, though she did submit documents from the case to the Elizebeth Smith Friedman Collection at the George C. Marshall Research Library at Virginia Military Institute. She was constrained by wartime secrecy, and in the post war period, by the government's continuing demand to stifle any discussion of its ability to break sophisticated codes and ciphers.

U.S. Attorney McNally gloated that getting evidence against Velvalee Dickinson "was one of the greatest jobs ever done by the United States Attorney's office in this district."[82] Certainly, the FBI played the lead role in investigating the Doll Woman, but had difficulty determining the hidden meaning of her letters. For the case to move forward, McNally had to seek out an expert—Elizebeth Friedman—to decode the suspicious correspondence. By his own admission, the Doll Woman codes "finally had been broken" by Elizebeth's analysis of the letters. Yet the FBI website makes no mention of her connection to the case and gives credit for solving the Doll Woman codes to the Bureau's own cryptographers. To set the record straight the FBI, whose own cryptanalysts were trained by Elizebeth,[83] would have to publicly acknowledge Elizebeth's influential impact in the Velvet case.

Seven decades after helping bring a notorious wartime spy to justice, Elizebeth Friedman deserves more than to be identified as a mere confidential informant.

=10=

Postwar Career and Elizebeth Friedman's Legacy

As World War II ended Elizebeth Friedman found herself with some free time, but without a job for the first time in nearly two decades. As the government combined cryptographic activities from various agencies, it downsized her code breaking position in the Coast Guard.

Far from being upset over the loss of her government position, however, Elizebeth recommended it. Then she set out to reinvent herself as a consultant, do some cherished research that she had put off for years and burnish the legacy in cryptology that both she and her husband would leave for posterity.

With victory in Europe secured in the summer of 1945, William Friedman went on an extensive inspection tour of facilities on the continent.[1] With her war-time nemesis, German spies in South America, at bay, Elizebeth discovered time to write her husband about how America was reacting to the European victory, engagements with friends at home and the war still being waged against Japan.

In a series of letters in July and August, Elizebeth worried that her correspondence sent by the armed services "V-mail" would never catch up to William as he moved from post to post. In her first letters she wrote about the mundane—slow progress in repairing the old auto, and the exciting—a car trip to Detroit to visit her sister.[2]

After living through war rationing and the ramshackle, summertime sweatshop at the Naval Communications Annex,[3] the end-of-the-war road trip brought a few serendipitous luxuries. Elizebeth enthused about a stop at the George Washington Hotel in western Pennsylvania, "It seems like coming into a new world—the beautiful mountains yesterday was such an uplift to my spirit, and then to find a completely-serviced and up-to-date hotel (bell-hops, managers, clerks etc. are college girls) and an hotel dining room serving butter! They brought the biggest bowl of ice to my room I've seen in years—even these things do my soul good—to get away from the eternal picayune details that we suffer under, living in D.C."[4]

On her return to Washington several days later, before the U.S. targeted a second atomic bomb on Nagasaki, she expressed doubts to Billy about the unfamiliar weapon first used on Hiroshima: "The atom bomb is the only thing people can talk about here today. I wonder if it is as much of a 'dud' as the Nazi robots and buzzbombs. Not that they were duds, certainly, but they certainly did NOT affect materially the course of the war. Yet everyone is saying this will end the war P.D.Q. I wonder! Much too good to be true, say I." Elizebeth also sent greetings to "all the good souls over there I should love to see too," an indication of the bonds she had formed with British cryptanalysts she had worked with in the war. Then she signed off "ALL MY LOVE, Elsbeth."[5]

When the official VJ day came eight days later, Elizebeth was sick at home nursing a stomach bug. She missed her husband and two children who all were away: "It seems tragic that I have no one of you precious three here with me to celebrate the unexpectedly early end of the war." She wrote about the crowd of 75,000 people around the White House celebrating the Japanese surrender. In honor of the end of the war, Elizebeth also informed her husband, President Truman had declared a two-day holiday for federal workers.[6]

Along with savoring the war's end, Elizebeth received a dozen roses and French perfume from her "too generous" husband for her birthday.[7] Also arriving from Bletchley Park, England's wartime cryptanalysis center, was a telegram from William: "ABSENCE ON YOUR BIRTHDAY DARLING SADDENS ME BUT HOPE FLORAL AMBASSADOR ARRANGED THROUGH MATHEW JONES WILL VOUCHSAFE UNDYING LOVE."[8]

Those heady gifts arrived just as the professional ground Elizebeth had been working on for three decades began to shift. She started scrutinizing the Coast Guard cryptanalytic unit she had created 15 years before. She was setting the wheels in motion to make the two-day federal employee holiday her own permanent furlough from the government.

On August 18, 1945, Army Chief of Staff George Marshall sent a memo to his counterpart in the Navy suggesting that a board investigate combining Army and Navy radio intercept and cryptanalytic activities: "United States Navy and Army signal intelligence agreements and commitments with the British and any other Allies, as well as with the Federal Bureau of Investigation, Office of Strategic Services, Treasury and the

Federal Communications Commission, will require reexamination and readjustment in the light of the post-hostilities situation."[9]

Another memo on communications intelligence on August 21st for the vice chief of Naval Operations doomed those in the cryptographic field, such as Elizabeth, who lacked expertise with machines to break codes and ciphers. "The days of intercept copy produced by individual radiomen following morse [sic] transmissions at hand speed on typewriters are nearly past: rapidly disappearing, too, are the fields of cryptography which can be defeated by individual cryptanalysts working with paper, pencil and intuition on small collections of traffic. Cryptography and cryptanalysis have become big businesses and highly mechanised [sic] ones."[10]

The next day an inter-service committee recommended that the OSS, FCC and Treasury Department be excluded from cryptanalytic activities in the post war. All those secret services would be merged in the Army and Navy with the FBI handling law enforcement code breaking.[11] Another memo seven months later indicated that "Coast Guard officers" might be detailed to continue communications intelligence service with the Navy,[12] leaving Elizabeth, who served as a civilian, without a cryptanalysis job with the government.

Elizabeth probably was not privy to those TOP SECRET memos, but as a cryptography veteran who had worked in the Navy's sophisticated, Bombe-based code breaking operation[13] during the war, she knew that her style of decrypting ciphers by hand and intuition was becoming antiquated. Those skills had served her well when she was busting rum runners and dope smugglers, but the science of cryptanalysis had taken giant strides in the war years. Code expert David Kahn wrote that World War II mechanized cryptography and mathematized cryptanalysis, "These trends, which were still just getting under way in 1939, accelerated with a rush during the war and culminated by 1945. This evolution transformed both cryptography and cryptanalysis and gave each a characteristic it still has."[14]

Ironically one of the people leading the mechanized charge into cryptography and cryptanalysis—and leading to the downsizing of Elizabeth's position—was her own husband. William Friedman was largely responsible for hiring mathematically inclined code breakers in the Army and ramping up its use of machines to encrypt messages for U.S forces and decrypt those of the enemy.[15] Those mechanized changes brought a new era of code breaking that Elizabeth could live without. "Everything is so damn big today. It's a curse. The problem with machines is that nobody ever gets the thrill of seeing a message come out," she told a newspaper reporter in 1972.[16]

The Navy officially returned all of its Coast Guard operations to the Department of Treasury on January 1, 1946.[17] Before she officially left the Navy's jurisdiction Elizebeth had to complete many archival tasks for her unit. "Papers, records were sorted; reams of 'work-sheets' were destroyed in the desire not to bury completely all posterity under a mammoth paper mausoleum; records deemed worthy of retaining for historical official archives were grouped, described, labeled, indexed, and irreverently dispatched to their sealed tombs in government vaults," she wrote in a four-page manuscript titled "Footnote to History." "I signed the pledge that was exacted of all departing from the sacred precincts of SECRECY, the pledge never to reveal (at least without authority from on high), or even to refer to, any of the projects with which I had dealt during the [sic] World War II."

When she walked out of the Nebraska Avenue Naval Communications Annex that housed her cryptographic group for the last time, Elizebeth stopped across the street and peered back at the structure, contemplating her two decades of code breaking. "It was the end of a Period an Era. I knew that as surely as I stood on two feet, I should never enter that reservation again or return to that particular form of endeavor again."

Elizebeth writes that she was committed to returning to the Treasury Department's jurisdiction, but the world had changed immensely from her days breaking rum runner codes and ciphers.

> Those "personages" who had been the organizers, the officials, the operators, the-followers, the hangers-on of the Smuggling Era, had all been forced to find other avenues of activity during the war, the physical fact of which was enough in itself to stop effectively smuggling activities of any importance. And now although the war had ended, I felt intuitively that the smugglers had certainly not rested during the war but had undoubtedly developed other and probably even more profitable pursuits. Therefore I was convinced that there would be no significant developments which would justify the Treasury Department maintaining a section to read hidden communications of smugglers.

Civil Service regulations entitled government personnel who served in war positions to return to their civilian positions. Elizebeth, however, did not envision a productive use of her skills any longer:

> How was I to convince them that for even our small unit to return in toto would be a waste of the tax-payers money?
> The years 1938 to December 1941 had been exciting, round-the-clock adventures, as we counter-spied into the minds and activities of the agents attempting to

spy into those of the United States. With the vast reorganizations following the end of the war, such titillating pursuits would be denied our Treasury unit, all such activities having now been allotted to other agencies.[18]

One reason that Treasury and Coast Guard would no longer be breaking codes was the realization by the powers-that-be that secret cryptanalysis operations and law enforcement were not a good mix. A 1943 Navy memo titled "The Friedman Publicity" noted that in the years leading up to the war 20 news articles about Elizebeth and William Friedman spilled the beans about American code breaking abilities to espionage agents. "Some of these stories reached the public because Mrs. Friedman had to testify in court as to the method by which evidence was obtained. Naturally, she had to divulge certain secret details, which were then no longer secret. This is one of the reasons why the use of police agencies in cryptanalysis is dangerous," the memo stated. "To publicize a deciphering success in military or diplomatic work is to dry up the cource [sic] of information for a long time."[19]

Elizebeth, with a decade of experience in the realm of national security code breaking, could not disagree with that assessment. She urged Coast Guard officials to abolish the cryptanalytic unit that she had created and managed since 1931. "The usefulness of my section was therefore in my opinion, ended. I wrote the letter abolishing the positions, including my own," she wrote.[20]

Elizebeth's stance seemed to be unanimous. Coast Guard officials anticipated their post-war mission would be more like their pre–Prohibition days: using ships and aircraft for air-sea rescue operations instead of interdicting smugglers.[21] As Coast Guard officers looked ahead, they realized that they would no longer have their own intelligence operation as they had during Prohibition and the pre-war years. They would need to rely on other agencies to provide the information to them.[22] It wasn't until after the terrorist attacks on September 11, 2001, and the Coast Guard became an agency within the Department of Homeland Security that the maritime law enforcement agency again became an official member of the U.S. intelligence community,[23] creating its own Cryptographic Group in 2007 within the National Security Agency (NSA) at Fort Meade, Maryland.[24]

After the Coast Guard returned to the Treasury Department, in March 1946, Elizebeth received her first civilian efficiency rating since her unit joined the Navy in 1941. It was an "excellent" score, with 12 "outstanding" designations and 16 categories receiving a checkmark for "adequate."[25]

The last months of Elizebeth's government service were spent compiling records and the history of the cryptanalytic unit's work, both in law enforcement and spy catching: "To re-live those two phases of my professional career as a cryptologist," she wrote, "to file them down to a manageable bulk for storage for posterity, I would now direct the activities which would be, I hoped, my last stint for the United States."[26]

The official *History of Coast Guard Unit 387*, the war time cryptanalysis unit that Elizebeth commanded at the start of the war, and then was relegated to second-in-command, does not cite any individual contributions. Its 300-plus pages outline the German clandestine radio circuits the unit monitored and how it broke various ciphers, including those produced with the Green Enigma device. No one is listed as the author of the Unit 387 history, but its publication date on September 17, 1946,[27] was just five days after Elizebeth's final day as a federal employee.[28] Elizebeth told a National Security Agency historian 30 years later that her superior, Commander L.T. Jones, "was writing a study," that was most likely the unit's history.[29] One can surmise, however, that she had a hand in preparing the history since her private files indicate that "storage for posterity" of the unit's records was her primary duty in her final months of service.

The historian who interviewed Elizebeth in 1976, Robert Louis Benson, wrote, "Mrs. Friedman provided some information that she indicated should be held in confidence and not included in histories or articles."[30] He concluded "The unit was probably even more secret than other Comint organizations because it dealt with counterespionage and double agent operations," therefore, many records of the unit were "lacking."[31]

The government kept the Unit 387 history secret for 62 years, finally declassifying the hefty, oversized volume in 2008. Elizebeth took her war secrets to the grave. Responding to a request for her to speak at a women's club in 1951, Elizebeth wrote "What we did during that time must remain buried in the secret archives."[32]

Her memoirs obliquely refer to her war contributions, merely indicating a certain pride that she did "the spy stuff!"[33] Yet Elizebeth's other writings are nostalgic about that period. In the winter of 1959, while visiting Cambridge, England, Elizebeth and William were invited to a luncheon where she encountered "two former colleagues, one an associate of World Wars I and II, the other more nearly a colleague of mine of World War II." She enjoyed seeing them again and reminiscing. At the end of the luncheon she wrote, "I saw the slight figure in uniform again gliding to and from my desk and then I recalled that one of the sad thoughts I had about V.E. Day was that I would not be seeing his cheery, ruddy face again. Then I remembered how I myself 'folded my tent to steal away' after V-J Day."[34]

Elizebeth's stealing away did not last long. Soon she had landed a job with the International Monetary Fund (IMF). A colleague of William's, Dr. Solomon Kullback, told NSA historians that the IMF position may have been just one that Elizebeth had consulting with "government agencies that wanted to establish secure communications systems" after the war. "But too much of the details of the activities we didn't know," Kullback added, "because of security, need-to-know, compartmentalization, even though it wasn't described in those terms in those days."[35]

Although her NSA biography and Elizebeth's own file list her work there, IMF officials report that after nearly seven decades their records have "no trace" of her time as a consultant. As a result, Elizebeth's consultations at the IMF remain very sketchy, seemingly as secretive as her World War II work.[36] A short, handwritten note in Elizebeth's papers says only that she was a "Consultant in Communications" for the agency from 1946 to 1949.[37] Her biography on the NSA's Cryptologic Hall of Honor website adds that she "created communications security systems" for the IMF.[38] Another source adds that she not only "devised," but "helped manage security systems protecting International Monetary Fund resources."[39]

One has to infer what Elizebeth's contributions to the IMF were by reviewing the scant information available. The International Monetary Fund was created by the Allies at the end of the war. It was obviously concerned about having secure communications among its members. Elizebeth's daughter, Barbara Atchison, remembered discussing the IMF position with her mother: "They said they had to have codes and ciphers in case, they had to keep it safe, in case they devalued the Franc, they had to keep it secret until, you know, it was formally announced."[40]

A discussion in 1946 demonstrated the need to protect sensitive financial information as it was being distributed to IMF participants: "Drafts of a formal request to members to communicate their proposed par values, together with measures to safeguard the confidentiality of the communications, were considered by the Board."[41]

In 1947 the IMF was concerned about determining dates of a member's "monetary reserves" for the preparation of the "calculation of a repurchase obligation." The only reference to a "cipher" in a published historical document of the IMF's first 20 years is regarding messages about that calculation. As the agency's communications consultant at the time, Elizebeth must have had a hand in the issuance of security instructions to members: "These instructions included the provision of a special code and cipher system and a test number, which had to be used when drawings were requested by cable. Each member was asked for an undertaking that the use of this system and number was equivalent to the provision of a signed commitment by the Government."[42] The procedure mimics the modus operandi that Elizebeth required of William Donovan's Coordinator of Information office when she set up the communications system for that fledgling government spy agency in 1941.

Once her stint with the IMF was finished, Elizebeth—with what William described as an "itchy foot and the cash to assuage the itch"—indulged herself with a three-month European vacation without her husband. Elizebeth had wanted Billy to accompany her, but her planned destinations of Switzerland, France and Italy held no intrigue for him, writing to a friend, "what have those places to offer me that I have not seen elsewhere in my travels? I say to hell with it; but if that is what she wants I am all for her spending the money that way."[43]

With that "itch" satisfied, Elizebeth turned her attention to projects that had languished on her "to do" list. As a result, the code couple returned to the puzzle that brought them together in the first place. The debate between the Stratfordians and Baconians was still raging four decades after Elizebeth began working with Elizabeth Wells Gallup at Riverbank Laboratories.

After the war the Friedmans moved from their Military Road home on the outskirts of the District of Columbia to the heart of the city, to a townhouse on 2nd Street Southeast, just a few blocks from the Capitol. They moved there because it was within walking distance of the Folger Shakespeare Library, where they could examine the Bard's portfolios. In the early 1950s, now that Elizebeth was retired from fulltime work,[44] the Friedmans earnestly sought to prove what they suspected at Riverbank, but had never been allowed to say openly because it offended the beliefs of their patron, Colonel George Fabyan: that there was nothing in Shakespeare's works to indicate any author other than William Shakespeare himself.

Scholars long had dubbed the controversy "The Greatest of Literary Problems." The Baconians, also known as the anti–Stratfordians, believed that Shakespeare, an uneducated peasant, could not have produced such a body of work that displayed such worldly knowledge.[45] "Shakespeare never, as far as we know, went very far from London or Stratford. So how would he know about Italy? How would he know about these historical sources that lie behind the plays that he writes?" commented University of York professor of Renaissance studies, Bill Sherman.[46]

Using the cryptographic skills they had learned over decades of work, the Friedmans decided it was time to put this pesky literary issue to rest. They worked feverishly—literally—both of them fighting viruses during the Christmas holiday to get a manuscript of their findings out for a literary competition by the last day of December 1954.[47] Their jointly-written thousand-page manuscript,[48] "The Cryptologist Looks at Shakespeare," won a $1,000 prize for literature from the Folger Library.[49] It was a bittersweet moment. The April morning that the local paper headlined "Washington Couple Win Folger Shakespeare Award," William suffered a heart attack while getting out of bed. Billy's recovery was slow—his discharge from the hospital was three months later.[50]

Several companies competed for the rights to publish the Friedmans' work. The couple chose Cambridge University Press, which demanded drastic cuts to the manuscript.[51] With William hospitalized, Elizabeth rejected the publisher's suggestion to work with a "collaborator for revision and consultation."[52] Instead, Elizabeth consulted William while he remained in the hospital, but worked at home alone to hone their tome.[53]

Under another working title, *Author! Author!*, William submitted the manuscript to the NSA for "security clearance."[54] When the substantially-edited manuscript came out as a book in 1957, however, the Friedmans disliked the new title given it by the publisher because it implied "that ciphers exist in Shakespeare," when the entire point of the book was to dismiss the notion that the Bard's works contained any secret writing.[55] Nevertheless, re-titled as *The Shakespearean Ciphers Examined*,[56] the book made a splash in the literary world that seemed to put to rest the long-standing Baconian controversy.[57]

Point-by-point through 288 pages—less than a third of the length of their Folger award-winning manuscript—the Friedmans' book dissected the claims of ciphers and codes hidden in both the language and the typefaces of various Shakespeare works. A review noted: "In 'The Shakespearean Ciphers Examined,' these systems succumb to the cool, surgical, irrefutable analyses of two of the world's leading cryptologists."[58]

Elizabeth and William delved into the history of the alleged codes discovered by the Baconians and the people who had perpetrated the secret-author theories. One such believer was Detroit physician Orville Ward Owen who wrote *Sir Francis Bacon's Cipher Story*. His favored tool to decipher Shakespeare was a wheel invented by Bacon. It contained "two spools, rather like over-sized cinema reels, pivoted to spin freely." As the spools rotated, they spun 1,000 feet of canvas to which were attached selected texts of Elizabethan writings.

The Friedmans did their best to follow Owen's instructions to decipher the works using the four key words that he described. First, the code couple described these key words as "generous," giving the decipherer too much "freedom of choice," and, in fact, generating "plenty" of false leads. Second, they wrote that Owen's quotations of passages was unfair, with no citations of the quotes. The Friedmans concluded that "if Owen was a fraud, he was a remarkably determined and consistent one."[59]

The book also proclaimed a high dose of skepticism for William Stone Booth's theories which misused the concept of a string cipher, the Friedmans observed. That type of encryption could use an acrostic, for example, a cipher which uses the first or last letter from a verse to form a message distinct from the actual verse. The Friedmans noted that even prior Baconians had pointed out the fallacy of Booth's string cipher system for its ambiguity. William and Elizebeth added that Booth's use of acrostic analysis lacked uniformity, requiring a haphazard zigzag down Shakespeare's pages to develop a bogus cipher instead of a uniform, logical pattern at the beginning or end of the sentences.[60]

Reaching back to their formative years at Riverbank, the Friedmans decided to experiment with Mrs. Gallup's insistence that the typefaces in some Shakespeare folios utilized the Bacon biliteral cipher. Their recollection from working with Mrs. Gallup was that she would often change "some of the assignments" of her keys to find a secret message. The Friedmans' independent testing showed that there could be multiple messages obtained from Gallup's method rather than one single, consistent meaning. As cryptologists, Elizebeth and William expressed "regret" at not finding any biliteral ciphers: "One could only accept a decipherment as testimony if it were demonstrable that the plain text was reached by the systematic and undeviating application of a genuine key," they wrote. "Mrs. Gallup applied her key so arbitrarily that her results only show what it was she was determined to find."[61]

"In the end, the Friedmans' careful, detailed, point-by-minute-point demolition of the Baconian cipher contentions buries these pseudo-cryptograms beneath a mass of evidence as crushing as an avalanche," David Kahn commented in a book review for the *New York Times*. "As far as cryptology is concerned, Shakespeare wrote Shakespeare."[62] The book—despite being cut down by two-thirds—won the Fifth Annual Shakespeare Award from the American Shakespeare Festival Theater and Academy.[63]

William and Elizebeth celebrate at a party honoring them on the publication of their book, *The Shakespeare Ciphers Examined.* The book was published in 1957 (courtesy Chris Atchison).

After the publication of *The Shakespearean Ciphers Examined* and after William was retired, but still consulting for the NSA,[64] the pair worked on another communications conundrum that had stumped experts. Elizebeth—spurred on by a master's degree in archaeology—long had been attracted to the mysterious Mayan hieroglyphs. When she vacationed in Mexico in 1940 she visited Mayan ruins in Oaxaca. At the same time, she indicated on a civil service form that if she were interested in another position it would be to study ancient languages, especially Mayan hieroglyphics, which academics studying the culture had been unable to read.

Both Elizebeth and William had dabbled in solving the strange Mesoamerican symbols for many years.[65] Their fascination even extended to using Mayan glyphs on bookplates from their private library; the symbols and the archaic language translated into English warned borrowers: "This book we entrusted you a while-ago. It not-being you-return-give it us, Is-being-sharpened our-axe by the expert."[66]

In 1958 the code couple traveled to Mexico to work on solving the symbols. Elizebeth wrote a friend, "It has been 25 years since we made a promise to ourselves to see the Mayan ruins. Now we are here. Having read and studied about them so much, it would have been the usual result to find them disappointing. On the contrary they are more impressive than one could possibly imagine."[67]

They never made a breakthrough on solving the hieroglyphs. After that three-month trip the Friedmans intended to return often to work on decrypting the symbols, but they never went back since the NSA demanded more time of William in his capacity as a consultant.[68]

Elizebeth must have been very proud of William's accomplishments in the cryptographic field, which began to outshine hers as his achievements were publicized after World War II. He previously had been recognized for writing *The Index of Coincidence and Its Applications to Cryptography*, as well as *Elements of Cryptanalysis*, which were pioneering texts in the new age of cryptography after World War I.[69]

Then William's secret World War II accomplishments began to emerge. Besides organizing and leading the team that broke the Japanese "Purple" cipher machine prior to the Pearl Harbor attack, he also helped develop the SIGABA, the "most secure cipher machine of the World War." After the war he became a major player in the Armed Forces Security Agency, which merged communications intelligence with the Navy, and later developed into the National Security Agency where he worked as an employee or consultant until his death in 1969.[70]

William Friedman's outstanding, though secret, contributions won him a War Department Medal for Exceptional Civilian Service, the Presidential Medal for Merit and the Presidential National Security Medal. He also received $100,000 in a special Congressional appropriation for his secret cryptologic inventions and patents that were prohibited from being produced in the commercial marketplace by the government.[71]

The adoration and praise also came with an uneasiness regarding the increasing secrecy required by security regulations in the Cold War. William and Elizebeth planned an overseas trip in early 1959; the NSA's director of security suggested that classified documents in the Friedmans' home "should be maintained for safekeeping" at the NSA until they returned to Washington. A memo on the subject indicates that William

"voiced no objection," even though "much of the material is widely disseminated" and "no grave Security problem would result by leaving this
material in the home of Mr. Friedman during his absence."[72]

As a result, two NSA employees came to the Friedmans' Capitol Hill
home on December 30, 1958[73] and confiscated 48 items from their personal library, including some that had been previously unclassified, but
now were being upgraded by the government. Both William and Elizebeth
became concerned about the "intolerable" and "nonsensical" security
restrictions.[74]

In an NSA oral history interview 24 years later, one of the NSA security officers tasked with removing the materials from the Friedmans' home
recalled that the highest classification of the material removed was "CON-
FIDENTIAL," and stored in a two-drawer safe, which officer Donald Coffey
described as "more than adequate for CONFIDENTIAL material, even in
a residence. I don't recall any implication that there was anything wrong
from a security sense as to how that material was handled or the fact that
it was there."[75]

Nevertheless, a follow-up letter from the NSA director determined
that even the list of confidential material taken by the agency "cannot
be disseminated in any manner which would bring them into the
public domain unless we first get clearance from DOD [Department of
Defense]."[76]

This was near the end of the McCarthy Era when snoops were looking
for Communist sympathizers in every corner of the government. "Mrs.
Friedman felt it was what one might have expected of Nazi Germany, but
not of the United States, particularly as it by implication suggested that
[William] Friedman had been careless, or worse, about security," wrote a
biographer who interviewed Elizebeth on the subject.[77]

Virginia Military Institute (VMI) historian Colonel Rose Mary Sheldon says the NSA's Friedman confiscations were required by updated security regulations in the Cold War. "It was not because anybody was trying
to be evil," she said. In 1958 DOD directive 5200.1 "made all material
related to cryptologic systems previously classified Restricted, now
upgraded to Confidential and they had to be taken back."[78]

In the hour it took the NSA agents to confiscate the documents from
the Friedmans' home, the couple cooperated fully. William even suggested
which items belonged to the government and should be removed. "He
said, 'Hey, this is yours. Take it,'" Coffey said in his oral history interview
on the subject. "As I say, he and his wife were cordial to us. They weren't
appreciative of the actions that were being taken, but they knew about it

and they weren't in agreement with it, but they were cordial to us as the representatives that had to carry this out."[79]

A few days later the NSA's director of security wrote the director that "it was quite obvious that he [Friedman] felt deeply hurt and that the material was being taken for reasons other than Security. He stated that this material deals with the history of cryptography and should belong to the American people."[80] A month later NSA's Classification Advisory Panel declared three of the items taken from the Friedmans' home "Confidential," ten others as "Confidential-Modified Handling Authorized," and six more as "For Official Use Only."[81]

Elizebeth's continuing involvement in the dispute was demonstrated by a handwritten letter in her files to "Dear General Carter," apparently Lieutenant General Marshall Carter, the director of the NSA from 1965 to 1969.[82] It is not clear whether the letter was typed and sent,[83] but Elizebeth laid out her thoughts about the legality of the NSA confiscations in the handwritten version dated only "Nov. 4." She writes that six lectures prepared by her husband under contract to the NSA "were unclassified; it was only after they went to NSA that they were classified, a rather long time after, I believe." Her letter goes on to name several items formerly in the Friedman library that were on the NSA's "so-called 'classified' list."[84] A different letter that she did send to General Carter called the NSA confiscation a "search-and-seizure act." That letter—a dozen years after the episode—went to Carter, who by 1971 had become director of the George C. Marshall Research Foundation at VMI.[85]

Despite the confiscations, William and Elizebeth Friedman continued to catalog their trove of papers to donate to the foundation's Marshall Library. An appraisal in 1968 valued the portions remaining in their cryptography collection at $49,500.[86] The couple considered donating the papers to the Library of Congress, but on a visit there, Elizebeth considered the items in too much disarray to be useful to researchers. The Marshall Library was the smallest facility certified to handle classified documents, thus the Friedmans' chose it for their valuable collection.[87]

After William died, Elizebeth devoted a great deal of her remaining years to preserving his legacy as the "Dean of American Cryptology." A few months after his death she wrote family and friends about her endeavor: "I have been working very steadily and hard—some days 8 to 10 hours a day—right here at his desk in our library. I have a typist, (paid by the Marshall Library), one to two days a week. Even so, it's not something one accomplishes with speed and dispatch." Elizebeth revealed that the legal agreement with the library stipulated that all of the Friedmans' papers must remain in her house until an annotated bibliography was completed. "After the Collection is shipped to the Marshall Library, I shall be free to sell the house. If I feel then the way I do now, I shall leave Washington. It is anything but a happy place for me to be right now."[88]

Elizabeth finalized the donation to the Marshall Library in 1971.[89] The Friedman Papers traveled to the Lexington, Virginia facility accompanied by armed NSA guards. The papers were not opened to the public until 1978.[90]

In 2005 a VMI history professor prepared an annotated bibliography of the Friedman Papers and noticed that the library contained only 2,800 of the 3,002 articles listed. "The items that were missing also had their descriptive cards missing," said Professor Rose Mary Sheldon, "which suggested that the collection had been sanitized, and that, of course, led me to the federal government."[91] "It seems bizarre," Colonel Sheldon also wrote, "that NSA took copies of certain books from the FC [Friedman Collection] and yet they are available in the Mendelsohn Collection and from the Library of Congress."[92]

The former NSA director, Marshall Carter, admitted the folly of the agency's action in a 1988 oral history. Carter said officials from the agency wanted to classify some papers that were already in the Marshall Library's possession. "The stupidity of that, from my viewpoint, since they had never been classified, since the papers had already been all gone through by NSA already didn't make any sense," Carter told the NSA historian. "But I said, 'Set those papers aside and don't keep them in the accessible files until we've got this thing ironed out.'"[93]

Many of the items were restored to the library after the NSA declassified and released 7,600 documents from William Friedman's files in April 2015.[94] At a ceremony celebrating the release of the documents, Colonel Sheldon noted that it will take time to update the bibliography to see how the items confiscated by the NSA correlate with the newly released files.[95] At that same ceremony, the NSA's Associate Director for Policy and Records, Dr. David Sherman, admitted that there are even more Friedman materials "to find" and release at the agency.[96] A year later, in a comprehensive article reviewing the struggle over releasing and then reclassifying the Friedman Papers, Dr. Sherman wrote that 13 percent of the papers remain redacted to protect national security.[97]

The Friedman Papers at the Marshall Library are considered to be the world's most extensive private collection of material on cryptography.[98] They are in a second floor room with portraits of William and Elizebeth hanging on the wall and their desk to give it a feel of the Friedman's own library in their Capitol Hill townhouse. One authority described Elizabeth's work cataloging the papers both at her home and at the library as enhancing the value of the collection.[99] "I think this library gives us an enormous amount of material to think about the role of secrecy in a modern democracy," said Renaissance studies scholar Bill Sherman.[100]

An author who compiled an unpublished biography of Elizabeth in 1991 interviewed her at the Marshall Library on several occasions. Katie Letcher Lyle wrote that Mrs. Friedman visited the Lexington archives "fairly frequently, to help arrange and catalogue her husband's collection of books and files, and later and to a much lesser extent, her own." Lyle, whose husband worked at the library, reported that she came to know Elizabeth very well. "We shared a love of dry martinis and good food, and she had dinner with us on several occasions. Her chief interest after Colonel Friedman's death was in making certain that her husband was correctly interpreted to the world."[101]

Such engagements helped Elizabeth emerge from despair over her husband's death. During that period she granted interviews to at least one NSA historian that dealt mostly with William's cryptographic achievements; they also covered some of her accomplishments, but did not touch on her World War II years. Elizabeth's children, Barbara and John, persuaded her to begin preserving her legacy as well. She began dictating her memoirs into a tape recorder to be transcribed.[102] The more than 100 pages of transcriptions have numerous handwritten edits and additions.

Those transcribed memoirs touch briefly on Elizabeth's legacy beyond the world of cryptography and on another area where she was a pioneer. She summarized her thoughts on the impact she had as the first female cryptanalyst, whose job it was to lead a cryptographic workplace filled with men.[103]

"Many times I've been asked as to how my direction, that is the direction and superior status of a woman as instructor, teacher, mentor, and slave driver to men, even to commissioned and non-commissioned officers, how these men accepted my authority. I must declare with all truth that with one exception, all of the men young or older who have worked for me and under me and with me, have been most helpful and have never been obstructionists in any way."

Elizabeth recalled that just before World War II she trained four non-commissioned Coast Guard officers in the work of classifying intercepted correspondence: "these men when they were leaving at the end of their course took particular pains to inform me that when they had received their orders to report to my office for training that they had great misgivings. But that the two years training had been one of pleasure and benefit and profit in every way and that they could not have asked for a more agreeable supervisor or person in authority above them."[104]

Elizebeth's influence may also have helped raise the pay of women being hired by the Army for cryptographic work. In *Battle of Wits: The Complete Story of Codebreaking in World War II*, author Stephen Budiansky observed that William Friedman was "enlightened" by his wife that women's abilities in cryptography deserved a $2,000 per year salary, five times what ladies doing the same work were paid by the British.[105]

In the modern era, women walking in Elizebeth's footsteps admire her accomplishments. "I think the fact that Elizebeth appears to have done free-lance or contracted work for the government while on breaks in service to have her two children has been inspirational to many women in the NSA workforce," wrote NSA historian Betsy Rohaly Smoot. "There is recognition that she had to be both intelligent and tough to accomplish what she did in a time when most women in the federal government served in clerical, rather than professional, positions."[106]

For women in the law enforcement community, Elizebeth made a sizeable crack in the glass ceiling before anyone acknowledged the existence of that ceiling. "Here she is in this tough, tough environment that she excelled in," remarked the historian of the Bureau of Alcohol, Tobacco, Firearms and Explosives, Barbara Osteika. "And I've got to say, every time I talk about her, she was used to being the smartest person in the room."[107]

Elizebeth's memoirs note that when she was called to testify in court, judges, U.S. attorneys and Customs officers treated her with respect. "I have never received anything but the upmost courtesy and in many cases even admiration. Their astonishment at the work I had been able to do and bring to a conclusion which was a powerful means of supporting the battle they were fighting was, I think, the greater, because I was a woman. In fact, in all those areas, wherever in this country or in Canada, I have appeared, I have found no jealousy whatsoever of the fact that this success had been won by a woman, that this or that feat had been accomplished by a woman, in fact it was quite the contrary."[108]

One such example followed the 1933 CONEXCO liquor smuggling conspiracy case, when the special prosecutor extolled the virtues of Elizebeth's testimony. "It would have been a misfortune of the first magnitude in the prosecution of this case not to have had a witness of Mrs. Friedman's qualifications and personality available," A.W.W. Woodcock wrote to the secretary of the Treasury.[109]

"It seems to me that her accomplishments were of the level to garner this kind of attention," Osteika said of Woodcock's praise of Elizebeth. "This is something: a woman to get recognized and respected at this level, I think is huge."[110]

Yet Elizebeth did experience some roadblocks because of her gender. When she wrote the proposal to beef-up the Coast Guard Cryptanalytic Unit in 1930, "it was Admiral Billard that actually took her writing and her vision and he was the one who testified in front of Congress," commented Osteika. "That's sort of one of the underpinnings of the theme of Elizebeth Friedman is that she was the brains running the outfit here. But (because) she was a woman and was well outside her lane in terms of being married and having children and still having a career; I mean that was unheard of. But by the same token, they couldn't do it without her."[111]

"Grammy had a voice like a lion," recalled Elizebeth's grandson, Chris Atchison. She was strong willed and could always get her point across in a take-charge manner, he said in remarks at a ceremony naming the ATF headquarters auditorium in honor of his grandmother. "It is impossible to say what the world would have been like without her."[112]

The ATF auditorium is actually the second federal government facility commemorating Elizebeth's work. One of the first structures built at the National Security Agency's Fort Meade headquarters site, the Operations 1 building, was renamed the William and Elizebeth Friedman Operations Building in 2002.[113]

According to NSA historian Smoot: "On a day-to-day basis NSA employees have the opportunity to reflect on her work while working in the William and Elizebeth Smith Friedman Building or attending events in our William and Elizebeth Friedman Auditorium. Though she did not work for NSA or its immediate predecessor organizations, she is a cryptologist of note and is remembered here."[114]

Just as the name on the NSA building is a joint recognition, it is difficult to separate Elizebeth's legacy from that of her husband—and she probably would not want them to be separated. They truly were a team when they started their cryptographic careers at Riverbank; they worked together not only as husband and wife throughout their married life, but time and again—when bureaucratic imperatives for secrecy did not forbid it—they collaborated on cryptographic projects.

"I think that they came in at a critical time and at the right time and the world would definitely be a different place without what they did," said Chris Atchison. "And they did that together and it's an awesome story if you think about it."[115]

"Although Mrs. Friedman worked closely with her husband William

William and Elizebeth Friedman's achievements are on display at the National Cryptologic Museum just outside NSA Headquarters in Fort Meade, Maryland (National Security Agency).

as part of a team, many of her contributions to cryptology were unique," says her biography on the NSA Cryptologic Hall of Honor website. It notes her success in breaking the increasingly complex ciphers of rum runners during Prohibition as well as the codes in Mandarin Chinese of opium smugglers. The Hall of Honor biography concludes: "the complexity or difficulty mattered not. After fifty years at her business, Elizebeth Smith Friedman had indeed proved to be a pioneer in code breaking."[116]

Her list of accomplishments has to include leading Coast Guard cryptanalysts at the start of World War II and then becoming second-in-command of that unit when the Navy put an officer in charge. Particularly noteworthy is the fact that Elizebeth's unit was the first U.S. team to break messages on the German Enigma cipher machine.[117] Also in World War

II she played a key, albeit, secret role in bringing the Japanese spy, the Doll Woman, to justice.[118]

Elizebeth's 1991 biographer, Katie Letcher Lyle, even argues that Elizebeth was indirectly responsible for helping solve the Japanese Purple code prior to World War II since she lured William into cryptanalysis at Riverbank and served as his lifelong "Divine Fire" inspiration.[119] Another indirect contribution by Elizebeth to solving the Purple code was that she supplied rum runner messages in the early 1930s that the Coast Guard already had solved to cryptanalytic trainees in William's Army group. "It was excellent training in learning how to break into a code system," one of the trainees, Solomon Kullback, told NSA historians.[120] In 1934 Kullback wrote a secret War Department technical paper, "General Solution for the Double Transposition Cipher," using some of the rum runners' intercepted messages as examples.[121] William organized Dr. Kullback and other civilian trainees into the team that in 1940 built the machine that broke the Japanese system.

All of this cooperation between them in the early years of their careers ultimately caused confusion about the legacies of both Friedmans. "This would lead to a misunderstanding which Elizebeth was at great pains to put right throughout her life: the concept that it was she who *taught* Friedman cryptography," Lyle wrote in her biography of Elizebeth.[122]

Smoot minimizes accounts that William Friedman got into cryptography because of his own interest in the subject. "The story we tend to believe most," the NSA historian remarked about the Friedmans' work on Shakespeare at Riverbank, "is that he met Elizebeth Smith, who is one of the young women working on the project and fell in love with her and then fell in love with her work."[123]

In fact, when asked how he became the father of American cryptology, William merely replied: "I was seduced."[124]

Elizebeth herself dismissed the idea that she was the leader of the Friedman team. They were co-equals: "We began at the same time in this field of analysis. We were teachers of ourselves, simultaneously, as well as of others, we were merely leaders."[125] An NSA history of cryptology spends several paragraphs on William's accomplishments, but acknowledges that "Elizebeth was his equal as a cryptologist."[126]

From the time they began working on the dubious codes in Shakespeare's writings, through their collaboration in the Hindu trials and World War I code breaking of the Riverbank years, then again, late in life as they settled the argument about the Shakespeare ciphers, and fought the NSA's intrusions into their private collection, Billy and Elizebeth

Friedman worked as a team. They were the first and penultimate code couple.

"They were stronger as a unit and I think they both knew it," Chris Atchison observed of his grandparents' relationship. "I think they recognized in each other certain strengths and certain weaknesses and they fit together very well and I think that they, without each other, I'm not sure each one would have accomplished what they accomplished. I think they drove each other; I think they helped each other and I think that as husband and wife, there was probably some magic there that really took it over the top. And I think that we're very fortunate that they got together."[127]

Yet from the time Elizebeth started working on rum runners' codes until her stint with the IMF, *officially* the Friedmans worked separately in

A memorial wall outside the Elizebeth Smith Friedman Auditorium at ATF headquarters in Washington, D.C., displays several photos and newspaper articles documenting her career (photograph by the author).

their cryptography assignments for different government agencies. That is where Elizabeth individually takes on the mantle of legendary code breaker.

The apparatus that Elizabeth helped pioneer in Prohibition—the "tip of the spear"[128]—is the model for the all-source intelligence approach to law enforcement today. "Now the foundation was built upon the effort pioneered by Elizabeth Friedman and that long lineage of Coast Guard efforts in the code breaking community," said Rear Admiral Christopher Tomney at the 2014 ceremony dedicating the ATF auditorium in Elizabeth's name. "Mrs. Elizabeth Friedman certainly is an American hero, is part of a long blue line of Coast Guard code breakers and intelligence professionals that have dedicated their lives to the notion that intel really needs to drive operations and really needs to inform our decision makers."[129]

"She was the driving force and it was really, the more she did, the more they realized could be done," according to Barbara Osteika, the ATF historian. "But it was really her inventing intelligence analysis, all-source intelligence analysis."

In addition, her months spent training fledgling FBI cryptanalysts prior to World War II gave that agency a foothold in the crime-breaking science that still endures today. "She is to federal law enforcement what he [William Friedman] is to military intelligence," said Osteika.[130] To honor the work of women following Elizabeth's path, WIFLE, Women in Federal Law Enforcement, created the Elizabeth Smith Friedman Intelligence Award of Excellence in 2014.[131]

Elizabeth was a visionary pioneer in an age when her field of expertise was just coming of age. She used her intuition and cryptographic skills to set a standard that is still hard to match. She left her mark in literature, law enforcement and national security.

Elizabeth died in a New Jersey nursing home on October 31, 1980.[132] At a memorial service for her at Washington's Cosmos Club, Alfred Friendly, a family friend who had been a World War II cryptologist and a managing editor at the *Washington Post*, declared: "The list of her triumphs, known to most of you, is staggering simply when set down on paper, yet they are almost past conception if you try to think of the consequences to the public—to us—of every unsavory secret she laid bare."[133]

Elizabeth is buried alongside her beloved Billy at Arlington National Cemetery. Engraved on their tombstone is the Baconian motto that the code couple lived by: "Knowledge is Power." The farmer's daughter who became a "dynamo in low heels,"[134] Elizabeth Smith Friedman empowered the world with the hidden knowledge that she revealed—often unsavory, but always enlightening—about Shakespeare, smugglers and spies.

Chapter Notes

Prologue

1. Remarks by Rear Adm. Christopher J. Tomney, USCG, at Elizebeth Smith Friedman Auditorium Dedication Ceremony, ATF National Headquarters, Washington, D.C., June 17, 2014.

2. Chas. S. Root, "Memorandum for the Commandant," Dec. 28, 1929, RG 26, Entry 297, Box 73, file 1, National Archives Building, Washington, D.C.

3. "Elizebeth Smith Friedman 1892–1980," *Cryptologic Spectrum*, December 1980, reprinted in "The Friedman Legacy: A Tribute to William and Elizebeth Friedman," Center for Cryptologic History, National Security Agency, 1992. https://www.nsa.gov/resources/everyone/digital-media-center/video-audio/historical-audio/friedman-legacy/assets/files/friedman-legacy-transcript.pdf, accessed June 17, 2016, 206.

4. The U.S. secretary of state recommended payment of $50,666.50 in reparations but nothing would be paid for damages to the ship or the loss of the *I'm Alone's* cargo. "I'm Alone" Case, Joint Final Report of the Commissioners, Jan. 19, 1935, RG 26, Entry 297, Box 75, file 2, National Archives Building, Washington, D.C., 5.

5. Donna Howell, "She Helped Break Rumrunners; Crackdown: Elizebeth Smith Friedman's code breaking upheld the law," *Investor's Business Daily*, May 19, 2005, A03.

6. Undated resume. Elizebeth Friedman personnel file, National Archives, St. Louis.

7. Author interview with Barbara Osteika, Jan. 16, 2014.

8. Remarks by ATF Director B. Todd Jones at Elizebeth Smith Friedman Auditorium Dedication Ceremony, ATF National Headquarters, Washington, D.C., June 17, 2014.

9. "National Network of Fusion Centers Fact Sheet," Department of Homeland Security, http://www.dhs.gov/national-network-fusion-centers-fact-sheet#1, accessed June 27, 2014.

10. Jones remarks.

11. William Friedman is known as the "Dean of American Cryptology." The National Security Agency, declassified and released most of its records on William on April 20, 2015, 46 years after his death in 1969.

12. James R. Chiles, "Breaking Codes Was This Couple's Lifetime Career," *Smithsonian*, June 1987, reprinted in "The Friedman Legacy: A Tribute to William and Elizebeth Friedman," Center for Cryptologic History, National Security Agency, 1992. https://www.nsa.gov/resources/everyone/digital-media-center/video-audio/historical-audio/friedman-legacy/assets/files/friedman-legacy-transcript.pdf, accessed June 17, 2016, 201–202.

13. E. Friedman resume.

14. Elizebeth Friedman memoirs; Elizebeth S. Friedman Collection, Box 12, file 1–2, George C. Marshall Library, Virginia Military Institute, 47–78.

15. Chiles, "Breaking Codes..." 200.

16. Robert Louis Benson, "A History of U.S. Communications Intelligence during World War II: Policy and Administration" United States Cryptologic History, Series IV, World War II, Volume 8, https://www.nsa.gov/about/cryptologic-heritage/historical-figures-publications/publications/wwii/assets/files/history_us_comms.pdf, accessed June 17, 2016, 9.

17. Lt. Cmdr. Michael Bennett, "Guardian Spies: The Story of Coast Guard Intelligence in World War II (Part 2)," *American Intelligence Journal*, Spring 2010, Vol. 28, No. 1.

18. "Elizebeth Smith Friedman 1892–1980," 206.

19. E. Friedman memoirs, 98.

20. Margaret Santry, "Dialogue of Radio

Interview," NBC Radio, May 25, 1934, Elizebeth S. Friedman Collection, Box 11, file 15, George C. Marshall Library, Virginia Military Institute, 6.

21. David Kahn, *The Code-Breakers, The Story of Secret Writing*, Scribner, 1967, xv–xvi.

22. *Ibid.*

23. Santry, "Dialogue of Radio Interview."

24. *Ibid.*

25. E. Friedman memoirs, 100.

26. Comments by Albert Friendly, "In Memoriam Elizebeth Smith Friedman," *Cryptologic Spectrum*, NSA, December 1980, The Friedman papers, Box 16, file 24, George C. Marshall Library, Virginia Military Institute.

27. Santry, "Dialogue of Radio Interview."

28. E. Friedman memoirs, 84–85.

29. Author interview with Barbara Atchison, July 16–17, 2012.

30. Elizebeth S. Friedman (1892–1980) Cryptologic Hall of Honor 1999 Inductee, NSA, https://www.nsa.gov/about/cryptologic-heritage/historical-figures-publications/hall-of-honor/1999/efriedman.shtml, accessed Aug. 11, 2016.

31. "Elizebeth Smith Friedman 1892–1980."

32. Jennifer Wilcox, "Sharing the Burden: Women in Cryptology during World War II," Center for Cryptologic History, March 1998, https://www.nsa.gov/about/cryptologic-heritage/historical-figures-publications/publications/wwii/assets/files/sharing_the_burden.pdf, accessed June 17, 2016.

33. The Navy's OP-20-G maintained a list of names of its cryptographic workers and made them sign it acknowledging President Truman's Aug. 28, 1945 directive. RG 38 A1 1030, Box 1, OP-20-G Headquarters personnel, National Archives at College Park, MD.

34. Tory Cooney, "Cracking the Code: Hillsdale alum aided U.S. intelligence during world wars," *The Hillsdale Collegian*, March 21, 2014, http://www.hillsdalecollegian.com/2014/03/cracking-the-code-hillsdale-alum-aided-u-s-intelligence-during-world-wars/, accessed July 7, 2014.

35. David Mowry, "German Clandestine Activities in South America in World War II," NSA, 1989, declassified April 13, 2009, https://www.nsa.gov/news-features/declassified-documents/cryptologic-histories/assets/files/german_clandestine_activities.pdf, accessed June 17, 2016, 17–19.

36. Henry Morgenthau Diaries, Roll 114 411, Franklin D. Roosevelt Library, 67–69.

37. Summary of interview of Mrs. E. S. Friedman by R. Louis Benson, Jan. 9, 1976, NSA-OH-1976–22, DOC ID 4237384, approved for release by NSA July 30, 2015,

https://www.nsa.gov/news-features/declassified-documents/oral-history-interviews/assets/files/nsa-OH-1976–22-efriedman.pdf, accessed June 17, 2016, 3.

38. Frank W. Lewis, "German Agent Systems of World War II," undated, Approved for Release by NSA June 5, 2009, DOCID: 3565448, https://www.nsa.gov/news-features/declassified-documents/tech-journals/assets/files/german-agent-systems.pdf, accessed June 17, 2016.

39. CG Unit 387 was deactivated after the war. See a Feb. 6, 1946 Coast Guard memo. RG 26, Entry 338 (A-1) Box 4, National Archives Building, Washington, D.C.

40. "Elizebeth Smith Friedman 1892–1980," 205.

41. Remarks by Col. Rose Mary Sheldon at "Declassification and Release of William Friedman's Official Papers," George C. Marshall Foundation, April 25, 2015, https://www.youtube.com/watch?v=qxqgK8QCchw&app=desktop, accessed June 2, 2015.

42. "Hall of Honor Inductees: 1999," http://www.nsa.gov/about/cryptologic_heritage/hall_of_honor/1999/index.shtml.

43. "National Cryptologic Museum," http://www.nsa.gov/about/cryptologic_heritage/museum/index.shtml.

44. "A New Kind of Detective Work 1920–1933," date unknown, NSA, https://www.nsa.gov/about/cryptologic-heritage/historical-figures-publications/publications/pre-wwii/assets/files/new_detective_work.pdf, accessed June 17, 2016, 2.

Chapter 1

1. "Personal History Statement," July 1, 1930, Elizebeth Friedman personnel file, National Archives, St. Louis.

2. "A little while with Elizabeth [sic] Friedman," March 25, 1975 interview with unknown person. The Friedman papers, Box 12, file 1, George C. Marshall Library, Virginia Military Institute, 3.

3. "Elizebeth Friedman Autobiography at Riverbank Laboratories, Geneva, Illinois," listed as "ESF Oral History Pt. 2" at Center for Cryptologic History, National Security Agency, 1.

4. Elizebeth Friedman memoirs; Elizebeth S. Friedman Collection, Box 12, file 1–2, George C. Marshall Library, Virginia Military Institute, 2.

5. Oral history of Elizebeth Smith Friedman, Nov. 11, 1976, NSA-OH-1976–16, DOCID: 4237384, approved for release July 30, 2015, https://www.nsa.gov/news-features/declassified-documents/oral-history-

interviews/assets/files/nsa-OH-1976–16-efriedman.pdf, accessed June 17, 2016, 8.

6. E. Friedman memoirs, 2.

7. Oral history NSA-OH-1976–16, 8.

8. E. Friedman memoirs, 2.

9. James R. Chiles, "Breaking Codes Was This Couple's Lifetime Career," *Smithsonian*, June 1987, reprinted in "The Friedman Legacy: A Tribute to William and Elizebeth Friedman," Center for Cryptologic History, National Security Agency, 1992. https://www.nsa.gov/resources/everyone/digital-media-center/video-audio/historical-audio/friedman-legacy/assets/files/friedman-legacy-transcript.pdf, accessed June 17, 2016, 195.

10. Lambros D. Callimahos, "The Legendary William F. Friedman," *Cryptologic Spectrum*, Winter 1974, reprinted in "The Friedman Legacy: A Tribute to William and Elizebeth Friedman," Center for Cryptologic History, National Security Agency, 1992, https://www.nsa.gov/resources/everyone/digital-media-center/video-audio/historical-audio/friedman-legacy/assets/files/friedman-legacy-transcript.pdf, accessed June 17, 2016, 193.

11. Oral history NSA-OH-1976–16, 8.

12. E. Friedman memoirs, 3

13. *Ibid.*

14. John Marion Smith's Civil War history courtesy of Gail Heiser and http://www.civilwararchive.com/Unreghst/unininf8.htm.

15. Author interview with Barbara Atchison, July 16–17, 2012.

16. Author interview with Barbara Atchison, May 1, 2013.

17. Katie Letcher Lyle, "Divine Fire, Elizebeth Smith Friedman, Cryptanalyst," unpublished manuscript, 1991, Center for Cryptologic History, National Security Agency, 168.

18. Many articles say Elizebeth was the youngest of nine children. A genealogy file in her papers at the George C. Marshall Library at VMI indicate, however, that one of John and Sopha Smith's children died in infancy; they had nine children who survived to adulthood. Elizebeth S. Friedman Collection, Box 11, file 20, George C. Marshall Library, Virginia Military Institute.

19. Atchison interview, July 16–17, 2012.

20. E. Friedman genealogy files.

21. E. Friedman memoirs, 2.

22. *Ibid.*

23. Lyle, "Divine Fire," 66.

24. Atchison interview, July 16–17, 2012.

25. Fran Becque, "Baconian Biliteral Cipher, on the Estate of Colonel Fabayon [sic], National Security, and a Fraternity Woman," Focus on Fraternity History & More, http://www.franbecque.com/2013/08/09/baconian-biliteral-cipher-on-the-estate-of-colonel-fabyon-national-security-and-a-fraternity-woman/, accessed July 7, 2014.

26. Dr. Forrest Pogue interview with Elizebeth Friedman, May 16, 1973, Elizebeth S. Friedman Collection, Box 16, file 19, George C. Marshall Library, Virginia Military Institute, 1.

27. E. Friedman memoirs, 3.

28. *Ibid.*, 9.

29. Riverbank Laboratories, City of Geneva website, http://www.geneva.il.us/riverbnk/riverpag.html, accessed April 15, 2013.

30. Bill Sherman remarks, "A Portrait of William F. Friedman," video, The George C. Marshall Foundation, 2014, http://marshallfoundation.org/library/digital-archive/shakespearean-ciphers-examined/, accessed July 7, 2014.

31. E. Friedman memoirs, 5.

32. Lyle, "Divine Fire," 26.

33. John R. Friedman, "DIVINE FIRE, A film story by John Friedman," unpublished film script, 1994, 3.

34. Chiles, "Breaking Codes," 195.

35. Lyle, "Divine Fire," 25.

36. Atchison interview, July 16–17, 2012.

37. E. Friedman memoirs, 6.

38. *Ibid.*

39. Chiles, "Breaking Codes," 197.

40. Riverbank Laboratories.

41. E. Friedman memoirs, 4.

42. Elizebeth Friedman Autobiography, 4.

43. "DIVINE FIRE, A film story by John Friedman."

44. Pogue interview, 6.

45. Chiles, "Breaking Codes," 196.

46. David Mowry, "Cryptologic Almanac 50th Anniversary Series, William F. Friedman," National Security Agency, declassified June 12, 2009, https://www.nsa.gov/news-features/declassified-documents/crypto-almanac-50th/assets/files/William_F_Friedman.pdf, accessed June 17, 2016.

47. E. Friedman memoirs, 8.

48. *Ibid.*, 7.

49. *Ibid.*, 105.

50. Chiles, "Breaking Codes," 197.

51. Leah Stock Helmick, "Key Woman of the T-Men," *Reader's Digest*, September 1937, 52.

52. E. Friedman memoirs, 13.

53. Sherman remarks, "A Portrait of William F. Friedman."

54. Pogue interview, 6.

55. Atchison interview, July 16–17, 2012.

56. *Ibid.*

57. Elizebeth letter to William, Jan. 29, 1917. Elizebeth S. Friedman Collection, Box 2, file 1, George C. Marshall Library, Virginia Military Institute.

58. Elizebeth letter to William, Jan. 31, 1917. Elizebeth S. Friedman Collection, Box 2, file 1, George C. Marshall Library, Virginia Military Institute.
59. Elizebeth letter to William, Feb. 7, 1917. Elizebeth S. Friedman Collection, Box 2, file 1, George C. Marshall Library, Virginia Military Institute.
60. Elizebeth letter to William, Feb. 6, 1917. Elizebeth S. Friedman Collection, Box 2, file 1, George C. Marshall Library, Virginia Military Institute.
61. John Friedman, unpublished documentary script, "Code Breaking Couple," 2006, sent to author by John Friedman, the Friedmans' son.
62. Lyle, "Divine Fire," 61–62.
63. Atchison interview, July 16–17, 2012.
64. E. Friedman memoirs, 105.
65. David Kahn, *The Code-Breakers, The Story of Secret Writing*, Scribner, 1967, 887.
66. E. Friedman memoirs, 105.
67. *Ibid.*, 106–107.

Chapter 2

1. Leah Stock Helmick, "Key Woman of the T-Men," *Reader's Digest*, September 1937, 53.
2. Author classified, "The Origination and Evolution of Radio Traffic Analysis: The World War I Era," NSA, date unspecified, but approved for release June 16, 2008, https://www.nsa.gov/news-features/declassified-documents/cryptologic-quarterly/assets/files/trafficanalysis.pdf, accessed June 17, 2016, 1.
3. *Ibid.*
4. "A little while with Elizebeth [sic] Friedman," March 25, 1975 interview with unknown person. Elizebeth S. Friedman Collection, Box 12, file 1, George C. Marshall Library, Virginia Military Institute, 106.
5. Remarks by Betsy Rohaly Smoot at "Declassification and Release of William Friedman's Official Papers," George C. Marshall Foundation, April 25, 2015, https://www.youtube.com/watch?v=qxqgK8QCchw&app=desktop, accessed June 2, 2015.
6. Riverbank Laboratories, City of Geneva website, http://www.geneva.il.us/riverbnk/riverpag.htm, accessed April 15, 2013.
7. James R. Chiles, "Breaking Codes Was This Couple's Lifetime Career," *Smithsonian*, June 1987, reprinted in "The Friedman Legacy: A Tribute to William and Elizebeth Friedman," Center for Cryptologic History, National Security Agency, 2006. https://www.nsa.gov/resources/everyone/digital-media-center/video-audio/historical-audio/friedman-

legacy/assets/files/friedman-legacy-transcript.pdf, accessed June 17, 2016, 197.
8. Oral history of Elizebeth Smith Friedman, Nov. 11, 1976, NSA-OH-1976–16, DOCID: 4237384, approved for release July 30, 2015, https://www.nsa.gov/news-features/declassified-documents/oral-history-interviews/assets/files/nsa-OH-1976–16-efriedman.pdf, accessed June 17, 2016, 10.
9. Elizebeth Friedman memoirs; Elizebeth S. Friedman Collection, Box 12, file 1–2, George C. Marshall Library, Virginia Military Institute, 99.
10. "Elizebeth Friedman Autobiography at Riverbank Laboratories, Geneva, Illinois," listed as "ESF Oral History Pt. 2" at Center for Cryptologic History, National Security Agency, 12.
11. William F. Friedman, "Lecture V," reprinted in "The Friedman Legacy: A Tribute to William and Elizebeth Friedman," Center for Cryptologic History, National Security Agency, 2006. https://www.nsa.gov/resources/everyone/digital-media-center/video-audio/historical-audio/friedman-legacy/assets/files/friedman-legacy-transcript.pdf, accessed June 17, 2016, 108.
12. "A little while with Elizebeth Friedman," 106.
13. W.F. Friedman "Lecture V," 109.
14. "A little while with Elizebeth Friedman," 107.
15. Memo from Capt. J.O. Mauborgne, to Chief of the War College, April 11, 1917, William Friedman Collection, George C. Marshall Foundation, http://marshallfoundation.org/library/friedman/documents/110_734_1_0034_0036_OCR.pdf, accessed March 16, 2014.
16. "A little while with Elizebeth Friedman," 107.
17. William F. Friedman, "A Brief History of U.S. Cryptologic Operations 1917–1929," undated National Security Agency publication, declassified July 16, 2008, https://www.nsa.gov/news-features/declassified-documents/cryptologic-spectrum/assets/files/Brief_History_U.S._Cryptologic_Operations.pdf, accessed June 18, 2016, 1.
18. Katie Letcher Lyle, "Divine Fire, Elizebeth Smith Friedman, Cryptanalyst," unpublished manuscript, 1991, Center for Cryptologic History, National Security Agency, 73.
19. Bill Sherman analyzes the biliteral cipher in the photo, "Knowledge is Power," video, The George C. Marshall Foundation, 2014, http://marshallfoundation.org/library/digital-archive/shakespearean-ciphers-examined/, accessed July 7, 2014.
20. William Friedman, "Communications

Intelligence and Security" lecture, April 26, 1960, William F. Friedman Collection: Correspondence, Memoranda, and Personnel File Records—NSA/CSS, approved for release Jan. 14, 2015, https://www.nsa.gov/resources/everyone/digital-media-center/video-audio/historical-audio/friedman-audio/assets/files/Communication_Intelligence_Security_26_Apr_1960_LtCol_W_F_Friedman_Transcript.pdf, accessed June 17, 2016, 12.

21. E. Friedman memoirs, 25.
22. Lyle, "Divine Fire," 15.
23. E. Friedman memoirs, 25.
24. *Ibid.*, 26.
25. *Ibid.*, 27.
26. *Ibid.*, 29.
27. "A little while with Elizabeth Friedman," 108.
28. Elizabeth Friedman Autobiography, 24.
29. E. Friedman memoirs, 30.
30. Chiles, "Breaking Codes," 195.
31. Lambros D. Callimahos, "The Legendary William F. Friedman," *Cryptologic Spectrum*, Winter 1974, reprinted in "The Friedman Legacy: A Tribute to William and Elizebeth Friedman," Center for Cryptologic History, National Security Agency, 2006 https://www.nsa.gov/resources/everyone/digital-media-center/video-audio/historical-audio/friedman-legacy/assets/files/friedman-legacy-transcript.pdf, accessed June 17, 2016, 190.
32. E. Friedman memoirs, 32.
33. Chiles, "Breaking Codes," 195.
34. E. Friedman memoirs, 33.
35. *Ibid.*
36. William Friedman, "Second Period, Communications Security," undated, William F. Friedman Collection: Correspondence, Memoranda, and Personnel File Records—NSA/CSS, DocRefID A63403, declassified March 24, 2014, https://www.nsa.gov/news-features/declassified-documents/friedman-documents/assets/files/lectures-speeches/FOLDER_169/41758999079813.pdf, accessed June 17, 2016, 49.
37. E. Friedman memoirs, 34.
38. Chiles, "Breaking Codes," 195.
39. E. Friedman memoirs, 34.
40. W. Friedman, "Second Period, Communications Security," 50.
41. E. Friedman memoirs, 34.
42. W.F. Friedman "Lecture V," 107.
43. Connie Lunnen, "She Has a Secret Side, Breaking Codes Was More Personal in Her Day, Elizebeth Friedman Says," *The Houston Chronicle*, May 24, 1972, Elizebeth S. Friedman Collection, Box 11, file 14, George C. Marshall Library, Virginia Military Institute.

44. E. Friedman memoirs, 16.
45. "A little while with Elizabeth Friedman," 110.
46. Elizabeth stated that she co-authored "numerous cipher books" with her husband while at Riverbank. "Personal History," Oct., 21, 1927 and again July 3, 1931, Elizebeth Friedman personnel file, National Archives, St. Louis.
47. E. Friedman memoirs, 31.
48. Lyle, "Divine Fire," 80.
49. John Friedman, unpublished documentary script, "Code Breaking Couple," 2006, sent to author by John Friedman, the Friedmans' son.
50. "A little while with Elizabeth Friedman," 110.
51. *Ibid.*
52. June 8, 1918 letter from William to Elizabeth, Elizebeth S. Friedman Collection, Box 2, file 13, George C. Marshall Library, Virginia Military Institute.
53. Undated 1918 letter from William to Elizabeth, Elizebeth S. Friedman Collection, Box 2, file 13, George C. Marshall Library, Virginia Military Institute.
54. W.F. Friedman "Lecture V," 109.
55. Aug. 8, 1918 letter from Fabyan to William, Elizebeth S. Friedman Collection, Box 1, file 42, George C. Marshall Library, Virginia Military Institute.
56. Margaret Santry, "Dialogue of Radio Interview," NBC Radio, May 25, 1934, Elizebeth S. Friedman Collection, Box 11, file 15, George C. Marshall Library, Virginia Military Institute, 3.
57. Lyle, "Divine Fire," 100.
58. E. Friedman memoirs, 35–36.
59. *Ibid.*, 45.
60. Nov. 2, 1918 letter from Fabyan to Elizabeth, Elizebeth S. Friedman Collection, Box 1, file 42, George C. Marshall Library, Virginia Military Institute.
61. Nov. 7, 1918 letter from Fabyan to Elizabeth, Elizebeth S. Friedman Collection, Box 1, file 42, George C. Marshall Library, Virginia Military Institute.
62. Jan. 6, 1919 letter from Fabyan to Elizabeth, Elizebeth S. Friedman Collection, Box 1, file 42, George C. Marshall Library, Virginia Military Institute.
63. Jan. 9, 1919 letter from Elizabeth to Fabyan, Elizebeth S. Friedman Collection, Box 1, file 43, George C. Marshall Library, Virginia Military Institute.
64. Jan. 2, 1919 letter from William to Elizabeth, Elizebeth S. Friedman Collection, Box 2, file 20, George C. Marshall Library, Virginia Military Institute.
65. Telegrams from March 4 to 13, 1919 from William to Elizabeth, Elizebeth S.

Friedman Collection, Box 2, file 20, George
C. Marshall Library, Virginia Military Institute.
66. E. Friedman memoirs, 46–49.
67. *Ibid.*, 91.
68. *Ibid.*, 92.
69. Lyle, "Divine Fire," 111.
70. E. Friedman memoirs, 92.
71. John R. Friedman, "DIVINE FIRE, A
film story by John Friedman," unpublished
film script, 1994, 10.
72. Maj. J.O. Mauborgne letter to "My
dear Friedman," Nov. 27, 1920, William Friedman Collection, George C. Marshall Foundation, http://marshallfoundation.org/library/
friedman/documents/110_734_1_0113_
0116_OCR.pdf, accessed March 16, 2014.
73. Lyle, "Divine Fire," 117.
74. E. Friedman memoirs, 49.
75. *Ibid.*
76. David Kahn, *The Code Breakers, The
Story of Secret Writing,* Scribner, 1967, 376.
77. E. Friedman memoirs, 50.
78. Kahn, The Code Breakers, 376.
79. E. Friedman memoirs, 50.
80. "DIVINE FIRE, A film story by John
Friedman," 12.
81. Callimahos, "The Legendary William
F. Friedman," 189.
82. Smoot remarks.
83. E. Friedman memoirs, 99.

Chapter 3

1. William F. Friedman, "A Brief History
of U.S. Cryptologic Operations 1917–1929,"
From Special Research History-029, "A Brief
History of the Signal Intelligence Service,"
June 29, 1942, declassified July 16, 2008,
https://www.nsa.gov/news-features/
declassified-documents/cryptologic-
spectrum/assets/files/Brief_History_U.S._
Cryptologic_Operations.pdf, accessed June
18, 2016, 2.
2. *Ibid.*
3. Elizebeth Friedman personnel file,
Nov. 30, 1920, National Archives, St. Louis.
4. William F. Friedman, "A Brief History..."
5. Elizebeth Friedman memoirs; Elizebeth S. Friedman Collection, Box 12, file 2,
George C. Marshall Library, Virginia Military Institute, 47.
6. Letter from Elizebeth Friedman to
Durward Howes, Nov. 14, 1934, Elizebeth S.
Friedman Collection, Box 1, file 6, George C.
Marshall Library, Virginia Military Institute.
7. E Friedman memoirs, 38.
8. *Ibid.*, 41–45.
9. Elizebeth Friedman personnel file,

Naval Communication Service memo, Jan.
25, 1923, National Archives, St. Louis.
10. Elizebeth Friedman personnel file,
U.S. Civil Service Commission memo, Feb.
2, 1923, National Archives, St. Louis.
11. Elizebeth Friedman personnel file,
Elizebeth S. Friedman acceptance and oath,
Feb. 12, 1923, National Archives, St. Louis.
12. Elizebeth Friedman personnel file,
Naval Communication Service memo, March
22, 1923, National Archives, St. Louis.
13. Elizebeth Friedman personnel file,
Naval Communication Service memo, June
6, 1923, National Archives, St. Louis.
14. *Ibid.*
15. E. Friedman memoirs, 92.
16. *Ibid.*, 39.
17. *Ibid.*, 93.
18. *Ibid.*
19. Undated letter from Elizebeth to
William, Elizebeth S. Friedman Collection,
Box 12, file 2, George C. Marshall Library,
Virginia Military Institute.
20. E. Friedman memoirs, 41–45.
21. *Ibid.*
22. *Ibid.*
23. *Ibid.*, 99–100.
24. "Constitution of the United States,
Amendments 11–27," http://www.archives.
gov/exhibits/charters/constitution_
amendments_11–27.html.
25. Lt. Eric S. Ensign, USCG, *Intelligence
in the Rum War at Sea, 1920–1933,* Joint Military Intelligence College, Washington, D.C.,
2001, 3.
26. *Ibid.*, 1–2.
27. *Ibid.*, 3–7.
28. Elizebeth S. Friedman, "History of
Work in Cryptanalysis, April 1927–June
1930," Elizebeth S. Friedman Collection, Box
4, file 17, George C. Marshall Library, Virginia Military Institute, 6.
29. David P. Mowry, "Listening to the
Rum Runners," Center for Cryptologic History, 1996 but made available by the National
Security Agency in 2001, https://www.nsa.
gov/about/cryptologic-heritage/historical-
figures-publications/publications/pre-wwii/
assets/files/rumrunners.pdf, accessed June
17, 2016, 1.
30. E. Friedman memoirs, 45.
31. *Ibid.*
32. Ensign, *Intelligence in the Rum War,*
16–19.
33. "Radio New York: The First Civilian
Intercept Station?" undated, approved for
release by NSA, Dec. 1, 2011, https://www.nsa.
gov/news-features/declassified-documents/
crypto-almanac-50th/assets/files/radio-new-
york.pdf, accessed June 18, 2016.
34. Ensign, *Intelligence in the Rum War,* 17.

35. *Ibid.*, 24.

36. Elizebeth Friedman personnel file, letter from the Secretary of the Treasury, Dec. 8, 1925, National Archives, St. Louis.

37. Ensign, *Intelligence in the Rum War*, 24–26.

38. Memo from Charles S. Root to Major Hamlin, April 22, 1927; Elizebeth S. Friedman Collection, Box 4, file 16, George C. Marshall Library, Virginia Military Institute.

39. During this period Elizebeth received several transfers within various Treasury Department agencies, but worked at the direction of the Coast Guard. See a June 1930 typewritten note with handwritten comments by Elizebeth, Elizebeth S. Friedman Collection, Box 4, file 17, George C. Marshall Library, Virginia Military Institute, as well as Elizebeth Friedman personnel file, various appointment memos of the period, National Archives, St. Louis.

40. Elizebeth Friedman personnel file, U.S. Civil Service Commission appointment letter, May 5, 1927, National Archives, St. Louis.

41. E. Friedman memoirs, 45.

42. Author interview with Barbara Atchison, July 16, 2012.

43. E. Friedman memoirs, 45.

44. Mowry, "Listening to the Rum Runners," 14.

45. E. S. Friedman, "History of Work in Cryptanalysis," 1.

46. E. Friedman memoirs, 51.

47. *Ibid.*, 47–48.

48. Typed list of codes and meanings. Elizebeth S. Friedman Collection, Item 784, file 1, George C. Marshall Library, Virginia Military Institute.

49. Ensign, *Intelligence in the Rum War*, 26–28.

50. Miriam Ottenberg, *The Federal Investigators*, Prentice-Hall, 1962. Elizebeth S. Friedman Collection, Item 933, file 1, George C. Marshall Library, Virginia Military Institute.

51. Ensign, *Intelligence in the Rum War*, 26.

52. E. S. Friedman, "History of Work in Cryptanalysis," 2.

53. F.J. Gorman, MEMORANDUM FOR THE COMMANDANT, Oct. 10, 1930, reprinted in *Cryptolog*, Aug-Sep 1986, NSA, declassified Oct. 16, 2012, https://www.nsa.gov/news-features/declassified-documents/cryptologs/assets/files/cryptolog_103.pdf, accessed June 29, 2016.

54. Remarks by Rear Adm. Christopher J. Tomney, USCG Asst. Commander for Intelligence and Criminal Investigations, at Elizebeth Smith Friedman Auditorium Dedication Ceremony, ATF National Headquarters, Washington, D.C., June 17, 2014.

55. Mowry, "Listening to the Rum Runners," 18.

56. Mary McCracken Jones, "Girl Code Decipherer Learned About Ciphers From Shakespeare," *New York Sun*, Nov. 10, 1933, Elizebeth S. Friedman Collection, Box 16, file 30, George C. Marshall Library, Virginia Military Institute, 30.

57. Elizebeth S. Friedman, "Memorandum upon a Proposed Central Organization at Coast Guard Headquarters for Performing Cryptanalytic Work," November, 1930. Elizebeth S. Friedman Collection, Box 5, file 6, George C. Marshall Library, Virginia Military Institute, 4.

58. E. S. Friedman, "History of Work in Cryptanalysis," 3.

59. E. S. Friedman, "Memorandum upon a Proposed Central Organization..." 2.

60. Memo from E.S. Friedman to Lt. Cmdr. Gorman, Dec. 23, 1930, Elizebeth S. Friedman Collection, Box 17, file 26, George C. Marshall Library, Virginia Military Institute.

61. Mowry, "Listening to the Rum Runners," 19.

62. E. S. Friedman, "Memorandum upon a Proposed Central Organization..." 3.

63. *Ibid.*, 5–6.

64. *Ibid.*

65. *Ibid.*, 7.

66. Gorman, MEMORANDUM FOR THE COMMANDANT.

67. "Facts & Figures: Income and Prices 1900–1999," U.S. Diplomatic Mission to Germany, http://usa.usembassy.de/etexts/his/e_prices1.htm, accessed June 16, 2015.

68. Elizebeth Friedman personnel file, Appointment of Elizabeth Friedman as Cryptanalyst in Charge of the Coast Guard, transferred from Customs Agency Service, June 30, 1931, National Archives, St. Louis.

69. Gorman, MEMORANDUM FOR THE COMMANDANT.

70. Treasury Department Telephone Directory, Elizebeth S. Friedman Collection, Box 17, file 26, George C. Marshall Library, Virginia Military Institute.

71. E. Friedman memoirs, 51–52.

72. *Ibid.*

73. R. Louis Benson, Interview of Mrs E. S. Friedman, Jan. 9, 1976, approved for release by NSA July 30, 2015, https://www.nsa.gov/news-features/declassified-documents/oral-history-interviews/assets/files/nsa-OH-1976-22-efriedman.pdf, accessed June 17, 2016, 1–2.

74. Ensign, *Intelligence in the Rum War*, 39–40.

75. Lt. Cmdr. Michael Bennett, "Guardian

Spies: The Story of Coast Guard Intelligence in World War II (Part 2)," *American Intelligence Journal*, Spring 2010, Vol. 28, No. 1.

76. Memo from William L. Thibadeau, December 18, 1930, RG 26, Entry 297, Box 48, codes and cipher file, National Archives Building, Washington, D.C.

77. Memo from E.S. Friedman to Lt. Cmdr. Gorman, Dec. 30, 1930, RG 26, Entry 297, Box 48, codes and cipher file, National Archives Building, Washington, D.C.

78. E. S. Friedman, "History of Work in Cryptanalysis," 6–7.

79. Ensign, *Intelligence in the Rum War*, 40–48.

80. E. S. Friedman, "History of Work in Cryptanalysis," 6–7.

81. Leah Stock Helmick, "Key Woman of the T-Men," *Reader's Digest*, September 1937, 53.

82. Connie Lunnen, "She Has a Secret Side, Breaking Codes Was More Personal in Her Day, Elizebeth Friedman Says," *The Houston Chronicle*, May 24, 1972, Elizebeth S. Friedman Collection, Box 11, file 14, George C. Marshall Library, Virginia Military Institute.

83. Atchison interview.

84. Author interview with Barbara Osteika, Jan. 16, 2014.

85. E. Friedman memoirs, 48–49.

86. Herbert Hoover: "Annual Message to Congress on the State of the Union," Dec. 3, 1929. Online by Gerhard Peters and John T. Woolley, *The American Presidency Project*. http://www.presidency.ucsb.edu/ws/?pid= 22021, accessed June 19, 2014.

87. Patrick Weadon, "A New Kind of Detective Work," Center for Cryptologic History, 2001, https://www.nsa.gov/about/ cryptologic-heritage/historical-figures-publications/publications/pre-wwii/assets/ files/new_detective_work.pdf, accessed June 17, 2016.

Chapter 4

1. A.L. Gamble memo, March 28, 1929. RG 26, Entry 297, Box 73, file 1, National Archives Building, Washington, D.C.

2. Statement by Boatswain Frank Paul, March 27, 1929. RG 26, Entry 297, Box 73, file 1, National Archives Building, Washington, D.C.

3. Affidavit by Melvin L. Matson, March 27, 1929. RG 26, Entry 297, Box 73, file 1, National Archives Building, Washington, D.C.

4. Paul statement.

5. "The Sinking of The I'm Alone," Source: Robert Thorne, Downhomer, October 2001, http://www.newfoundlandshipwrecks.com/ Im%20Alone/documents/rumrunner_im_ alone.htm, accessed April 19, 2013.

6. Paul statement.

7. Coast Guard radio dispatch from *WOLCOTT* to Pascagoula, March 20, 1929. RG 26, Entry 297, Box 73, file 2, National Archives Building, Washington, D.C.

8. Paul statement.

9. In 1926, the Coast Guard built several of the 100-foot class cutters for law enforcement patrols. Lt. Eric S. Ensign, USCG, *Intelligence in the Rum War at Sea, 1920–1933*, Joint Military Intelligence College, Washington, DD, 2001, 11.

10. Statement by Boatswain A.W. Powell, March 27, 1929. RG 26, Entry 297, Box 73, file 1, National Archives Building, Washington, D.C.

11. Statement by Capt. John Thomas Randell, March 24, 1929, RG 26, Entry 297, Box 77, file 2, National Archives Building, Washington, D.C.

12. Powell statement.

13. Randell statement.

14. George Smith, "Canadian Leader Denounces U.S. for 'Act of War,'" Chicago Tribune Press Service, May 21, 1929. Clipping from an unknown newspaper in Coast Guard files. RG 26, Entry 297, Box 77, file 12, National Archives Building, Washington, D.C.

15. "The Holiday Season," *The Montreal Daily Star*, July 9, 1929, Clipping in Coast Guard files. RG 26, Entry 297, Box 77, file 12, National Archives Building, Washington, D.C.

16. "Seizure of Diplomatic Liquor Creates Incident," Time Magazine, April 1, 1929, http://www.druglibrary.org/schaffer/history/ e1920/siameseincident.htm, accessed April 19, 2013, 68–69.

17. Text of speech to Mary Bartelme Club, Nov. 30, 1951, Elizebeth S. Friedman Collection, Box 17, file 10, George C. Marshall Library, Virginia Military Institute.

18. Vincent Massey, "Note from the Canadian Minister to the Secretary of State, April 9, 1929," RG 26, Entry 297, Box 74, file 2, National Archives Building, Washington, D.C.

19. Letter from unnamed intelligence officer, April 18, 1929, RG 26, Entry 297, Box 73, file 2, National Archives Building, Washington, D.C.

20. "Memorandum for Mr. Hickerson," April 11, 1929, RG 26, Entry 297, Box 73, file 2, National Archives Building, Washington, D.C.

21. Massey, "Note from the Canadian Minister."

22. Associated Press. "'I'm Alone' Traced to Ownership Here," Dec. 29, 1934, *The New York Times*, 31.
23. Elizebeth Friedman memoirs; Elizebeth S. Friedman Collection, Box 12, file 1, George C. Marshall Library, Virginia Military Institute, 2–6.
24. "Decoded messages used in 'I'm Alone' smuggling operations," RG 26, Entry 297, Box 76, file 8, National Archives Building, Washington, D.C.
25. "Affidavit of Elizebeth Smith Friedman," Nov. 30, 1934, *Joint Interim Report of the Commissioners*, Elizebeth S. Friedman Collection, Box 77, file 5, George C. Marshall Library, Virginia Military Institute.
26. E. Friedman memoirs, 5.
27. "History of the Operations of the British Schooner I'M ALONE, from 20 April, 1924," RG 26, Entry 297, Box 73, file 1, National Archives Building, Washington, D.C.
28. Randell statement.
29. Letter from Chas. S. Root to W.R. Vallance, Oct. 5, 1929, RG 26, Entry 297, Box 73, file 1, National Archives Building, Washington, D.C.
30. Randell statement.
31. Letter from C.D. Feak, Assistant Intelligence Officer, April 10, 1929, RG 26, Entry 297, Box 73, file 1, National Archives Building, Washington, D.C.
32. Nancy Galey Skoglund, "The *I'm Alone* Case: A Tale of Days of Prohibition," University of Rochester Library Bulletin, Vol. XXII, Spring 1968, No. 3, http://www.lib.rochester.edu/index.cfm?PAGE=1004, accessed July 17, 2012.
33. Merriam-Webster defines hawser as "a large rope for towing, mooring, or securing a ship." http://www.merriam-webster.com/dictionary/hawser.
34. C.D. Feak, "Memorandum," March 12, 1928, RG 26, Entry 297, Box 73, file 2, National Archives Building, Washington, D.C.
35. "The Former Liquor Smugglers 'I'm Alone' and 'Grace and Ruby,'" April 2, 1928, RG 26, Entry 297, Box 73, file 1, National Archives Building, Washington, D.C.
36. Randell statement.
37. E. Friedman memoirs, 6–7.
38. *Ibid.*, 7–8.
39. *Ibid.*, 8–9.
40. Chas. S. Root, "Memorandum for the Commandant," Dec. 28, 1929, RG 26, Entry 297, Box 73, file 1, National Archives Building, Washington, D.C.
41. Letter from Customs agent Grady Avant, Sept. 10, 1931, RG 26, Entry 297, Box 73, file 2, National Archives Building, Washington, D.C.

42. C.S. Root, "Memorandum to Division of Foreign Control," Oct. 25, 1929, RG 26, Entry 297, Box 73, file 1, National Archives Building, Washington, D.C.
43. "Memorandum, Eugene Creaser Shipping Co. Ltd," March 29, 1930, RG 26, Entry 297, Box 73, file 2, National Archives Building, Washington, D.C.
44. Skoglund, "The *I'm Alone* Case."
45. Memo to Chief, Division of Foreign Control, Oct. 24, 1929, RG 26, Entry 297, Box 73, file 1, National Archives Building, Washington, D.C.
46. Skoglund, "The *I'm Alone* Case."
47. E. Friedman memoirs, 13–14.
48. "Decoded messages used in 'I'm Alone' smuggling operations."
49. E. Friedman memoirs, 14–17.
50. Root memorandum.
51. Author interview with Barbara Osteika, June 17, 2014.
52. "Affidavit of Elizebeth Smith Friedman."
53. E. Friedman memoirs, 20–21.
54. Associated Press, "'I'm Alone' Traced to Ownership Here."
55. E. Friedman memoirs, 20.
56. PEPPER, Claude Denson (1900–1989) "Biographical Directory of the United States Congress," http://bioguide.congress.gov/scripts/biodisplay.pl?index=p000218, accessed July 30, 2013.
57. "Hearing on Claim of the British Ship 'I'm Alone,'" Elizebeth S. Friedman Collection, Box 6, file 16, George C. Marshall Library, Virginia Military Institute, 90–92.
58. E. Friedman memoirs, 20.
59. Associated Press, "'I'm Alone' Traced to Ownership Here."
60. E. Friedman memoirs, 31–33.
61. *Ibid.*, 21.
62. "'I'm Alone' Case," Joint Final Report of the Commissioners, Jan. 5, 1935, RG 26, Entry 297, Box 75, file 2, National Archives Building, Washington, D.C., 3–4.
63. *Ibid.*
64. "I'm Alone Skipper Describes Cruises," *The New York Times*, Dec. 30, 1934, 17.
65. Joint Final Report of the Commissioners.
66. "I'm Alone Apology Given to Canada" *The New York Times*, Jan. 22, 1935, 8.
67. Elizebeth S. Friedman, "Memorandum upon a Proposed Central Organization at Coast Guard Headquarters for Performing Cryptanalytic Work," November, 1930. Elizebeth S. Friedman Collection, Box 5, file 6, George C. Marshall Library, Virginia Military Institute, 6.
68. Letter from William R. Vallance, Jan. 10, 1935. Elizebeth S. Friedman Collection,

Box 6, file 22, George C. Marshall Library, Virginia Military Institute.

69. Root memorandum.

Chapter 5

1. Elizebeth Friedman personnel file, F.J. Gorman memo, July 18, 1931, National Archives, St. Louis.

2. Letter to Miss Josephine Coates, Jan. 23, 1930, Elizebeth S. Friedman Collection, Box 1, file 2, George C. Marshall Library, Virginia Military Institute.

3. Elizebeth Friedman's personnel file (National Archives, St. Louis) has several memos from the Coast Guard commandant issuing travel orders to appear as a witness before grand juries or in trials or to help investigators in an ongoing case.

4. National Security Agency photo gallery, https://www.nsa.gov/resources/everyone/digital-media-center/image-galleries/people/historical-figures/, accessed June 18, 2016.

5. Author interview of ATF historian Barbara Osteika, June 17, 2014.

6. F. J. Gorman memo, "Work of the Cryptanalysis Section of Headquarters for other branches of the Government," July 8, 1933, RG 26, Entry 297, Box 48, National Archives Building, Washington, D.C.

7. Elizebeth Friedman memo on the history of Pacific Coast smuggling, unspecific date in 1930, Elizebeth S. Friedman Collection, Box 4, file 24, George C. Marshall Library, Virginia Military Institute.

8. David P. Mowry, "Listening to the Rum Runners," Center for Cryptologic History, 1996 but made available by the National Security Agency in 2001, https://www.nsa.gov/about/cryptologic-heritage/historical-figures-publications/publications/pre-wwii/assets/files/rumrunners.pdf, accessed June 18, 2016, 26.

9. Gorman July 8, 1933 memo.

10. A.W.W. Woodcock memo, case number 236-S, Jan. 20, 1932, RG 26, Entry 297, Box 48, National Archives Building, Washington, D.C.

11. Commandant F.C. Billard memo to Mrs. E. S. Friedman, Cryptanalyst in Charge, Jan. 26, 1932, RG 26, Entry 297, Box 48, National Archives Building, Washington, D.C.

12. Gorman July 8, 1933 memo.

13. Ibid.

14. Osteika interview.

15. Mowry, "Listening to the Rum Runners," 23.

16. Elizebeth Friedman memoirs; Elizebeth S. Friedman Collection, Box 12, file 1, George C. Marshall Library, Virginia Military Institute, 64–65.

17. Mowry, "Listening to the Rum Runners," 22.

18. E. Friedman memoirs, 64–69.

19. Elizebeth Friedman memo to chief intelligence officer, February 1934, Elizebeth S. Friedman Collection, Box 5, file 20, George C. Marshall Library, Virginia Military Institute.

20. E. Friedman memoirs, 68.

21. Letter from A.W.W. Woodcock to the Sec. of the Treasury, June 28, 1933, RG 26, Entry 297, Box 48, National Archives Building, Washington, D.C.

22. Elizebeth Friedman personnel file, F.J. Gorman memo to the chief clerk, May 11, 1933, National Archives, St. Louis.

23. Gorman July 8, 1933 memo.

24. E. Friedman memoirs, 20–24.

25. Ibid., 50.

26. F.M. Meals memo to Commandant, "Subject Seizure of British Steamer HOLME-WOOD, of Bridgetown, Barbados, at Haverstraw, New York, 3 October, 1933," Elizebeth S. Friedman Collection, Box 6, file 24, George C. Marshall Library, Virginia Military Institute.

27. There is also disagreement about the spelling of the ship's name. Some Coast Guard memos spell it HOLMEWOOD, others HOMEWOOD.

28. "NOTES ON THE SOLUTION OF CIPHER AND CODE USED BY THE HOLM-WOOD," Oct. 11, 1934, Elizebeth S. Friedman Collection, Box 6, file 24, George C. Marshall Library, Virginia Military Institute.

29. Ibid.

30. F.J. Gorman memo to Commandant, Oct. 11, 1933, Elizebeth S. Friedman Collection, Box 6, file 24, George C. Marshall Library, Virginia Military Institute.

31. "NOTES ON THE SOLUTION OF CIPHER AND CODE USED BY THE HOLM-WOOD."

32. Gorman Oct. 11, 1933 memo.

33. "Rum Ship Captain Quits at His Goal," Oct. 5, 1933, New York Times, 4, http://timesmachine.nytimes.com/timesmachine/1933/10/05/99934201.html?pageNumber=4.

34. Gorman Oct. 11, 1933 memo.

35. "NOTES ON THE SOLUTION OF CIPHER AND CODE USED BY THE HOLM-WOOD."

36. "MILLIONS ARE SAVED TO NATION BY DECODER OF SMUGGLERS' NOTES," article in unknown newspaper, May 28, 1934, Elizebeth S. Friedman Collection, Box 11, file 15, George C. Marshall Library, Virginia Military Institute.

37. Margaret Santry, "Dialogue of Radio

Interview," NBC Radio, May 25, 1934, Elizabeth S. Friedman Collection, Box 11, file 15, George C. Marshall Library, Virginia Military Institute, 4.

38. Lt. Eric S. Ensign, USCG, *Intelligence in the Rum War at Sea, 1920–1933*, Joint Military Intelligence College, Washington, D.C., 2001, 58.

39. *Ibid.*

40. H.G. Hamlet, "Effect of continued operation of the international smuggling syndicates on federal revenues," Treasury Dept., Aug. 17, 1933, RG 26, Entry 297, Box 77, National Archives Building, Washington, D.C.

41. Ensign, *Intelligence in the Rum War*, 58.

42. Mary McCracken Jones, "Girl Code Decipherer Learned About Ciphers from Shakespeare," *New York Sun*, Nov. 10, 1933, Elizebeth S. Friedman Collection, Box 16, file 30, George C. Marshall Library, Virginia Military Institute.

43. Santry, "Dialogue of Radio Interview," 4.

44. Mowry, "Listening to the Rum Runners," 29.

45. F.J. Gorman memo for A.E.S. Shamhart, June 9, 1933, RG 26, Entry 297, Box 48, National Archives Building, Washington, D.C.

46. E.S. Friedman memo to Commander Gorman, June 9, 1933, RG 26, Entry 297, Box 48, National Archives Building, Washington, D.C.

47. Elizebeth Friedman narrative on the Ezra Brothers, Elizebeth S. Friedman Collection, Box 6, file 25, George C. Marshall Library, Virginia Military Institute.

48. Elizebeth Friedman memo to Commander Gorman, Aug. 22, 1933, Elizebeth S. Friedman Collection, Box 6, file 25, George C. Marshall Library, Virginia Military Institute.

49. E.S. Friedman, "Memorandum for Commander Gorman," undated but refers to files sent in June 1933, RG 26, Entry 297, Box 48, National Archives Building, Washington, D.C.

50. Elizebeth Friedman narrative on Ezras.

51. Elizebeth Friedman memo, Aug. 22, 1933.

52. Leah Stock Helmick, "Key Woman of the T-Men," *Reader's Digest*, September 1937, 53.

53. Winifred Mallon, "Woman Wins Fame as Cryptanalyst," *The New York Times*, Feb. 12, 1937, Elizebeth S. Friedman Collection, Box 17, file 2, George C. Marshall Library, Virginia Military Institute.

54. Elizebeth Friedman narrative on Ezras.

55. "MEMORANDUM FOR MR.

OWENS," Sept. 26, 1933, Elizebeth S. Friedman Collection, Box 6, file 25, George C. Marshall Library, Virginia Military Institute.

56. Elizebeth Friedman narrative on Ezras.

57. Helmick, "Key Woman of the T-Men," 54.

58. Elizebeth Friedman personnel file, Oath of Office, July 15, 1930, National Archives, St. Louis.

59. Elizebeth Friedman memo on Lew Kim Yuen case, Feb. 16, 1937, Elizebeth S. Friedman Collection, Box 6, file 26, George C. Marshall Library, Virginia Military Institute.

60. Elizebeth Friedman narrative on Lew Kim Yuen case, Elizebeth S. Friedman Collection, Box 6, file 26, George C. Marshall Library, Virginia Military Institute.

61. Elizebeth Friedman memo on Lew Kim Yuen case.

62. *Ibid.*

63. Elizebeth Friedman letter to Dr. Arthur Hummel, Feb. 24, 1937, Elizebeth S. Friedman Collection, Box 6, file 26, George C. Marshall Library, Virginia Military Institute.

64. Harold N. Graves letter to Rear Adm. R.R. Waesche, Feb. 26, 1937, Elizebeth S. Friedman Collection, Box 6, file 26, George C. Marshall Library, Virginia Military Institute.

65. A measure of weight in eastern Asia, *Merriam-Webster Dictionary*, http://www.merriam-webster.com/dictionary/tael.

66. Elizebeth Friedman narrative on Ezras.

67. Elizebeth Friedman personnel file, "Important case, Month of January, 1939," news release from Bureau of Narcotics, January 1939, National Archives, St. Louis.

68. Elizebeth Friedman personnel file, memo from Commandant R.R. Waesche, Oct. 15, 1938, National Archives, St. Louis.

69. Mallon, "Woman Wins Fame as Cryptanalyst."

70. E. Friedman memoirs, 83–86.

71. Mallon, "Woman Wins Fame as Cryptanalyst."

Chapter 6

1. "The Single Intelligence School," The Friedman papers, Box 13, file 9, George C. Marshall Library, Virginia Military Institute, 1–2.

2. Message No. 5, The Friedman papers, Box 13, file 9, George C. Marshall Library, Virginia Military Institute.

3. Katie Letcher Lyle, "Divine Fire, Elizebeth Smith Friedman, Cryptanalyst," unpublished manuscript, Center for Cryptologic History, National Security Agency, 1991, 122.

4. United States Civil Service Classification Sheet, July 16, 1931, RG 38, Entry 1030, Box 175, Folder 12000/2 National Archives Building, Washington, D.C.
5. Personnel recommendation, Elizebeth Friedman personnel file, Jan. 29, 1940, National Archives, St. Louis.
6. Letter from William Friedman to Elizebeth, June 4, 1940. The Friedman papers, Box 3, file 7, George C. Marshall Library, Virginia Military Institute.
7. Author interview with Barbara Atchison, July 16–17, 2012.
8. "Elizebeth Friedman Autobiography at Riverbank Laboratories, Geneva, Illinois," listed as "ESF Oral History Pt. 2" at Center for Cryptologic History, National Security Agency, 68.
9. *Ibid.*
10. Elizebeth Friedman memoirs; Elizebeth S. Friedman Collection, Box 12, file 1–2, George C. Marshall Library, Virginia Military Institute, 57.
11. Elizebeth Friedman Autobiography, 63.
12. Passenger list of the *SS Leviathan*, Elizebeth S. Friedman Collection, Box 16, file 1, George C. Marshall Library, Virginia Military Institute.
13. E. Friedman memoirs, 59.
14. Postcard to John Ramsey Friedman, Oct. 3, 1932, Elizebeth S. Friedman Collection, Box 1, file 4, George C. Marshall Library, Virginia Military Institute.
15. Letter to Mrs. E.S. Dinieus, Nov. 26, 1932, Elizebeth S. Friedman Collection, Box 1, file 4, George C. Marshall Library, Virginia Military Institute.
16. E. Friedman memoirs, 60.
17. *Ibid.*, 64.
18. Letter from F.E. Pollio, Sept. 14, 1937, Elizebeth S. Friedman Collection, Box 6, file 28, George C. Marshall Library, Virginia Military Institute.
19. L.C. Covell, travel orders for Elizebeth Friedman, Oct. 16, 1937, Elizebeth Friedman personnel file, National Archives, St. Louis.
20. R.R. Waesche, travel orders for Elizebeth Friedman, Oct. 16, 1937, Elizebeth Friedman personnel file, National Archives, St. Louis.
21. Postcard to John Ramsey Friedman, Oct. 17, 1937, Elizebeth S. Friedman Collection, Box 6, file 28, George C. Marshall Library, Virginia Military Institute.
22. Oral history of Elizebeth Smith Friedman, Nov. 11, 1976, NSA-OH-1976–17, DOCID: 4229028, approved for release July 30, 2015, https://www.nsa.gov/news-features/declassified-documents/oral-history-interviews/assets/files/nsa-OH-1976–17-efriedman.pdf, accessed June 17, 2016, 11.

23. The Associated Press, "Airliner Crashes on Utah Mountain; 19 Believed Dead," Oct. 19, 1937, *The New York Times*, http://timesmachine.nytimes.com/timesmachine/1937/10/19/96753580.html?pageNumber=1, 1.
24. John Friedman, unpublished documentary script, "Code Breaking Couple," 2006, sent to author by John Friedman, the Friedmans' son.
25. Elizebeth Friedman narrative of the Gordon Lim case, Elizebeth S. Friedman Collection, Box 6, file 29, George C. Marshall Library, Virginia Military Institute, 18.
26. Letter from William Friedman to Elizebeth, Oct. 18, 1937, Elizebeth S. Friedman Collection, Box 3, file 6, George C. Marshall Library, Virginia Military Institute.
27. John Friedman, "Code Breaking Couple."
28. Oral history, NSA-OH-1976–17, 11.
29. Postal telegraph from Elizebeth to William, Oct. 18, 1937, Elizebeth S. Friedman Collection, Box 6, file 28, George C. Marshall Library, Virginia Military Institute.
30. Gordon Lim case narrative, 1–18.
31. Oral history, NSA-OH-1976–17, 12.
32. Elizebeth Friedman memo to chief intelligence officer, Oct. 30, 1937, Elizebeth S. Friedman Collection, Box 6, file 2, George C. Marshall Library, Virginia Military Institute.
33. Gordon Lim case narrative, 18–20.
34. Memo by R.L. Cadiz, Oct. 27, 1937, Elizebeth Friedman personnel file, National Archives, St. Louis.
35. Letter from C.H.L. Sharman to Commissioner of Narcotics in Washington, Nov. 4, 1937, Elizebeth S. Friedman Collection, Box 6, file 27, George C. Marshall Library, Virginia Military Institute.
36. Letter from Charles G. Power to Rear Adm. Russell R. Waesche, Nov. 6, 1937, Elizebeth S. Friedman Collection, Box 6, file 27, George C. Marshall Library, Virginia Military Institute.
37. Memo from Adm. Waesche to Elizebeth Friedman, Nov. 11, 1937, Elizebeth S. Friedman Collection, Box 6, file 27, George C. Marshall Library, Virginia Military Institute.
38. Commandant Waesche memo to the GAO, July 5, 1938, Elizebeth Friedman personnel file, National Archives, St. Louis.
39. Letter from Elizebeth Friedman to G. W. Fish, Nov. 7, 1937, Elizebeth S. Friedman Collection, Box 6, file 27, George C. Marshall Library, Virginia Military Institute.
40. Memo from Thomas Gorman to the Coast Guard commandant, Jan. 11, 1938. Elizebeth Friedman personnel file, National Archives, St. Louis.

41. Temporary duty, travel orders for Elizebeth Friedman, Jan. 11, 1938, Elizebeth Friedman personnel file, National Archives, St. Louis.

42. Gordon Lim case narrative, 16–24.

43. "Woman Solves Chinese Code to Nip Opium Ring," *Washington Post*, Feb. 9, 1938, Elizebeth Friedman personnel file, National Archives, St. Louis.

44. Letter from Elizebeth Friedman to G.W. Fish, Feb. 12, 1938, Elizebeth S. Friedman Collection, Box 6, file 32, George C. Marshall Library, Virginia Military Institute.

45. Memo from Elizebeth Friedman to Coast Guard commandant, Feb. 14, 1938, Elizebeth S. Friedman Collection, Box 1, file 9, George C. Marshall Library, Virginia Military Institute.

46. Letter G.W. Fish to Elizebeth Friedman, Feb. 22, 1938, Elizebeth S. Friedman Collection, Box 6, file 32, George C. Marshall Library, Virginia Military Institute.

47. Memo from Elizebeth Friedman to the chief intelligence officer, March 28, 1938, Elizebeth S. Friedman Collection, Box 6, file 32, George C. Marshall Library, Virginia Military Institute.

48. Gordon Lim case narrative, 25–27.

49. These requests can be found in various boxes and files in the Elizebeth S. Friedman Collection at the George C. Marshall Library, Virginia Military Institute.

50. Letter from Elizebeth Friedman to Mary Field Parton, April 7, 1938, Elizebeth S. Friedman Collection, Box 6, file 28, George C. Marshall Library, Virginia Military Institute.

51. E. Friedman memoirs, 83.

52. "Code Expert to Get Doctorate," *The New York Times*, June 11, 1938, 16.

53. Western Union Telegram from William Friedman to Elizebeth, June 12, 1938, Elizebeth S. Friedman Collection, Box 3, file 6, George C. Marshall Library, Virginia Military Institute.

54. Letter from William to Elizebeth Friedman, June 16, 1938, Elizebeth S. Friedman Collection, Box 3, file 7, George C. Marshall Library, Virginia Military Institute.

55. E. Friedman memoirs, 81.

56. Federal government form for education and experience, no date, Elizebeth Friedman personnel file, National Archives, St. Louis.

57. E. Friedman memoirs, 100.

58. Letter from Adm. R.R. Waesche to Elizebeth Friedman, Oct. 15, 1938, Elizebeth Friedman personnel file, National Archives, St. Louis.

59. Letter from William Friedman to Elizebeth, Jan. 18, 1938, Elizebeth S. Friedman Collection, Box 3, file 7, George C. Marshall Library, Virginia Military Institute.

60. E. Friedman memoirs, 100.

Chapter 7

1. Elizebeth Friedman memoirs; Elizebeth S. Friedman Collection, Box 12, file 1, George C. Marshall Library, Virginia Military Institute, 89.

2. Stanley E. Hilton, *Hitler's Secret War in South America 1939–1945*, Louisiana State University Press, Baton Rouge, 1981, 192–193.

3. Henry Morgenthau, Jr. letter to FDR, Nov. 14, 1941, Henry Morgenthau Diaries, Roll 127, Diary 462, Franklin D. Roosevelt Library, 109–100, http://www.fdrlibrary.marist.edu/_resources/images/morg/md0625.pdf, accessed May 10, 2016.

4. Lt. Cmdr. Michael E Bennett, USCG, "Guardian Spies: The Story of Coast Guard Intelligence in World War II" *American Intelligence Journal*, Volume 27, Number 1, Fall 2009, 21.

5. David P. Mowry, "Listening to the Rum Runners," Center for Cryptologic History, 1996 but made available by the National Security Agency in 2001, https://www.nsa.gov/about/cryptologic-heritage/historical-figures-publications/publications/pre-wwii/assets/files/rumrunners.pdf, accessed June 18, 2016.

6. E. Friedman memoirs.

7. Summary of interview of Mrs. E. S. Friedman by R. Louis Benson, Jan. 9, 1976, NSA-OH-1976–22, DOC ID 4237384, approved for release by NSA July 30, 2015, https://www.nsa.gov/news-features/declassified-documents/oral-history-interviews/assets/files/nsa-OH-1976–22-efriedman.pdf, accessed June 17, 2016, 2.

8. Author redacted, "The Origination and Evolution of Radio Traffic Analysis, The Period Between the Wars," *Cryptologic Quarterly*, Spring 1987, declassified by NSA June 16, 2008, https://www.nsa.gov/news-features/declassified-documents/cryptologic-quarterly/assets/files/the_period_between_wars.pdf, accessed June 18, 2016.

9. "Oral History of Frank Rowlett," NSA-OH-1976(1–10), DOCID: 4223202, date unspecified, declassified July 14, 2015, https://www.nsa.gov/news-features/declassified-documents/oral-history-interviews/assets/files/nsa-OH-1976–1–10-rowlett.pdf, accessed June 17, 2016, 69.

10. Colin B. Burke, "It Wasn't All Magic: The early Struggle to Automate Cryptanalysis, 1930s-1960s," Center for Cryptologic

History, National Security Agency, December 1994, declassified May 29, 2013, https:// www.nsa.gov/news-features/declassified-documents/cryptologic-histories/assets/files/magic.pdf, accessed June 18, 2016.

11. H.F. Kingman, "MEMORANDUM FROM OFFICE OF NAVAL OPERATIONS RE UNDESIRABLE PUBLICITY IN CONNECTION WITH CRYPTANALYTICAL ACTIVITIES BY GOVERNMENT AGENCIES," June 2, 1934, William F. Friedman Collection: Correspondence, Memoranda, and Personnel File Records—NSA/CSS, DocRefID A72637, approved for release by NSA Sept. 18, 2013, https://www.nsa.gov/news-features/declassified-documents/friedman-documents/assets/files/reports-research/FOLDER_044/41719919075920.pdf, accessed June 18, 2016

12. "Cryptologic Almanac 50th Anniversary Series, Joseph N. Wenger," DOCID: 3575736, approved for release June 12, 2009, https://www.nsa.gov/news-features/declassified-documents/crypto-almanac-50th/assets/files/Joseph_N._Wenger.pdf, accessed June 20, 2016.

13. J.N. Wenger, memo Aug. 16, 1937, William F. Friedman Collection: Correspondence, Memoranda, and Personnel File Records—NSA/CSS, DocRefID A72632, declassified Sept. 18, 2013, https://www.nsa.gov/news-features/declassified-documents/friedman-documents/assets/files/reports-research/FOLDER_044/41719869075915.pdf, accessed June 18, 2016.

14. William Friedman, memo about Coast Guard M-138 strip cipher, March 13, 1936, William F. Friedman Collection: Correspondence, Memoranda, and Personnel File Records—NSA/CSS, DocRefID A67563, declassified Sept. 9, 2013, https://www.nsa.gov/news-features/declassified-documents/friedman-documents/assets/files/patent-equipment/FOLDER_084/41702549074187.pdf, accessed June 20, 2016.

15. J.N. Wenger Aug. 16, 1937 memo.

16. Memo for the commandant from Elizebeth Friedman, Aug. 31, 1937, Elizebeth S. Friedman Collection, Box 6, file 26, George C. Marshall Library, Virginia Military Institute.

17. Elizebeth said there was "no truth" at all about William and her sharing information. Interview with Mrs. William F. Friedman by Dr. Forrest C. Pogue, May 16, 1973, Elizebeth S. Friedman Collection, Box 16, file 17, George C. Marshall Library, Virginia Military Institute, 23.

18. Leah Stock Helmick, "Key Woman of the T-Men," *Reader's Digest,* September 1937, 55.

19. Ronald Clark, *The Man Who Broke Purple,* Little, Brown and Company, Boston, Toronto, 1977, 179–180.

20. John R. Friedman, "DIVINE FIRE, A film story by John Friedman," unpublished film script, 1994, 18.

21. Author interview with Barbara Atchison, July 16–17, 2012.

22. Elizebeth Friedman memo to Mr. Schwartz, Oct. 20, 1938, Elizebeth S. Friedman Collection, Box 1, file 9, George C. Marshall Library, Virginia Military Institute.

23. W.K. Clark, "The Woman All Spies in U.S. Fear," article in unspecified newspaper, date unknown, though it appears to be the same article Elizebeth was referring to in her letter to Mr. Schwartz on Oct. 6, 1939. The article may have been a wire service feature used in several papers.

24. Letter from Elizebeth Friedman to Mr. Schwartz, Oct. 6, 1939, RG 56, Box 173, Entry 193, National Archives at College Park, MD.

25. Forward to *History of Coast Guard Unit 387,* 1946, declassified 2008, RG 38, Naval Security Group Crane, Box 57, National Archives at College Park, MD.

26. Elizebeth Friedman, "Footnote to History," 1946, Elizebeth S. Friedman Collection, Box 17, file 16, George C. Marshall Library, Virginia Military Institute.

27. Friedman to Schwartz letter, Oct. 6, 1939.

28. "Report for: U.S. Army-Naval Communication Intelligence Coordinating Committee. Special Report No. 1," June 9, 1944, approved for release by NSA Dec. 12, 2007, https://www.nsa.gov/news-features/declassified-documents/nsa-60th-timeline/assets/files/pre-nsa/19440609_PreNSA_Doc_3263556_USArmyNaval.pdf, accessed June 20, 2016.

29. Letter from Charles Schwartz to Elizebeth Friedman, Oct. 9, 1939, RG 56, Box 173, Entry 193, National Archives at College Park, MD.

30. Letter from William Friedman to Elizebeth, Jan. 18, 1938, Elizebeth S. Friedman Collection, Box 3, file 7, George C. Marshall Library, Virginia Military Institute.

31. U.S. Civil Service Commission Elizebeth Friedman personnel information sheet, June 15, 1940, Elizebeth Friedman personnel file, National Archives, St. Louis.

32. Atchison interview.

33. Elizebeth Friedman personnel information sheet.

34. Elizebeth Friedman letter to L.G. Fry, Dec. 7, 1937, Elizebeth S. Friedman Collection, Box 17, file 1, George C. Marshall Library, Virginia Military Institute.

35. Atchison interview.
36. Letter from William Friedman to Elizebeth, June 4, 1940, Elizebeth S. Friedman Collection, Box 3, file 7, George C. Marshall Library, Virginia Military Institute.
37. Letter from Elizebeth to William Friedman, June 10, 1940, Elizebeth S. Friedman Collection, Box 2, file 5, George C. Marshall Library, Virginia Military Institute.
38. *Ibid.*
39. Letter from William to Elizebeth Friedman, June 10, 1940, Elizebeth S. Friedman Collection, Box 3, file 7, George C. Marshall Library, Virginia Military Institute.
40. William F. Friedman, "A Brief History of U.S. Cryptologic Operations 1917–1929," June 29, 1942, declassified by the NSA July 16, 2008, https://www.nsa.gov/news-features/declassified-documents/cryptologic-spectrum/assets/files/Brief_History_U.S._Cryptologic_Operations.pdf, accessed June 18, 2016, 5.
41. Col. Rose Mary Sheldon remarks, "A Portrait of William F. Friedman," video, 2014, The George C. Marshall Foundation, http://marshallfoundation.org/library/digital-archive/shakespearean-ciphers-examined/, accessed July 7, 2014.
42. Summary of interview of Mrs. E. S. Friedman, 4–5.
43. "DIVINE FIRE, A film story by John Friedman.
44. Oral history of Elizebeth Smith Friedman, Nov. 11, 1976, NSA-OH-1976–17, DOCID: 4229028, approved for release July 30, 2015, https://www.nsa.gov/news-features/declassified-documents/oral-history-interviews/assets/files/nsa-OH-1976–17-efriedman.pdf, accessed June 18, 2016, 16.
45. E. Friedman memoirs, 95.
46. James R. Chiles "Breaking Codes was this Couple's Lifetime Career," *Smithsonian*, June 1987, Elizebeth S. Friedman Collection, Box 17, file 8, George C. Marshall Library, Virginia Military Institute, 141.
47. Atchison interview.
48. Clark, *The Man Who Broke Purple*, 158–159.
49. Col. Rose Mary Sheldon, "William F. Friedman: A Very Private Cryptographer and His Collection," Cryptologic Quarterly, 2015–01, Vol. 34, 15.
50. Memo to Mr. Wood, Nov. 15, 1933, RG 56 Box 173, Entry 193, National Archives at College Park, MD.
51. Malcolm F. Willoughby, *The U.S. Coast Guard in World War II*, United States Naval Institute, Annapolis Maryland, 1957, 136–137.
52. Memo from Navy Commander J.N. Wenger, June 30, 1937, RG 457, Box 1386,

A1 9032 folder 4419, National Archives at College Park, MD.
53. "A New View to Pearl Harbor: United States Navy Communications Intelligence 1924–1941," United States Cryptologic History, Series IV, World War II, Volume 2, No date. Declassified April 24, 1995.
54. Willoughby, *The U.S. Coast Guard in WWII*, 8.
55. Minutes of staff meeting of Secretary Morgenthau, Nov. 5, 1941, Henry Morgenthau Diaries, Roll 127, Diary 456, Franklin D. Roosevelt Library, 261–264.
56. J.F. Farley letter to Commander John R. Redman, March 6, 1942, *History of Coast Guard Unit 387*, RG 38 Naval Security Group Crane, Box 57, National Archives at College Park, MD.
57. Elizebeth Friedman handwritten memo to Commander Anthony, unspecific date in 1945, Elizebeth S. Friedman Collection, Box 17, file 26, George C. Marshall Library, Virginia Military Institute.
58. "DIVINE FIRE, A film story by John Friedman," 19.
59. Personnel classification sheet for Elizebeth Friedman, date uncertain, but appears to be 1938 or 1939. RG 38, Entry 1030 A1, Box 81, Folder 12000/3, National Archives at College Park, MD.
60. Lt. F.E. Pollio memo to chief personnel officer of the Coast Guard, March 26, 1937, Elizebeth S. Friedman Collection, Box 6, file 1, George C. Marshall Library, Virginia Military Institute.
61. Robert Louis Benson, "A History of U.S. Communications Intelligence during World War II: Policy and Administration" United States Cryptologic History, Series IV, World War II, Volume 8, https://www.nsa.gov/about/cryptologic-heritage/historical-figures-publications/publications/wwii/assets/files/history_us_comms.pdf, accessed June 18, 2016, 9.
62. Summary of interview of Mrs. E. S. Friedman, 2.
63. Notes of a telephone conversation between Secretary Morgenthau and William Donovan, June 20, 1941, Henry Morgenthau Diaries, Roll 114, 411, Franklin D. Roosevelt Library, 67–69.
64. Treasury Department memo, July 21, 1941, RG 26, Entry 335 (A-1), Box 2, Donovan Folder, National Archives, Washington, D.C.
65. "War Report of the OSS," Sept. 5, 1947, republished 1976, by Walker and Company, New York, 90.
66. Memos from Donovan to Wallace B. Phillips, Nov. 17, 1941, RG 226, OSS Donovan office microfilm files, 0465, File 5–

13–3, National Archives at College Park, MD.

67. Mowry, "Listening to the Rum Runners."

68. William F. Friedman, "Lecture VI," reprinted in "The Friedman Legacy: A Tribute to William and Elizebeth Friedman," Center for Cryptologic History, National Security Agency, 1992. https://www.nsa.gov/resources/ everyone/digital-media-center/video-audio/ historical-audio/friedman-legacy/assets/files/ friedman-legacy-transcript.pdf, accessed June 17, 2016, 148–149.

69. Summary of interview of Mrs. E. S. Friedman, 2.

70. Colin Burke, "What OSS Black Chamber? What Yardley? What "Dr." Friedman? Ah, Grombach?" http://userpages.umbc. edu/~burke/whatossblack.pdf, accessed Jan. 22, 2013.

71. William Friedman writing a review of the Pearl Harbor Attack believed there was information available to avoid the attack, but "nobody in either the Army or the Navy" was responsible for looking at the "whole story," only individual pieces of the puzzle. William Friedman, "Certain Aspects of Magic in the Cryptological Background of the Various Official Investigations Into the Attack on Pearl Harbor," 1957, NSA, Center for Cryptologic History, SRH-125, www.ibiblio.org/ hyperwar/PTO/Magic/SRH-125/index.html, accessed Jan. 26, 2014, also available RG 457, National Archives at College Park, MD.

72. Atchison interview.

73. E. Friedman memoirs, 95–96.

74. William Donovan memo to Office of the Signal Corps, Dec. 8, 1941 RG 226, OSS Donovan office microfilm files, 0389, File 4–7–1, National Archives at College Park, MD.

75. W.A. Kimbel memo to Coordinator of Information, Dec. 8, 1941, RG 226, OSS Donovan office microfilm files, 0389, File 5–10, National Archives at College Park, MD.

76. Lt. Jones trained under William Friedman. During the war while under Navy authority, took over command of Coast Guard Unit 387 from Elizebeth Friedman. David Mowry, "German Clandestine Activities in South America in World War II," National Security Agency, 1989, declassified April 13, 2009, https://www.nsa.gov/news-features/ declassified-documents/cryptologic-histories/ assets/files/german_clandestine_activities. pdf, accessed June 18, 2016.

77. W.A. Kimbel memo to Coordinator of Information, Dec. 13, 1941, RG 226, OSS Donovan office microfilm files, 0593, File 4–1, National Archives at College Park, MD.

78. Letter from William Donovan to Secretary Morgenthau, Dec. 14, 1941, Henry Morgenthau Diaries, Roll 127, Diary 456, Franklin D. Roosevelt Library, 36–38.

79. Minutes of staff meeting of Secretary Morgenthau, Dec.15, 1941, Henry Morgenthau Diaries, Roll 127, Diary 456, Franklin D. Roosevelt Library, 36–38.

80. Letter from Assistant Sec. of the Navy to Chief of Civilian Personnel, Coast Guard, Dec. 19, 1941, Elizebeth Friedman personnel file, National Archives, St. Louis.

81. Colin Burke, "What OSS Black Chamber? What Yardley? What "Dr." Friedman? Ah, Grombach?"

82. Clark, *The Man Who Broke Purple*, 178–180.

83. Memo from Capt. M.B. Coburn to Col. Donovan, Dec. 24, 1941, RG 226, OSS Donovan office microfilm files, 0491, File 5–8, National Archives at College Park, MD.

84. Elizebeth Friedman letter to Colonel Donovan, Dec. 29, 1941, Elizebeth S. Friedman Collection, Box 17, file 15, George C. Marshall Library, Virginia Military Institute.

85. William Donovan letter to Office of the Signal Corps, Dec. 30, 1941, RG 226, OSS Donovan office microfilm files, 0502, File 4–7–2, National Archives at College Park, MD.

86. William Donovan memo to J.R. Hayden, Jan. 3, 1942, RG 226, OSS Donovan office microfilm files, microfilm 7–6–1, file 4–4., National Archives at College Park, MD.

87. William Donovan letter to the Secretary of War, Feb. 3, 1942, RG 226, OSS Donovan office microfilm files, 0187, File 4–13–1, National Archives at College Park, MD.

88. "War Report of the OSS," 90.

89. Lt. Eric S. Ensign, USCG, *Intelligence in the Rum War at Sea, 1920–1933*, Joint Military Intelligence College, Washington, D.C., 2001, 53.

90. Affidavit signed by Elizebeth Friedman, June 23, 1941, Elizebeth Friedman personnel file, National Archives, St. Louis.

91. Lt. Jones later was put in command of OP-20-GU, but OSS documents in the National Archives show he was still assigned to and working at the OSS through early April 1942. See Donovan letter, Feb. 3, 1942, op. cit. and Lt. Jones' memos on "Security of Dispatch" at OSS from March 9th through April 4, 1942, RG 226, Entry 92, Box 98, Folder 22, National Archives at College Park, MD.

Chapter 8

1. Stanley E. Hilton, *Hitler's Secret War in South America 1939–1945*, Louisiana State University Press, Baton Rouge, 1981, 220–221.

2. " Interviewee: Radioman First Class Glen Boles, USCGR, World War II Coast Guard Veteran," Nov. 27, 2005, U.S. Coast Guard Oral History Program, https://www.uscg.mil/history/weboralhistory/glenboles_oralhistory.asp, accessed July 27, 2016.

3. *Hitler's Secret War in South America 1939–1945*, 220–221.

4. R.E. Gordon, "MEMORANDUM FOR DR. KULLBACK," July 15, 1941, declassified Dec. 19, 2013, https://www.nsa.gov/news-features/declassified-documents/friedman-documents/assets/files/reports-research/FOLDER_060/41707809074712.pdf, accessed June 29, 2016.

5. *History of Coast Guard Unit 387*, Sept. 17, 1946, declassified, Dec. 17, 2008, RG 38, Naval Security Group Crane, Box 57, National Archives at College Park, MD.

6. *Hitler's Secret War in South America 1939–1945*, 48.

7. *Ibid.*, 69.

8. *Ibid.*, 45–47.

9. *Ibid.*, 25–26.

10. "German Espionage and Sabotage Against the United States in World War II," *O.N.I. Review* [Office of Naval Intelligence] 1, no.3 (January 1946), [declassified, formerly "confidential"], http://www.history.navy.mil/research/library/online-reading-room/title-list-alphabetically/g/german-espionage-and-sabotage.html, accessed June 20, 2016.

11. Samuel Eliot Morison, *History of United States Naval Operations in World War II, Vol. 1, The Battle of the Atlantic, September 1939-May 1943*," Little, Brown and Company, Boston, 1947, 410.

12. Michael Gannon, *Operation Drumbeat, The Dramatic True Story of Germany's First U-Boat Attacks Along the American Coast in World War II*, Harper & Row, New York, 1990, 390.

13. *History of United States Naval Operations in World War II, Vol. 1*," 308–310.

14. For an analysis of the Enigma, see Jennifer Wilcox, "Solving the Enigma: History of the Cryptanalytic Bombe," Center for Cryptologic History, National Security Agency, 2006, https://www.nsa.gov/about/cryptologic-heritage/historical-figures-publications/publications/wwii/assets/files/solving_enigma.pdf, accessed June 18, 2016.

15. Colin B. Burke, "It Wasn't All Magic: The early Struggle to Automate Cryptanalysis, 1930s-1960s," Center for Cryptologic History, NSA, December 1994, declassified May 29, 2013, https://www.nsa.gov/news-features/declassified-documents/cryptologic-histories/assets/files/magic.pdf, accessed June 18, 2016, 98.

16. Wilcox, "Solving the Enigma: History of the Cryptanalytic Bombe," 17.

17. Elizebeth Friedman memoirs; Elizebeth S. Friedman Collection, Box 12, file 1, George C. Marshall Library, Virginia Military Institute, 96.

18. *Ibid.*, 97.

19. *History of Coast Guard Unit 387*, 124.

20. Steven Budiansky, *Battle of Wits, The Complete Story of Codebreaking in World War II*, The Free Press, New York, 2000, 228.

21. Interview of Frank Raven," Jan. 24, 1980, NSA-OH-03–72, DOCID: 4222266, approved for release July 13, 2015, https://www.nsa.gov/news-features/declassified-documents/oral-history-interviews/assets/files/nsa-OH-1980–03-raven.pdf, accessed June 17, 2016, 19.

22. Tiltman was one of the organizers of the British CG&CS. See John F. Clabby, "Brigadier John Tiltman, A Giant Among Cryptanalysts," Center for Cryptologic History, NSA, 2007, https://www.nsa.gov/about/cryptologic-heritage/historical-figures-publications/publications/misc/assets/files/tiltman.pdf, accessed June 20, 2016, 12.

23. "Report by Lieut. Colonel J.H. Tiltman on his visit to North America during March and April 1942," HW 14/46, The National Archives of the UK (TNA), 2.

24. Abstract of Duty Assignments for Capt. Leonard T. Jones, USCG, Nov. 28, 1962. Courtesy: Cmdr. Michael E. Bennett, USCG.

25. Elizebeth Friedman letter to Colonel Donovan, Dec. 29, 1941, Elizebeth S. Friedman Collection, Box 17, file 15, George C. Marshall Library, Virginia Military Institute.

26. Capt. Raymond J. Brown, USCG, "Coast Guard Codebreakers: Inspire Those Who Serve," *Proceedings Magazine*, Naval Institute Press, December 1998, Vol. 124/12/1, 150, http://www.usni.org/magazines/proceedings/1998–12/coast-guard-codebreakers-inspire-those-who-serve, accessed Jan. 9, 2013.

27. There are several memos from Leonard Jones while working at COI from March 9-April 4, 1942, RG 226, Entry 92, Box 98, Folder 22, National Archives at College Park, MD.

28. The author sought the personnel records for Jones from the National Archives at St. Louis, but was unable to get them since they are not yet available to the public.

29. "Report of meeting of Standing Committee for Coordination of Cryptanalytical Work," Office of the Chief of Naval Operations, Aug. 25, 1942, declassified July 3, 2012, https://www.nsa.gov/news-features/declassified-documents/nsa-60th-timeline/assets/files/pre-nsa/19420909_PreNSA_

Doc_3984124_Meeting.pdf, accessed June 20, 2016.

30. Commander Jones received a Legion of Merit for his work in World War II. An online reference for that award records his service date with the Division of Naval Communications starting May 15, 1942. Military Times Hall of Valor, http://valor.militarytimes.com/recipient.php?recipientid=312360, accessed July 21, 2016.

31. Michael Bennett, Lt. Cmdr. USCG, "GUARDIAN SPIES: The Story of Coast Guard Intelligence in World War II (Part two)," *American Intelligence Journal*, Spring 2010, Volume 28, No. 1.

32. Summary of interview of Mrs. E. S. Friedman by R. Louis Benson, Jan. 9, 1976, NSA-OH-1976–22, DOC ID 4237384, approved for release by NSA July 30, 2015, https://www.nsa.gov/news-features/declassified-documents/oral-history-interviews/assets/files/nsa-OH-1976–22-efriedman.pdf, accessed June 17, 2016, 3.

33. *History of Coast Guard Unit 387.*

34. Bennett, "GUARDIAN SPIES."

35. Elizebeth's speech to Mary Bartelme Club, Nov. 30, 1951, Elizebeth S. Friedman Collection, Box 17, file 10, George C. Marshall Library, Virginia Military Institute.

36. Summary of interview of Mrs. E. S. Friedman, 1.

37. Memo from Commandant to Mrs. Elizabeth S. Friedman," RG 38, Entry 1030 A1, Box 81, Folder 12000/3, National Archives at College Park, MD.

38. *Rules for Handling Mail and Files at Units of the United States Coast Guard*, Treasury Department, 1936, http://www.archives.gov/research/military/coast-guard/1936-rules-for-handling-mail.pdf, accessed April 29, 2013, 23.

39. Kurt F. Jensen, "Cautious Beginnings: Canadian Foreign Intelligence, 1939–51," http://books.google.com/books?id=0YLJFlVQFoAC&pg=PA50&lpg=PA50&dq=intelligence+section+oliver+strachey&source=bl&ots=HaBhI3s4aq&sig=p6IxKVku O96bQyUZW0f9zVeOkjg&hl=en&sa=X&ei=UVJ7U8SeNdOMyATR1oKoBg&ved=0CFAQ6AEwCQ#v=onepage&q=intelligence%20section%20oliver%20strachey&f=false, accessed May 20, 2014.

40. Summary of interview of Mrs. E. S. Friedman, 5.

41. Oliver Strachey, Wikipedia, https://en.wikipedia.org/wiki/Oliver_Strachey, accessed Nov. 1, 2015.

42. John F. Bratzel & Leslie Be Rout, "Abwehr Ciphers in Latin America," *Cryptologia*, 1983, 7:2, 382. Jones, "Clandestine Radio Intelligence," 138.

43. Oliver Strachey letter to Elizebeth Friedman, March 16, 1942, Elizebeth S. Friedman Collection, Box 6, file 7, George C. Marshall Library, Virginia Military Institute.

44. "Final Report, British-Canadian-American Radio Intelligence Discussions, Washington, D.C., April 1–17," 1942, HW 14/46, The National Archives of the UK (TNA).

45. *Ibid.*, 23–31.

46. *Ibid.*, 43–44.

47. "Final Report British-Canadian-American Radio Intelligence Discussions, Washington, D.C., April 6–17, 1942," Library and Archives of Canada, RG 24, Vol. 29163, 26–27.

48. Remarks by Rear Adm. Christopher J. Tomney, USCG Asst. Commander for Intelligence and Criminal Investigations, at Elizebeth Smith Friedman Auditorium Dedication Ceremony, ATF National Headquarters, Washington, D.C., June 17, 2014.

49. *Hitler's Secret War in South America 1939–1945*, 196.

50. CDR L.T. Jones, USCG, "Clandestine Radio Intelligence," Sept. 7, 1944, approved for release by NSA, Sept. 26, 2012, FOIA Case #19053, 1–3.

51. Robert Louis Benson, "A History of U.S. Communications Intelligence during World War II: Policy and Administration" United States Cryptologic History, Series IV, World War II, Volume 8, https://www.nsa.gov/about/cryptologic-heritage/historical-figures-publications/publications/wwii/assets/files/history_us_comms.pdf, accessed June 20, 2016, 3.

52. *Ibid.*

53. "The Co-ordination of IW/T Intelligence in the Western, Hemisphere, April, 1942," KV 4/218, The National Archives of the UK (TNA), 5.

54. *Ibid.*, 25–26.

55. *Ibid.*, 27–28.

56. Jones, "Clandestine Radio Intelligence," 3.

57. "The Co-ordination of IW/T Intelligence in the Western, Hemisphere, April, 1942," 27–28.

58. *Ibid.*, 36.

59. Summary of interview of Mrs. E. S. Friedman, 2.

60. "Report of Conference Appointed to Study Allocation of Cryptanalysis," June 30, 1942, declassified July 3, 2012, https://www.nsa.gov/news-features/declassified-documents/nsa-60th-timeline/assets/files/pre-nsa/19420630_PreNSA_Doc_3983157_ReportStudy.pdf, accessed June 20, 2016.

61. A.D. Kramer, Lt. Cmdr. "Memorandum for 20-G, Subject, Cryptanalysis; F.B.I.

activities and liaison with the British," June 8, 1942, https://www.nsa.gov/news-features/declassified-documents/ukusa/assets/files/early_papers_1940–1944.pdf, accessed Aug. 9, 2016.

62. "Report of Conference Appointed to Study Allocation of Cryptanalysis."

63. Jones, "Clandestine Radio Intelligence," 4.

64. David Mowry, "German Clandestine Activities in South America in World War II," NSA, 1989, declassified April 13, 2009, https://www.nsa.gov/news-features/declassified-documents/cryptologic-histories/assets/files/german_clandestine_activities.pdf, accessed June 18, 2016, 1.

65. David Kahn, *Hitler's Spies: German Military Intelligence in World War II*, McMillan Publishing Company, Inc., New York, 1978, 292.

66. *History of Coast Guard Unit 387*, 2–74.

67. Bratzel "Abwehr Ciphers in Latin America," 142

68. Jones, "Clandestine Radio Intelligence," 2.

69. Mowry, "German Clandestine Activities in South America in World War II, 23.

70. "Argentine Ships Will Still Sail Unguarded; Citizens of Americas Linked to Axis Spying," The New York Times, Feb. 12, 1944, P. 7.

71. Mowry, "German Clandestine Activities in South America in World War II, 51.

72. David P. Mowry, "Cryptologic Aspects of German Intelligence Activities in South American during WWII," 2011, United States Cryptologic History, Series IV, World War II, Volume 11, Center for Cryptologic History, NSA, https://www.nsa.gov/about/cryptologic-heritage/historical-figures-publications/publications/wwii/assets/files/cryptologic_aspects_of_gi.pdf, accessed June 18, 2016, 25.

73. Letter from Lt. Col. J.H. Tiltman to William Friedman, May 29, 1942, HW 14/46, The National Archives of the UK (TNA).

74. Letter from "Geoffrey" to "Dear John," apparently Tiltman, July 31, 1942, HW 14/47, The National Archives of the UK (TNA).

75. Summary of interview of Mrs. E. S. Friedman, 5.

76. Robert L. Benson, "The Origin of U.S.-British Communications Intelligence Cooperation (1940–41)," no date, NSA, https://www.nsa.gov/news-features/declassified-documents/cryptologic-spectrum/assets/files/origin_us_british.pdf, accessed June 20, 2016, 7–8.

77. Summary of interview of Mrs. E. S. Friedman, 5.

78. Many letters can be found in this Marshall Library box. This is a letter from Elizebeth to William, Mary 13, 1943, Elizebeth S. Friedman Collection, Box 2, file 7, George C. Marshall Library, Virginia Military Institute.

79. "Bletchley Park Diary, William F. Friedman" Edited with Notes and Bibliography By Colin MacKinnon, 2013, http://www.colinmackinnon.com/files/The_Bletchley_Park_Diary_of_William_F._Friedman_E.pdf, accessed May 20, 2014, 61.

80. Elizebeth letter to William, May 31, 1943, Elizebeth S. Friedman Collection, Box 2, file 7, George C. Marshall Library, Virginia Military Institute.

81. "Bletchley Park Diary, William F. Friedman," 110.

82. "Most Secret," June 25, 1942, HW 19/323, The National Archives of the UK (TNA).

83. Memo to Colonels Clark and McCormick about German clandestine radio traffic, Nov. 17, 1942, RG 457, Entry A1 9032, Box 1279, Folder German Clandestine Radio Traffic, National Archives at College Park, MD.

84. Memo from Major G. G. Stevens, "Clandestine," Dec. 24, 1942, HW 14/62, The National Archives of the UK (TNA).

85. Bratzel "Abwehr Ciphers in Latin America," 142

86. Summary of interview of Mrs. E. S. Friedman, 2–3.

87. Mowry, "German Clandestine Activities in South America in World War II, 14.

88. Memo from Major G. G. Stevens, "Clandestine."

89. Summary of interview of Mrs. E. S. Friedman, 4.

90. Jones, "Clandestine Radio Intelligence," 9.

91. "Historical Review of OP-20-G," RG 38, Naval Security Group Crane, Box 110, FOLDER 5750/150, National Archives at College Park, MD.

92. David Brinkley, *Washington Goes to War*, Alfred A. Knopf, New York, 1988, 117–118.

93. Mowry, "German Clandestine Activities in South America in World War II, 25.

94. Summary of interview of Mrs. E. S. Friedman, 2.

95. Elizebeth Friedman, "Footnote to History," Elizebeth S. Friedman Collection, Box 17, file 16, George C. Marshall Library, Virginia Military Institute, 1.

96. Report on OP-20-G general conference meeting, March 11, 1943, RG 38, Entry 1030 A1, Box 81, Folder 5050/41, National Archives at College Park, MD.

97. Mowry, "Cryptologic Aspects of Ger-

man Intelligence Activities in South American during WWII," 84–85.

98. *Ibid.*, 88.

99. Wilcox, "Solving the Enigma: History of the Cryptanalytic Bombe," 9.

100. There are at least four war diaries of OP-20-G-4–1 that indicated Coast Guard set ups for the Hypo or M-8, RG 38, Naval Security Group Crane, Box 110, Folder 5750/159–160, National Archives at College Park, MD.

101. *History of Coast Guard Unit 387*, 146.

102. Mowry, "Cryptologic Aspects of German Intelligence Activities in South American during WWII," 85–86.

103. *Ibid.*, 86–87.

104. *History of Coast Guard Unit 387*, 230.

105. "Wiring for E-machine, as obtained from Coast Guard," March 12, 1943, William F. Friedman Collection: Correspondence, Memoranda, and Personnel File Records—NSA/CSS, Doc Ref ID: A4146632, Declassified and approved for release by NSA Oct. 21, 2014, https://www.nsa.gov/news-features/declassified-documents/friedman-documents/assets/files/patent-equipment/FOLDER_520/41790129082914.pdf, accessed June 18, 2016.

106. *History of Coast Guard Unit 387*, 262–265.

107. OP-20-GI-A, "THE 'JOLLE' OPERATION," Aug. 25, 1944, RG 38, Naval Security Group Crane, Box 25, National Archives at College Park, MD.

108. OP-20-G, "Plan to German landing on Argentine Coast," June 5, 1944, RG 457, Entry A1 9032, Box 1368, Folder German Espionage, Jolle Operation, National Archives at College Park, MD.

109. Harold C. Deutsch, "The Historical Impact of Revealing the Ultra Secret," *Journal of the U.S. Army War College*, NSA, https://www.nsa.gov/news-features/declassified-documents/cryptologic-spectrum/assets/files/ultra_secret.pdf, accessed Aug. 9, 2016.

110. From Berlin to Argentine, Serial CG3–1540, Aug. 2, 1943, RG 38, Naval Security Group Crane, Box 79, National Archives at College Park, MD.

111. From Berlin to Argentina, Serial CG4–1544, Aug. 10, 1944, RG 38, Naval Security Group Crane, Box 79, National Archives at College Park, MD.

112. Summary of interview of Mrs. E. S. Friedman, 3.

113. David P. Mowry, "The Cryptology of the German Intelligence Services," NSA, 1989, declassified April 13, 2009, https://www.nsa.gov/news-features/declassified-documents/cryptologic-histories/assets/files/cryptology_of_gis.pdf, accessed June 4, 2016, 22–25.

114. Mowry, "German Clandestine Activities in South America in World War II," 13.

115. William F. Friedman, "EXAMPLES OF INTELLIGENCE OBTAINED FROM CRYPTANALYSIS," Aug. 1, 1946, William F. Friedman Collection: Correspondence, Memoranda, and Personnel File Records—NSA/CSS, DocRefID A67564, declassified Oct. 29, 2013, https://www.nsa.gov/news-features/declassified-documents/friedman-documents/assets/files/correspondence/FOLDER_152/41747769078696.pdf, accessed June 20, 2016.

116. Mowry, "German Clandestine Activities in South America in World War II," 13–14.

117. Brown, "Coast Guard Codebreakers: Inspire Those Who Serve."

118. "History of Martinique," Wikipedia, https://en.wikipedia.org/wiki/History_of_Martinique#World_War_II, accessed Jan. 29, 2016.

119. Elizebeth Friedman memoirs; Elizebeth S. Friedman Collection, Box 12, file 1, George C. Marshall Library, Virginia Military Institute, 97.

120. "Cryptologic Almanac 50th Anniversary Series, The World at the End of the War," January-February 2002, NSA, approved for release June 12, 2009, https://www.nsa.gov/news-features/declassified-documents/crypto-almanac-50th/assets/files/End_of_the_War.pdf, accessed June 20, 2016, 1.

121. Mowry, "German Clandestine Activities in South America in World War II," 57–58.

122. J.N. Wenger, "Correction to historical review," Oct. 8, 1945, RG 38, Naval Security Group Crane, Box 108, FOLDER 5750/99, National Archives at College Park, MD, 3.

123. Brown, "Coast Guard Codebreakers: Inspire Those Who Serve."

124. Boles, oral history interview.

125. Brown, "Coast Guard Codebreakers: Inspire Those Who Serve."

126. David Hatch, "Enigma and Purple: How the Allies Broke German and Japanese Codes During the War," no date, http://www.usna.edu/Users/math/wdj/_files/documents/papers/cryptoday/hatch_purple.pdf, accessed Oct. 10, 2015, 61.

127. Jones, "Clandestine Radio Intelligence."

128. *Ibid.*, 10–11.

129. "Evaluation and Dissemination of Information of Japanese Cryptanalytic or T/'A Results," Jan. 1, 1944, William F. Friedman Collection: Correspondence, Memoranda, and Personnel File Records—NSA/

CSS, Doc Ref ID: A65531, Declassified and approved by release by NSA April 28, 2014, https://www.nsa.gov/news-features/declassified-documents/friedman-documents/assets/files/reports-research/FOLDER_461/41755639079479.pdf, accessed June 20, 2016.

130. "How can more cohesive working be achieved between MIS and SSA," April 1945, https://www.nsa.gov/news-features/declassified-documents/friedman-documents/assets/files/reports-research/FOLDER_461/41755639079479.pdf, accessed June 29, 2016, 1.

131. "Coast Guard Intelligence," *Intelligence*, Coast Guard Publication 2–0, May 2010, http://www.uscg.mil/doctrine/CGPub/CG_Pub_2_0.pdf, accessed Jan. 22, 2013.

132. Civil Service Commission classification sheet, June 26, 1943, Elizebeth Friedman personnel file, National Archives, St. Louis.

133. Conference for Supervisors, March 8, 1943, Elizebeth Friedman personnel file, National Archives, St. Louis.

134. Civil Service Commission classification sheet, June 26, 1943.

135. Efficiency rating of Elizebeth Friedman by Lt. Cmdr. Jones, March 31, 1943, Elizebeth Friedman personnel file, National Archives, St. Louis.

136. Efficiency rating of Elizebeth Friedman by Cmdr. Jones, March 31, 1944, Elizebeth Friedman personnel file, National Archives, St. Louis.

137. Efficiency rating of Elizebeth Friedman by Cmdr. Jones, March 31, 1945, Elizebeth Friedman personnel file, National Archives, St. Louis.

138. Personnel file for Leonard T. Jones, National Archives, St. Louis, courtesy: Cmdr. Michael E. Bennett, USCG.

139. Author interview with Barbara Atchison, July 16, 2012.

140. There are also a few references in the records to Elizebeth and Lt. Cmdr. Jones being in Coast Guard Unit 191, which may be a Coast Guard headquarters detachment, but the author has been unable to track down anything about that unit.

141. U.S. Navy personnel action form, June 16, 1943, Elizebeth Friedman personnel file, National Archives, St. Louis.

142. Payroll record for Elizebeth Friedman, July 1954, Elizebeth Friedman personnel file, National Archives, St. Louis.

Chapter 9

1. Letter from Maud Bowman Jan. 27, 1942, Elizebeth S. Friedman Collection, File 1124, George C. Marshall Library, Virginia Military Institute.

2. Letter from Maud Bowman Jan. 27, 1942 decoded by Elizebeth Friedman in 1944, Elizebeth S. Friedman Collection, File 1124, George C. Marshall Library, Virginia Military Institute.

3. Velvalee Dickinson, the "Doll Woman," FBI Website, https://www.fbi.gov/history/famous-cases/velvalee-dickinson-the-doll-woman, accessed July 20, 2016.

4. *Ibid.*

5. "PERSONAL HISTORY OF MRS. VELVALEE DICKINSON," FBI FOIA CASE 1210674–000, File HQ-100–81112-Section 21, CD 224.

6. Letter to Mrs. Elizebeth Friedman from U.S. Atty. James B.M. McNally, March 21, 1944, Elizebeth S. Friedman Collection, File 1124, George C. Marshall Library, Virginia Military Institute.

7. "PERSONAL HISTORY OF MRS. VELVALEE DICKINSON," CD 224.

8. John Jenkisson, "The FBI vs New York Spies," *New York World-Telegram*, June 23, 1945, 17.

9. Letter to Mrs. Friedman from McNally.

10. "PERSONAL HISTORY OF MRS. VELVALEE DICKINSON," CD 224.

11. Jenkisson, "The FBI vs New York Spies," 17.

12. "PERSONAL HISTORY OF MRS. VELVALEE DICKINSON," CD 224..

13. "Doll Woman," FBI Website.

14. Synopsis of Velvalee Dickinson case, Oct. 9, 1944, FBI FOIA CASE 1210674–000, File HQ-100–81112-Section 21, CD 221.

15. F.S. Penny, "Memorandum for Mr. D.M. Ladd, July 25, 1944, FBI FOIA CASE 1210674–000, File HQ-100–81112-Section 20, CD 37.

16. Memo from Conroy to the Director, Aug. 2, 1944, FBI FOIA CASE 1210674–000, File HQ-100–81112-Section 20, CD 118.

17. Report of Special Agent L. Vernon Ewing, Sept. 19, 1944, FBI FOIA CASE 1210674–000, File HQ-100–81112-Section 21, CD 14–15.

18. Memo from Conroy, Aug. 2, 1944, CD 118.

19. Special Agent Ewing report, Sept. 19, 1944, CD 14–15.

20. Letter to Mrs. Friedman from McNally.

21. *Ibid.*

22. *Ibid.*

23. RE: Velvalee Dickinson, Attention: Crime Records, Sept. 6, 1944, FBI FOIA CASE 1210674–000, File HQ-100–81112-Section 20, CD 240–241.

24. Memo from E.E. Conroy, SAC to Director, FBI, May 15, 1944, FBI FOIA CASE

1210674–000, File HQ-100–81112-Section 18, CD 155.

25. RE: Velvalee Dickinson, Attention: Crime Records, CD 242.

26. Letter to Mrs. Friedman from McNally.

27. RE: Velvalee Dickinson, Attention: Crime Records, CD 250.

28. "Woman Accused of Using Letters On Dolls to Convey Military Data," *New York Times*, Jan. 22, 1944, 1.

29. Jenkisson, "The FBI vs New York Spies," 17.

30. "Woman Accused of Using Letters On Dolls to Convey Military Data," 1.

31. Letter from J. Edgar Hoover to M.J. Lynch, May 10, 1944, FBI FOIA CASE 1210674–000, File HQ-100–81112-Section 18, CD 34.

32. "PERSONAL HISTORY OF MRS. VELVALEE DICKINSON," CD 224.

33. Hoover letter, May 10, 1944, CD 34.

34. Indictment, Feb. 11, 1944, U.S. v Dickinson, CASE # C116–362, 0021 Records of District Courts of the United States, National Archives, New York.

35. Synopsis of case, Oct. 9, 1944, 226.

36. Memo from REDACTED to D.M. Ladd, Aug. 19, 1944, FBI FOIA CASE 1210674–000, File HQ-100–81112-Section 21, CD 154.

37. "Open Codes," 1997, Approved for release by NSA, Dec. 1, 2011, https://www.nsa.gov/news-features/declassified-documents/crypto-almanac-50th/assets/files/open-codes.pdf, accessed June 20, 2016.

38. Memo from REDACTED, CD 154.

39. Memo from D.M. Ladd to The Director, Aug. 19, 1944, FBI FOIA CASE 1210674–000, File HQ-100–81112-Section 20, CD 151.

40. Letter to Edward Wallace, from the Office of the Chief of Naval Operations, March 13, 1944, Elizebeth S. Friedman Collection, File 1124, George C. Marshall Library, Virginia Military Institute.

41. Elizebeth Friedman is named as Confidential Informant T4 in the index to an FBI memo on March 15, 1944, FBI FOIA CASE 1210674–000, File HQ-100–81112-Section 18, CD 110.

42. Report by L. Vernon Ewing, April 22, 1944, recommends a cryptographer "who might possibly open up a new avenue of thought," FBI FOIA CASE 1210674–000, File HQ-100–81112-Section 18, CD 96.

43. Letter to Mrs. Friedman from McNally.

44. Ewing report, April 22, 1944, CD 96.

45. Letter from Dr. Elizabeth Smith Friedman to Edward Wallace, March 29, 1944, Elizebeth S. Friedman Collection, Box 7, File 1, George C. Marshall Library, Virginia Military Institute.

46. Elizebeth Friedman travel orders, April 3 and April 11, 1944, Elizebeth Friedman personnel file, National Archives, St. Louis.

47. Memo of working notes by Elizebeth Friedman on the Dickinson case, Elizebeth S. Friedman Collection, File 1124, George C. Marshall Library, Virginia Military Institute.

48. Letter from Dr. Elizabeth Smith Friedman to Edward Wallace, April 1, 1944, Elizebeth S. Friedman Collection, Box 7, File 1, George C. Marshall Library, Virginia Military Institute.

49. Ewing report, April 22, 1944, CD 97.

50. *Ibid.*, CD 97–101.

51. William Rice and Art Smith, "Doll Woman Yawns When Held for Trial as Paid Spy of Japs," *New York Daily News*, May 5, 1944, Elizebeth S. Friedman Collection, Box 7, File 1, George C. Marshall Library, Virginia Military Institute.

52. "Doll Dealer Held as Japanese Spy; Was Seized in Censorship Case," *New York Times*, May 6, 1944, 17.

53. *Ibid.*

54. "Doll Woman's Trial Set," *New York Times*, July 11, 1944, 8.

55. "Doll Woman," FBI Website.

56. "Doll Woman Enters Guilty Plea In Censor Case; Faces 10 Years," *New York Times*, July 29, 1944, 1.

57. *Ibid.*

58. Docket notes, July 28, 1944, U.S. v Dickinson, CASE # C116–362, 0021 Records of District Courts of the United States, National Archives, New York.

59. Conroy memo, Aug. 2, 1944, CD 118.

60. Hoover letter, May 10, 1944, CD 34.

61. Interview with Mrs. Velvalee Dickinson, April 27, 1944, FBI FOIA CASE 1210674–000, File HQ-100–81112-EBF 1007, CD 4.

62. Hoover letter, May 10, 1944 CD 34.

63. Special Agent Ewing report, Sept. 19, 1944, CD 15–16.

64. Conroy memo to Director, Aug. 4, 1944, FBI FOIA CASE 1210674–000, File HQ-100–81112-Section 20, CD 116–117.

65. Special Agent Ewing report, Sept. 19, 1944, CD 15–16.

66. *Ibid.*, CD 22.

67. Memo from L.B. Nichols to D.M. Ladd, Oct. 2, 1944, FBI FOIA CASE 1210674–000, File HQ-100–81112-Section 21, CD 153.

68. Conroy memo, Aug. 2, 1944, CD 118.

69. *Ibid.*

70. Synopsis of case, Oct. 9, 1944, CD 215.

71. "Doll Woman Sentenced to Prison For 10 Years and Fined $10,000," *The New York Times*, Aug. 15, 1944, 19.

72. Judgment and Commitment, Aug. 14, 1944, U.S. v Dickinson, CASE # C116–362, 0021 Records of District Courts of the United States, National Archives, New York.

73. "Doll Woman Sentenced to Prison," 19.
74. Docket notes, March 4, 1946, U.S. v Dickinson.
75. "Doll Woman," FBI Website.
76. Memo from Kelly to Director, July 13, 1955, FBI FOIA CASE 1210674–000, File HQ-100–81112-Section 22, CD 97.
77. Letter from L. Patrick Gray, III, Acting Director, Sept. 22, 1972, FBI FOIA CASE 1210674–000, File HQ-100–81112-Section 22, CD 129.
78. Memo from M.A. Jones to Mr. Nichols, Sept. 23, 1944, FBI FOIA CASE 1210674–000, File HQ-100–81112-Section 21, CD 175–178.
79. Memo from John Edgar Hoover to SAC, New York, Oct. 21, 1944, FOIA CASE 1210674–000, File HQ-100–81112-Section 21, CD 180.
80. Memo from John Edgar Hoover to SAC, New York, July 12, 1945, FOIA CASE 1210674–000, File HQ-100–81112-Section 21, CD 256.
81. "Doll Woman," FBI Website.
82. D.M. Ladd memo Aug. 19, 1944 memo, CD 154.
83. Robert Louis Benson, "A History of U.S. Communications Intelligence during World War II: Policy and Administration" United States Cryptologic History, Series IV, World War II, Volume 8, https://www.nsa.gov/about/cryptologic-heritage/historical-figures-publications/publications/wwii/assets/files/history_us_comms.pdf, accessed June 18, 2016, 9.

Chapter 10

1. William left July 14 and returned Sept. 12, 1945. He kept a diary in a spiral-bound stenographer's book, William F. Friedman Papers, Box 13, file 13, George C. Marshall Library, Virginia Military Institute.
2. Elizebeth letter to William, July 24, 1945, Elizebeth S. Friedman Collection, Box 2, file 8, George C. Marshall Library, Virginia Military Institute.
3. She notes that the temperatures in the building often were over 100 and once reached 114. Elizebeth Friedman, "Footnote to History," undated typed manuscript, Elizebeth S. Friedman Collection, Box 17, file 16, George C. Marshall Library, Virginia Military Institute, 1.
4. Elizebeth letter to William, July 26, 1945, Elizebeth S. Friedman Collection, Box 2, file 8, George C. Marshall Library, Virginia Military Institute.
5. Elizebeth letter to William, Aug. 7, 1945, Elizebeth S. Friedman Collection, Box

2, file 8, George C. Marshall Library, Virginia Military Institute.
6. Elizebeth letter to William, Aug. 15, 1945, Elizebeth S. Friedman Collection, Box 2, file 8, George C. Marshall Library, Virginia Military Institute.
7. Elizebeth letter to William, Aug. 26, 1945, Elizebeth S. Friedman Collection, Box 2, file 8, George C. Marshall Library, Virginia Military Institute.
8. Mackay Radio Radiogram from William to Elizebeth, Aug. 28, 1945, Elizebeth S. Friedman Collection, Box 3, file 9, George C. Marshall Library, Virginia Military Institute.
9. Memo from G.C. Marshall to Admiral King, Aug. 18, 1945, declassified June 12, 2012, https://www.nsa.gov/news-features/declassified-documents/nsa-60th-timeline/assets/files/pre-nsa/19450818_PreNSA_Doc_3978305_SignalIntelligence.pdf, accessed June 20, 2016.
10. MEMORADUM FOR THE VICE CHIEF OF STAFF, Aug. 21, 1945, declassified July 3, 2012, https://www.nsa.gov/news-features/declassified-documents/nsa-60th-timeline/assets/files/pre-nsa/19450821_PreNSA_Doc_3984126_MemoRe.pdf, accessed June 20, 2016.
11. MEMORANDUM FOR GENERAL MARSHALL and ADMIRAL KING, Aug. 22, 1945, declassification date unspecified in 2004, https://www.nsa.gov/news-features/declassified-documents/nsa-60th-timeline/assets/files/pre-nsa/19450822_PreNSA_Doc_3978329_SignalIntelligence.pdf, accessed June 20, 2016.
12. Joint Meeting of State-Army-Navy Communication Intelligence Board, Feb. 15, 1946, https://www.nsa.gov/news-features/declassified-documents/ukusa/assets/files/STANCIB_STANCICC_15feb46.pdf, accessed June 29, 2016, 8.
13. The Navy contracted with the National Cash Register Company to produce Bombes in March 1942. Jennifer Wilcox, "Solving the Enigma: History of the Cryptanalytic Bombe," Center for Cryptologic History, National Security Agency, 2006, https://www.nsa.gov/about/cryptologic-heritage/historical-figures-publications/publications/wwii/assets/files/solving_enigma.pdf, accessed June 18, 2016, 19.
14. David Kahn, *The Code-Breakers, The Story of Secret Writing*, Scribner, 1967, 612.
15. "Cryptologic Almanac 50th Anniversary Series, William F. Friedman," National Security Agency, declassified June 12, 2009, https://www.nsa.gov/news-features/declassified-documents/crypto-almanac-50th/assets/files/William_F_Friedman.pdf, accessed June 20, 2016.

16. Connie Lunnen, "She Has a Secret Side, Breaking Codes Was More Personal In Her Day, Elizebeth Friedman Says" The Houston Chronicle, May 24, 1972, Elizebeth S. Friedman Collection, Box 12, file 1, George C. Marshall Library, Virginia Military Institute.

17. Malcolm F. Willoughby, The U.S. Coast Guard in World War II, United States Naval Institute, Annapolis, 1957, 10.

18. Elizebeth Friedman, "Footnote to History," 1–4.

19. EXTRACT FROM: R.I.P. NO. 98, COPY 1, April 5, 1943,William F. Friedman Collection: Correspondence, Memoranda, and Personnel File Records—NSA/CSS, DocRefID A66485, declassified May 14, 2014, https://www.nsa.gov/news-features/declassified-documents/friedman-documents/assets/files/reports-research/FOLDER_377/41754199079335.pdf, accessed June 20, 2016.

20. Elizebeth Friedman, handwritten note on the back of a Coast Guard envelope, October 1946, Elizebeth S. Friedman Collection, Box 6, file 8, George C. Marshall Library, Virginia Military Institute.

21. James B. Hutchison, "Air-Sea Safety Patrol To Be Retained IN Peace Admiral Gorman Discloses," Gannett News Service, The Massena Observer, Nov. 1, 1945, http://news.nnyln.net/massena-observer/massena-observer-1945-august-1946-january/massena-observer-1945-august-1946-january%20-%200322.pdf, accessed Aug. 20, 2013, 6.

22. MEMORANDUM FOR ACTING COMMANDANT, Oct. 12, 1945, RG 26, Entry 344 (A1), Box 3, Folder 3, National Archives Building, Washington, D.C.

23. Remarks by Rear Adm. Christopher J. Tomney, USCG, at Elizebeth Smith Friedman Auditorium Dedication Ceremony, ATF National Headquarters, Washington, D.C., June 17, 2014.

24. NSA Observes Armed Forces Week-Coast Guard, May 15, 2015, https://www.nsa.gov/news-features/news-stories/2015/nsa-celebrates-armed-forces-week-coast-guard.shtml, accessed June 20, 2016.

25. Elizebeth Friedman efficiency rating, March 31, 1946, Elizebeth Friedman personnel file, National Archives, St. Louis.

26. Elizebeth Friedman, "Footnote to History," 4.

27. "History of Coast Guard Unit 387," Sept. 17, 1946, declassified, Dec. 17, 2008, RG 38, Naval Security Group Crane, Box 57, National Archives at College Park, MD.

28. Time and attendance report for Elize-

beth Friedman, Sept. 21, 1946, Elizebeth Friedman personnel file, National Archives, St. Louis.

29. Summary of interview of Mrs. E. S. Friedman by R. Louis Benson, Jan. 9, 1976, NSA-OH-1976–22, DOC ID 4237384, approved for release by NSA July 30, 2015, https://www.nsa.gov/news-features/declassified-documents/oral-history-interviews/assets/files/nsa-OH-1976–22-efriedman.pdf, accessed June 17, 2016, 5.

30. Ibid., 1.

31. Ibid., 3.

32. Elizebeth Friedman letter to "Anne," Oct. 24, 1951, Elizebeth S. Friedman Collection, Box 1, file 17, George C. Marshall Library, Virginia Military Institute.

33. Elizebeth Friedman memoirs, Elizebeth S. Friedman Collection, Box 12, file 1, George C. Marshall Library, Virginia Military Institute, 97.

34. Elizebeth Friedman, "Forward," Elizebeth S. Friedman Collection, Box 17, file 20, George C. Marshall Library, Virginia Military Institute.

35. Dr. Solomon Kullback, Oral History Interview, NSA OH-17–82, Aug. 26, 1982, DOCID: 4235410, declassified Aug. 28, 2015, https://www.nsa.gov/news-features/declassified-documents/oral-history-interviews/assets/files/nsa-oh-17–82-kullback.pdf, accessed June 20, 2016, 11.

36. After the author sent two letters to the IMF requesting information on Elizebeth Friedman's work there, an official in the Communications Department, David Danir, called the author on Sept. 10, 2014 to say that after an extensive records search, "no trace" of Elizebeth Friedman's work as a consultant or employee could be found.

37. Elizebeth Friedman handwritten note, an apparent resume for making a speech in 1951, Elizebeth S. Friedman Collection, Box 17, file 10, George C. Marshall Library, Virginia Military Institute.

38. Elizebeth S. Friedman (1892–1980) Cryptologic Hall of Honor 1999 Inductee, NSA, http://www.nsa.gov/about/cryptologic_heritage/hall_of_honor/1999/friedman_e.shtml.

39. "Clandestine Women: Spies in American History," National Women's History Museum website, https://www.nwhm.org/online-exhibits/spies/13.htm, accessed July 7, 2014.

40. Author interview with Barbara Atchison, July 16, 2012.

41. J. Keith Horsefield, The International Monetary Fund 1945–1965, Vol. I: Chronicle, International Monetary Fund, Washington, D.C., 1969, http://www.elibrary.imf.org/

staticfiles/IMF_History/IMF_45–65_vol1. pdf, accessed July 7, 2014, 155–156.

42. *Ibid.*

43. William Friedman letter to Brig. Gen. Carter Clarke, April 23, 1952, William F. Friedman Collection: Correspondence, Memoranda, and Personnel File Records—NSA/CSS, DocRefID A70092, approved for release March 25, 2014, https://www.nsa.gov/news-features/declassified-documents/friedman-documents/assets/files/correspondence/FOLDER_364/41734719077395.pdf, accessed June 20, 2016.

44. Barbara Atchison interview.

45. James Phinney Baxter, *The Greatest of Literary Problems*, Houghton Mifflin Company, Boston, 1917, https://archive.org/details/greatestoflitera00baxtrich, accessed July 17, 2014, 62.

46. Bill Sherman remarks, "The Friedmans on Shakespeare," video, The George C. Marshall Foundation, 2014, http://marshallfoundation.org/library/digital-archive/shakespearean-ciphers-examined/, accessed July 7, 2014.

47. Elizabeth Friedman letter to Charles Herring, April 22, 1955, Elizabeth S. Friedman Collection, Box 1, file 20, George C. Marshall Library, Virginia Military Institute.

48. Ronald Clark, *The Man Who Broke Purple*, Little Brown and Company, Boston, 1977, 222.

49. "FOLGER AWARDS MADE," United Press via *The New York Times*, April 3, 1955, http://timesmachine.nytimes.com/timesmachine/1955/04/03/88793350.html, accessed July 15, 2014, 84.

50. Clark, *The Man Who Broke Purple*, 222–223.

51. *Ibid.*, 224.

52. Elizabeth [sic] Smith Friedman, letter to F. Ronald Mansbridge, April 6, 1955, William F. Friedman Collection: Correspondence, Memoranda, and Personnel File Records—NSA/CSS, DocRefID A62971, approved for release by NSA June 19, 2014, https://www.nsa.gov/news-features/declassified-documents/friedman-documents/assets/files/correspondence/FOLDER_031/41721399076066.pdf, accessed June 20, 2016.

53. Clark, *The Man Who Broke Purple*, 224.

54. William F. Friedman, "MEMORANDUM FOR DIRECTOR, NATIONAL SECURITY AGENCY," undated, REF ID: A64948, https://www.nsa.gov/news-features/declassified-documents/friedman-documents/assets/files/correspondence/FOLDER_030/41777119081620.pdf, accessed June 20, 2016.

55. Kahn, *The Code-Breakers*, 879.

56. William F. Friedman and Elizebeth S. Friedman, *The Shakespearean Ciphers Examined*, Cambridge University Press, 1957.

57. The Friedmans' book may have put the Baconian controversy to rest, but did not end other avenues of Shakespeare speculation. The Friedmans mentioned the theory that the Earl of Oxford, Edward de Vere, truly was Shakespeare, but did not investigate that hypothesis since it was a lifestyle-based theory instead of a cryptologic one.

58. David Kahn, "Decoding the Bard," *The New York Times*, Oct. 6, 1957, http://timesmachine.nytimes.com/timesmachine/1957/10/06/91167527.html, accessed July 7, 2014, 277.

59. William F. Friedman and Elizebeth S. Friedman, *The Shakespearean Ciphers Examined*, 63–69.

60. *Ibid.*, 114–136.

61. *Ibid.*, 263–278.

62. Kahn, "Decoding the Bard," 296.

63. Official Curriculum Vitae, William F. Friedman, Elizebeth S. Friedman Collection, Box 13, file 23, George C. Marshall Library, Virginia Military Institute.

64. *Ibid.* William retired from the NSA in 1955 but continued consulting with the agency until his death in 1969.

65. Barbara Atchison interview.

66. "Umol-huun tah-tiyal," inside cover of *The Road to Pearl Harbor* by Herbert Feis, William F. Friedman Papers, Item 645, George C. Marshall Library, Virginia Military Institute.

67. Elizabeth Friedman, letter to "Dear Kay," Feb. 9, 1958, Elizebeth S. Friedman Collection, Box 1, file 23, George C. Marshall Library, Virginia Military Institute.

68. Clark, *The Man Who Broke Purple*, 243–244.

69. "Biographical Sketch," "The Friedman Legacy: A Tribute to William and Elizebeth Friedman," Center for Cryptologic History, National Security Agency, 1992. https://www.nsa.gov/resources/everyone/digital-media-center/video-audio/historical-audio/friedman-legacy/assets/files/friedman-legacy-transcript.pdf, accessed June 17, 2016, viii.

70. "Cryptologic Almanac 50th Anniversary Series, William F. Friedman."

71. *Ibid.*

72. S Wesley Reynolds, "Classified Documents in Possession of William F. Friedman," NSA, Dec. 5, 1958, A99778, approved for release May 13, 2014, https://www.nsa.gov/news-features/declassified-documents/friedman-documents/assets/files/correspondence/ACC4282/41783879082293.pdf, accessed July 11, 2016.

73. Oral History Interview NSA OH 23–82 with Donald F. Coffey, Nov. 4, 1982, approved for release Sept. 8, 2014, FOIA Case # 78498, 1–3.

74. Clark, *The Man Who Broke Purple*, 249–252.

75. Coffey oral history interview, 5.

76. Letter from Lt. Gen. John Samford, USAF to William Friedman, May 13, 1959, Elizebeth S. Friedman Collection, Box 12, George C. Marshall Library, Virginia Military Institute.

77. Katie Letcher Lyle, "Divine Fire, Elizebeth Smith Friedman, Cryptanalyst," unpublished manuscript, 1991, Center for Cryptologic History, National Security Agency, 181–183.

78. Remarks by Col. Rose Mary Sheldon at "Declassification and Release of William Friedman's Official Papers," George C. Marshall Foundation, April 25, 2015, https://www.youtube.com/watch?v=qxqgK8QC chw&app=desktop, accessed June 2, 2015.

79. Coffey oral history interview, 4–5.

80. Memo from [first initial blurred] Wesley Reynolds, Director of Security, Jan. 2, 1959, approved for release May 13, 2014, https://www.nsa.gov/news-features/declassified-documents/friedman-documents/assets/files/correspondence/ACC4282/41783909082296.pdf, accessed June 20, 2016.

81. Disposition Form, "Classification of Materials Received from Mr. Friedman," Feb. 6, 1959, approved for release May 13, 2014, https://www.nsa.gov/news-features/declassified-documents/friedman-documents/assets/files/correspondence/ACC4282/41784059082311.pdf, accessed June 20, 2016.

82. "Former Directors," National Security Agency, http://www.nsa.gov/about/leadership/former_directors.shtml, accessed July 18, 2014.

83. A typed letter does not appear in Elizebeth's files. The author also did not receive such a letter from the NSA when requested under FOIA Case #78498, though the NSA did reveal the Donald Coffey interview in that FOIA request as already noted.

84. Elizebeth Friedman, handwritten letter to "Dear General Carter," Nov. 4, year unspecified, Elizebeth S. Friedman Collection, Box 17, file 25, George C. Marshall Library, Virginia Military Institute.

85. Elizebeth Friedman letter to Gen. Marshall Carter, Jan. 8, 1971, William F. Friedman Collection: Correspondence, Memoranda, and Personnel File Records—NSA/CSS, DocRefID A2918420, approved for release June 16, 2015, https://www.nsa.gov/

news-features/declassified-documents/friedman-documents/assets/files/supplemental-collection/43014/42291749133021.pdf, accessed June 20, 2016.

86. Appraisal of Friedman papers, 1968, William F. Friedman Papers, Folder 2046, George C. Marshall Library, Virginia Military Institute.

87. "Declassification of the Friedman Papers," non-attributable source under rules of the 2015 Cryptologic History Symposium, Oct. 22, 2015.

88. Letter from Elizebeth Friedman, Jan. 28, 1970, Elizebeth S. Friedman Collection, Box 13, file 31, George C. Marshall Library, Virginia Military Institute.

89. Comments to author by Marshall Library director Paul Barron.

90. "Declassification of the Friedman Papers," non-attributable source under rules of the 2015 Cryptologic History Symposium, Oct. 22, 2015.

91. Sheldon remarks, April 25, 2015.

92. Col. Rose Mary Sheldon, "The Friedman Collection: An Analytical Guide," http://marshallfoundation.org/library/wp-content/uploads/sites/16/2014/09/Friedman_Collection_Guide_September_2014.pdf, accessed June 20, 2016.

93. NSA Oral History of Lt. Gen. Marshall S. Carter, Oct. 3, 1988, approved for release Oct. 30, 2015, https://www.nsa.gov/news-features/declassified-documents/oral-history-interviews/assets/files/NSA-OH-15–88-Carter.pdf, accessed June 20, 2016.

94. "George C. Marshall Foundation and National Security Agency Debut," April 24, 2015, NSA, https://www.nsa.gov/news-features/press-room/press-releases/2015/marshall-foundation-and-nsa-debut-friedman-collection.shtml, accessed June 20, 2016.

95. Sheldon remarks, April 25, 2015.

96. Remarks by Dr. David Sherman, NSA Associate Dir. For Policy and Records, at "Declassification and Release of William Friedman's Official Papers," George C. Marshall Foundation, April 25, 2015, https://www.youtube.com/watch?v=qxqgK8QC chw&app=desktop, accessed June 2, 2015.

97. Dr. David Sherman, "The National Security Agency and the William F. Friedman Collection," *Cryptologia*, June 29, 2016, http://dx.doi.org/10.1080/01611194.2016.1169458, accessed July 11, 2016.

98. "Elizebeth Smith Friedman 1892–1980," *Cryptologic Spectrum*, December 1980, reprinted in "The Friedman Legacy: A Tribute to William and Elizebeth Friedman," Center for Cryptologic History, National Security Agency, 1992. https://www.nsa.gov/

resources/everyone/digital-media-center/ video-audio/historical-audio/friedman-legacy/assets/files/friedman-legacy-transcript.pdf, accessed June 17, 2016, 207.

99. "Declassification of the Friedman Papers," non-attributable source under rules of the 2015 Cryptologic History Symposium, Oct. 22, 2015.

100. Bill Sherman remarks, "A Portrait of William F. Friedman," video, The George C. Marshall Foundation, 2014, http://marshall-foundation.org/library/digital-archive/ shakespearean-ciphers-examined/, accessed July 7, 2014.

101. Lyle, "Divine Fire," 198.

102. *Ibid.*, 199.

103. Undated resume, Elizebeth Friedman personnel file, National Archives, St. Louis.

104. E. Friedman memoirs, 54.

105. Stephen Budiansky, *Battle of Wits, The Complete Story of Codebreaking in World War II*, The Free Press, New York, 2000, 163.

106. Betsy Rohaly Smoot written comments requested by author, Aug. 7, 2014.

107. Author interview of Barbara Osteika, Jan. 16, 2014.

108. E. Friedman memoirs, 54–55.

109. Letter from A.W.W. Woodcock to the Sec. of the Treasury, June 28, 1933, RG 26, Entry 297, Box 48, National Archives Smoot, "Thoughts on Elizebeth Smith Friedman's Legacy," Building, Washington, D.C.

110. Osteika interview, Jan. 16, 2014.

111. *Ibid.*

112. Remarks by Chris Atchison at Elizebeth Smith Friedman Auditorium Dedication Ceremony, ATF National Headquarters, Washington, D.C., June 17, 2014.

113. "Cryptologic Hall of Honor, Elizebeth S. Friedman," National Security Agency website, https://www.nsa.gov/about/ cryptologic-heritage/historical-figures-publications/hall-of-honor/1999/efriedman. shtml, accessed June 20, 2016.

114. Smoot, "Thoughts on Elizebeth Smith Friedman's Legacy."

115. Author interview of Chris Atchison, July 17, 2011.

116. Elizebeth S. Friedman Cryptologic Hall of Honor website.

117. *"History of Coast Guard Unit 387."*

118. See Chapter 9.

119. Lyle, "Divine Fire," 6.

120. Kullback interview, 7–9.

121. Solomon Kullback, Ph.D., "General Solution for the Double Transposition Cipher," War Dept., Office of the Chief Signal Officer, William F. Friedman Collection: Correspondence, Memoranda, and Personnel File Records—NSA/CSS, DocRefID A57071, declassified May 19, 2014, https://www.nsa. gov/news-features/declassified-documents/ friedman-documents/assets/files/publica tions/FOLDER_439/41751169079035.pdf, accessed June 20, 2016.

122. Lyle, "Divine Fire," footnote #3, 204.

123. Betsy Rohaly Smoot remarks, "A Portrait of William F. Friedman," video, The George C. Marshall Foundation, 2014, http:// marshallfoundation.org/library/digital-archive/shakespearean-ciphers-examined/, accessed July 7, 2014.

124. "Cryptologic Almanac, William F. Friedman," National Security Agency, https:// www.nsa.gov/news-features/declassified-documents/crypto-almanac-50th/assets/ files/William_F_Friedman.pdf, accessed June 20, 2016.

125. E. Friedman memoirs, 86.

126. "Cryptologic Excellence: Yesterday, Today, and Tomorrow," National Security Agency, undated, circa 2002, https://www. nsa.gov/about/_files/cryptologic_heritage/ publications/misc/50th_anniversary.pdf, accessed Dec. 9, 2014, 9.

127. Chris Atchison interview.

128. See Prologue.

129. Tomney remarks.

130. Author interview of Barbara Osteika, June 17, 2014.

131. WIFLE Newsletter, March 2014, http://www.wifle.org/newsletters/march 2014/index.htm, accessed Dec. 19, 2015.

132. Maureen Joyce, "Elizebeth Friedman, U.S. Cryptanalyst, Pioneer in Science of Code-Breaking Dies," *The Washington Post*, Nov. 2, 1980, Elizebeth S. Friedman Collection, Box 16, file 23, George C. Marshall Library, Virginia Military Institute, B8.

133. Comments by Albert Friendly, "In Memoriam Elizebeth Smith Friedman," *Cryptologic Spectrum*, NSA, December 1980, The Friedman papers, Box 16, file 24, George C. Marshall Library, Virginia Military Institute.

134. *Ibid.*

Bibliography

There is a section on "Web sources" for information accessed through the World Wide Web, but in some cases, where it seems more appropriate to list the source under another section, articles or documents accessed online are included in that section along with the Web address.

Unpublished Documents and Other Primary Sources

Author's Interviews and Correspondence

Atchison, Barbara. Daughter of William and Elizebeth Friedman.
Atchison, Chris. Grandson of William and Elizebeth Friedman.
Barron, Paul. Director, George C. Marshall Research Library.
Danir, David. International Monetary Fund, telephone call, Sept. 10, 2014.
Osteika, Barbara. Historian, Bureau of Alcohol, Tobacco, Firearms and Explosives.
Smoot, Betsy Rohaly. Historian, National Security Agency, email questionnaire.

Federal Bureau of Investigation

Conroy, E.E., memo, SAC to Director, FBI, May 15, 1944, FBI FOIA CASE 1210674–000, File HQ-100–81112-Section 18, CD 155.
Conroy, E.E., memo to the Director, Aug. 2, 1944, FBI FOIA CASE 1210674–000, File HQ-100–81112-Section 20, CD 118.
Conroy, E.E., memo to the Director, Aug. 4, 1944, FBI FOIA CASE 1210674–000, File HQ-100–81112-Section 20, CD 116–117.
Ewing, L. Vernon, report, April 22, 1944, recommends a cryptographer "who might possibly open up a new avenue of thought," FBI FOIA CASE 1210674–000, File HQ-100–81112-Section 18, CD 96.
Ewing, L. Vernon, report, Sept. 19, 1944, FBI FOIA CASE 1210674–000, File HQ-100–81112-Section 21, CD 14–15.
Gray, L. Patrick, letter, Sept. 22, 1972, FBI FOIA CASE 1210674–000, File HQ-100–81112-Section 22, CD 129.
Hoover, J. Edgar, letter to M.J. Lynch, May 10, 1944, FBI FOIA CASE 1210674–000, File HQ-100–81112-Section 18, CD 34.
Hoover, John Edgar, memo to SAC, New York, Oct. 21, 1944, FOIA CASE 1210674–000, File HQ-100–81112-Section 21, CD 180.
Hoover, John Edgar, memo to SAC, New York, July 12, 1945, FOIA CASE 1210674–000, File HQ-100–81112-Section 21, CD 256.

Index to an FBI memo on March 15, 1944, FBI FOIA CASE 1210674–000, File HQ-100–81112-Section 18, CD 110.

Interview with Mrs. Velvalee Dickinson, April 27, 1944, FBI FOIA CASE 1210674–000, File HQ-100–81112-EBF 1007, CD 4.

Jones, M.A., memo to Mr. Nichols, Sept. 23, 1944, FBI FOIA CASE 1210674–000, File HQ-100–81112-Section 21, CD 175–178.

Kelly, memo to the Director, July 13, 1955, FBI FOIA CASE 1210674–000, File HQ-100–81112-Section 22, CD 97.

Ladd, D.M., memo to the Director, Aug. 19, 1944, FBI FOIA CASE 1210674–000, File HQ-100–81112-Section 20, CD 151.

Memo from REDACTED to D.M. Ladd, Aug. 19, 1944, FBI FOIA CASE 1210674–000, File HQ-100–81112-Section 21, CD 154.

Nichols, L.B., memo to D.M. Ladd, Oct. 2, 1944, FBI FOIA CASE 1210674–000, File HQ-100–81112-Section 21, CD 153.

Penny, F.S., memorandum for Mr. D.M. Ladd, July 25, 1944, FBI FOIA CASE 1210674–000, File HQ-100–81112-Section 20, CD 37.

"PERSONAL HISTORY OF MRS. VELVALEE DICKINSON," FBI FOIA CASE 1210674–000, File HQ-100–81112-Section 21, CD 224.

RE: Velvalee Dickinson, Attention: Crime Records, Sept. 6, 1944, FBI FOIA CASE 1210674–000, File HQ-100–81112-Section 20, CD 240–241.

Synopsis of Velvalee Dickinson case, Oct. 9, 1944, FBI FOIA CASE 1210674–000, File HQ-100–81112-Section 21, CD 221.

George C. Marshall Research Library, Virginia Military Institute, Lexington, Virginia

"Affidavit of Elizebeth Smith Friedman," Nov. 30, 1934, *Joint Interim Report of the Commissioners*, Elizebeth S. Friedman Collection, Box 77, file 5.

Appraisal of Friedman papers, 1968, William F. Friedman Papers, Folder 2046.

Bowman, Maud, letter, Jan. 27, 1942, decoded by Elizebeth Friedman in 1944, Elizebeth S. Friedman Collection, File 1124.

Chief of Naval Operations letter to Edward Wallace, March 13, 1944, Elizebeth S. Friedman Collection, File 1124.

Fabyan, George, various letters to Elizebeth or William Friedman, Elizebeth S. Friedman Collection, Box 1, file 42.

Feis, Herbert. *The Road to Pearl Harbor* William F. Friedman Papers, Item 645.

Fish, G.W, letter to Elizebeth Friedman, Feb. 22, 1938, Elizebeth S. Friedman Collection, Box 6, file 32.

Friedman, Dr. Elizebeth Smith, letter to Edward Wallace, March 29, 1944, Elizebeth S. Friedman Collection, Box 7, File 1.

Friedman, Dr. Elizebeth Smith, letter to Edward Wallace, April 1, 1944, Elizebeth S. Friedman Collection, Box 7, File 1.

Friedman, Elizebeth. "Footnote to History," 1946, Elizebeth S. Friedman Collection, Box 17, file 16.

Friedman, Elizebeth. "Forward," Elizebeth S. Friedman Collection, Box 17, file 20.

Friedman, Elizebeth, genealogy files, Elizebeth S. Friedman Collection, Box 11, file 20.

Friedman, Elizebeth, handwritten letter to "Dear General Carter," Nov. 4, year unspecified, Elizebeth S. Friedman Collection, Box 17, file 25.

Friedman, Elizebeth, handwritten note on the back of a Coast Guard envelope, October 1946, Elizebeth S. Friedman Collection, Box 6, file 8.

Friedman, Elizebeth, handwritten memo to Commander Anthony, unspecific date in 1945, Elizebeth S. Friedman Collection, Box 17, file 26.

Friedman, Elizebeth. "History of Work in Cryptanalysis, April 1927-June 1930," Elizebeth S. Friedman Collection, Box 4, file 17.

Friedman, Elizebeth, letter, Jan. 28, 1970, Elizebeth S. Friedman Collection, Box 13, file 31.

Friedman, Elizebeth, letter to "Anne," Oct. 24, 1951, Elizebeth S. Friedman Collection, Box 1, file 17.

Friedman, Elizebeth, letter to Miss Josephine Coates, Jan. 23, 1930, Elizebeth S. Friedman Collection, Box 1, file 2.

Friedman, Elizebeth, letter to "Dear Kay," Feb. 9, 1958, Elizebeth S. Friedman Collection, Box 1, file 23.

Friedman, Elizebeth, letter to Mrs. E.S. Dinieus, Nov. 26, 1932, Elizebeth S. Friedman Collection, Box 1, file 4.

Friedman, Elizebeth, letter to Colonel Donovan, Dec. 29, 1941, Elizebeth S. Friedman Collection, Box 17, file 15Friedman, Elizebeth, letter to William Friedman, May 13, 1943, Elizebeth S. Friedman Collection, Box 2, file 7.

Friedman, Elizebeth, letter to G. W. Fish, Nov. 7, 1937, Elizebeth S. Friedman Collection, Box 6, file 27.

Friedman, Elizebeth, letter to G.W. Fish, Feb. 12, 1938, Elizebeth S. Friedman Collection, Box 6, file 32.

Friedman, Elizebeth, letter to Durward Howes, Nov. 14, 1934, Elizebeth S. Friedman Collection, Box 1, file 6.

Friedman, Elizebeth, letter to Dr. Arthur Hummel, Feb. 24, 1937, Elizebeth S. Friedman Collection, Box 6, file 26.

Friedman, Elizebeth, letter to Mary Field Parton, April 7, 1938, Elizebeth S. Friedman Collection, Box 6, file 28.

Elizebeth Friedman, letter to William Friedman, June 10, 1940, Elizebeth S. Friedman Collection, Box 2, file 5.

Friedman, Elizebeth, letter to William Friedman, May 31, 1943, Elizebeth S. Friedman Collection, Box 2, file 7.

Friedman, Elizebeth, letter to William Friedman, July 24, 1945, Elizebeth S. Friedman Collection, Box 2, file 8.

Friedman, Elizebeth, letter to William Friedman, July 26, 1945, Elizebeth S. Friedman Collection, Box 2, file 8.

Friedman, Elizebeth, letter to William Friedman, Aug. 7, 1945, Elizebeth S. Friedman Collection, Box 2, file 8.

Friedman, Elizebeth, letter to William Friedman, Aug. 15, 1945, Elizebeth S. Friedman Collection, Box 2, file 8.

Friedman, Elizebeth, letter to William Friedman, Aug. 26, 1945, Elizebeth S. Friedman Collection, Box 2, file 8.

Friedman, Elizebeth, letter to L.G. Fry, Dec. 7, 1937, Elizebeth S. Friedman Collection, Box 17, file 1.

Friedman, Elizebeth, letter to Charles Herring, April 22, 1955, Elizebeth S. Friedman Collection, Box 1, file 20.

Friedman, Elizebeth, memo for the commandant, Aug. 31, 1937, Elizebeth S. Friedman Collection, Box 6, file 26.

Friedman, Elizebeth, memo of working notes by Elizebeth Friedman on the Dickinson case, Elizebeth S. Friedman Collection, File 1124.

Friedman, Elizebeth, memo on the history of Pacific Coast smuggling, unspecific date in 1930, Elizebeth S. Friedman Collection, Box 4, file 24.

Friedman, Elizebeth, memo on Lew Kim Yuen case, Feb. 16, 1937, Elizebeth S. Friedman Collection, Box 6, file 26.

Friedman, Elizebeth, memo to chief intelligence officer, February 1934, Elizebeth S. Friedman Collection, Box 5, file 20.

Friedman, Elizebeth, memo to chief intelligence officer, Oct. 30, 1937, Elizebeth S. Friedman Collection, Box 6, file 26.

Friedman, Elizebeth, memo to the chief intelligence officer, March 28, 1938, Elizebeth S. Friedman Collection, Box 6, file 32.

Friedman, Elizebeth, memo to Coast Guard commandant, Feb. 14, 1938, Elizebeth S. Friedman Collection, Box 1, file 9.

Friedman, Elizebeth, memo to Commander Gorman, Aug. 22, 1933, Elizebeth S. Friedman Collection, Box 6, file 25.

Friedman, E.S., memo to Lt. Cmdr. Gorman, Dec. 23, 1930, Elizebeth S. Friedman Collection, Box 17, file 26.

Friedman, Elizebeth, memo to Mr. Schwartz, Oct. 20, 1938, Elizebeth S. Friedman Collection, Box 1, file 9.

Friedman, Elizebeth, memoirs, Elizebeth S. Friedman Collection, Box 12, file 1–2.

Friedman, Elizebeth. "MEMORANDUM FOR MR. OWENS," Sept. 26, 1933, Elizebeth S. Friedman Collection, Box 6, file 25.

Friedman, Elizebeth. S. "Memorandum upon a Proposed Central Organization at Coast Guard Headquarters for Performing Cryptanalytic Work," November 1930. Elizebeth S. Friedman Collection, Box 5, file 6.

Friedman, Elizebeth, narrative of the Gordon Lim case, Elizebeth S. Friedman Collection, Box 6, file 29.

Friedman, Elizebeth, narrative on the Ezra Brothers, Elizebeth S. Friedman Collection, Box 6, file 25.

Friedman, Elizebeth, postal telegraph message to William Friedman, Oct. 18, 1937, Elizebeth S. Friedman Collection, Box 6, file 28,.

Friedman, Elizebeth, postcard to John Ramsey Friedman, Oct. 3, 1932, Elizebeth S. Friedman Collection, Box 1, file 4.

Friedman, Elizebeth, postcard to John Ramsey Friedman, Oct. 17, 1937, Elizebeth S. Friedman Collection, Box 6, file 28.

Friedman, Elizebeth, text of speech to Mary Bartelme Club, Nov. 30, 1951, Elizebeth S. Friedman Collection, Box 17, file 10.

Friedman, Elizebeth, various letters in 1917 to William Friedman, Elizebeth S. Friedman Collection, Box 2, file 1 and Box 12, file 2.

Friedman, William, diary, July 14-Sept. 12, 1945, William F. Friedman Papers, Box 13, file 13.

Friedman, William, letter to Elizebeth, Oct. 18, 1937, Elizebeth S. Friedman Collection, Box 3, file 6.

Friedman, William, letter to Elizebeth, Jan. 18, 1938, Elizebeth S. Friedman Collection, Box 3, file 7.

Friedman, William, letter to Elizebeth, June 16, 1938, Elizebeth S. Friedman Collection, Box 3, file 7.

Friedman, William, letter to Elizebeth, June 4, 1940, Elizebeth S. Friedman Collection, Box 3, file 7.

Friedman, William, letter to Elizebeth, June 10, 1940, Elizebeth S. Friedman Collection, Box 3, file 7.

Friedman, William, Mackay Radio Radiogram to Elizebeth, Aug. 28, 1945, Elizebeth S. Friedman Collection, Box 3, file 9.

Friedman, William, various letters and telegrams to Elizebeth Friedman, Elizebeth S. Friedman Collection, Box 2, file 13 or file 20.

Friedman, William, Western Union telegram to Elizebeth, June 12, 1938, Elizebeth S. Friedman Collection, Box 3, file 6.

Graves, Harold N, letter to Rear Adm. R.R. Waesche, Feb. 26, 1937, Elizebeth S. Friedman Collection, Box 6, file 26.

"Hearing on Claim of the British Ship "I'm Alone,"" Elizebeth S. Friedman Collection, Box 6, file 16.

"A little while with Elizabeth [sic] Friedman," March 25, 1975, interview with unknown person. Elizebeth S. Friedman Collection, Box 12, file 1.

Mauborgne, Capt. J.O., memo to Chief of the War College, April 11, 1917, William Friedman Collection, George C. Marshall Foundation, http://marshallfoundation.org/ library/friedman/documents/110_734_1_0034_0036_OCR.pdf.

Mauborgne, Maj. J.O, letter to "My dear Friedman," Nov. 27, 1920, William Friedman Collection, George C. Marshall Foundation, http://marshallfoundation.org/library/ friedman/documents/110_734_1_0113_0116_OCR.pdf.

McNally, James B.M. letter to Elizabeth Friedman, March 21, 1944, Elizebeth S. Friedman Collection, File 1124.

Meals, F.M, memo to Commandant, "Subject Seizure of British Steamer HOLMEWOOD, of Bridgetown, Barbados, at Haverstraw, New York, 3 October, 1933," Elizebeth S. Friedman Collection, Box 6, file 24.

Message No. 5, Elizebeth S. Friedman Collection, Box 13, file 9.

"NOTES ON THE SOLUTION OF CIPHER AND CODE USED BY THE HOLMWOOD," Oct. 11, 1934, Elizebeth S. Friedman Collection, Box 6, file 24.

Official Curriculum Vitae, William F. Friedman, Elizebeth S. Friedman Collection, Box 13, file 23.

Passenger list of the *SS Leviathan*, Elizebeth S. Friedman Collection, Box 16, file 1.

Pogue, Dr. Forrest, interview with Elizebeth Friedman, May 16, 1973, Elizebeth S. Friedman Collection, Box 16, file 19.

Pollio, F.E., letter, Sept. 14, 1937, Elizebeth S. Friedman Collection, Box 6, file 28.

Pollio, Lt. F.E., memo to chief personnel officer of the Coast Guard, March 26, 1937, Elizebeth S. Friedman Collection, Box 6, file 1.

Power, Charles G., letter to Rear Adm. Russell R. Waesche, Nov. 6, 1937, Elizebeth S. Friedman Collection, Box 6, file 27.

Root, Charles S., memo to Major Hamlin, April 22, 1927; Elizebeth S. Friedman Collection, Box 4, file 16.

Samford, Lt. Gen. John, letter to William Friedman, May 13, 1959, Elizebeth S. Friedman Collection, Box 12.

Santry, Margaret. "Dialogue of Radio Interview," NBC Radio, May 25, 1934, Elizebeth S. Friedman Collection, Box 11, file 15.

Sharman, C.H.L, letter to Commissioner of Narcotics in Washington, Nov. 4, 1937, Elizebeth S. Friedman Collection, Box 6, file 27.

"The Single Intelligence School," Elizebeth S. Friedman Collection, Box 13, file 9.

Strachey, Oliver, letter to Elizebeth Friedman, March 16, 1942, Elizebeth S. Friedman Collection, Box 6, file 7.

Treasury Department Telephone Directory, Elizebeth S. Friedman Collection, Box 17, file 26.

Typed list of codes and meanings. Elizebeth S. Friedman Collection, Item 784, file 1.

Vallance, William R, letter, Jan. 10, 1935. Elizebeth S. Friedman Collection, Box 6, file 22.

Waesche, Adm. Russell, memo to Elizebeth Friedman, Nov. 11, 1937, Elizebeth S. Friedman Collection, Box 6, file 27.

Library and Archives of Canada, Ottawa

"Final Report British-Canadian-American Radio Intelligence Discussions, Washington, D.C., April 6–17, 1942," Library and Archives of Canada, RG 24, Vol. 29163.

National Archives of the United Kingdom, Kew Gardens

"The Co-ordination of IW/T Intelligence in the Western, Hemisphere, April, 1942," KV 4/218,.

"Final Report, British-Canadian-American Radio Intelligence Discussions, Washington, D.C., April 1–17," 1942, HW 14/46.

"Geoffrey" letter to "Dear John," apparently Col. Tiltman, July 31, 1942, HW 14/47.

"Most Secret," June 25, 1942, HW 19/323.

"Report by Lieut. Colonel J.H. Tiltman on his visit to North America during March and April 1942," HW 14/46.

Stevens, Major G. G. "Clandestine," memo, Dec. 24, 1942, HW 14/62.

Tiltman, Lt. Col. J.H, letter to William Friedman, May 29, 1942, HW 14/46.

National Security Agency

Benson, R. Louis. "Summary of interview of Mrs. E. S. Friedman," Jan. 9, 1976, NSA-OH-1976–22, DOC ID 4237384, approved for release by NSA July 30, 2015.

Disposition Form, "Classification of Materials Received from Mr. Friedman," Feb. 6, 1959, approved for release May 13, 2014, https://www.nsa.gov/news-features/declassified-documents/friedman-documents/assets/files/correspondence/ACC4282/41784059082311.pdf.

"Evaluation and Dissemination of Information of Japanese Cryptanalytic or T/'A Results," Jan. 1, 1944, DocRefID: A65531, Declassified and approved by release by NSA April 28, 2014.

"EXTRACT FROM: R.I.P. NO. 98, COPY 1," April 5, 1943, DocRefID A66485, declassified May 14, 2014.

Friedman, Elizebeth, letter to Gen. Marshall Carter, Jan. 8, 1971, DocRefID A2918420, approved for release June 16, 2015.

Friedman, Elizabeth [sic] Smith, letter to F. Ronald Mansbridge, April 6, 1955, DocRefID A62971, approved for release by NSA June 19, 2014.

Friedman, William F. "EXAMPLES OF INTELLIGENCE OBTAINED FROM CRYPT-ANALYSIS," Aug. 1, 1946, William F. Friedman Collection: Correspondence, Memoranda, and Personnel File Records—NSA/CSS, DocRefID A67564, declassified Oct. 29, 2013.

Friedman, William, letter to Brig. Gen. Carter Clarke, April 23, 1952, DocRefID A70092, approved for release March 25, 2014.

Friedman, William, memo about Coast Guard M-138 strip cipher, March 13, 1936, DocRefID A67563, declassified Sept. 9, 2013.

Friedman, William F. "MEMORANDUM FOR DIRECTOR, NATIONAL SECURITY AGENCY," undated, REF ID: A64948, Approved for release by NSA July 7, 2014.

Friedman, William. "Second Period, Communications Security," undated, DocRefID A63403, declassified March 24, 2014.

Gordon, R.E. "MEMORANDUM FOR DR. KULLBACK," July 15, 1941, declassified Dec. 19, 2013, https://www.nsa.gov/news-features/declassified-documents/friedman-documents/assets/files/reports-research/FOLDER_060/41707809074712.pdf.

Gorman, F.J. MEMORANDUM FOR THE COMMANDANT, Oct. 10, 1930, reprinted in *Cryptolog*, Aug-Sep 1986, NSA, declassified Oct. 16, 2012, https://www.nsa.gov/news-features/declassified-documents/cryptologs/assets/files/cryptolog_103.pdf.

"How can more cohesive working be achieved between MIS and SSA," April 1945, https://www.nsa.gov/news-features/declassified-documents/friedman-documents/assets/files/reports-research/FOLDER_461/41755639079479.pdf.

"Interview of Frank Raven," Jan. 24, 1980, NSA-OH-03–72, DOCID: 4222266, approved for release July 13, 2015, https://www.nsa.gov/news-features/declassified-documents/oral-history-interviews/assets/files/nsa-OH-1980–03-raven.pdf.

Joint Meeting of State-Army-Navy Communication Intelligence Board, Feb. 15, 1946, https://www.nsa.gov/news-features/declassified-documents/ukusa/assets/files/STANCIB_STANCICC_15feb46.pdf.

Jones, CDR L.T. (USCG). "Clandestine Radio Intelligence," Sept. 7, 1944, approved for release by NSA, Sept. 26, 2012, FOIA Case #19053.

Kingman, H.F. "MEMORANDUM FROM OFFICE OF NAVAL OPERATIONS RE UNDESIRABLE PUBLICITY IN CONNECTION WITH CRYPTANALYTICAL ACTIVITIES BY GOVERNMENT AGENCIES," June 2, 1934, DocRefID A72637, approved for release by NSA Sept. 18, 2013.

Kramer, Lt. Cmdr. A.D. "Memorandum for 20-G, Subject, Cryptanalysis; F.B.I. activities and liaison with the British," June 8, 1942, https://www.nsa.gov/news-features/declassified-documents/ukusa/assets/files/early_papers_1940–1944.pdf.

Kullback, Solomon. "General Solution for the Double Transposition Cipher," War Dept., Office of the Chief Signal Officer, DocRefID A57071, declassified May 19, 2014.

Marshall, Gen. G.C, memo to Admiral King, Aug. 18, 1945, declassified June 12, 2012, https://www.nsa.gov/news-features/declassified-documents/nsa-60th-timeline/assets/files/pre-nsa/19450818_PreNSA_Doc_3978305_SignalIntelligence.pdf.

"MEMORANDUM FOR GENERAL MARSHALL and ADMIRAL KING," Aug. 22, 1945, declassification date unspecified in 2004, https://www.nsa.gov/news-features/declassified-documents/nsa-60th-timeline/assets/files/pre-nsa/19450822_PreNSA_Doc_3978329_SignalIntelligence.pdf.

"MEMORADUM FOR THE VICE CHIEF OF STAFF," Aug. 21, 1945, declassified July 3, 2012, https://www.nsa.gov/news-features/declassified-documents/nsa-60th-timeline/assets/files/pre-nsa/19450821_PreNSA_Doc_3984126_MemoRe.pdf.

"Oral History of Elizebeth Smith Friedman," Nov. 11, 1976, NSA-OH-1976–16, DOCID: 4237384, approved for release July 30, 2015.

"Oral History of Frank Rowlett," NSA-OH-1976(1–10), DOCID: 4223202, date unspecified, declassified July 14, 2015.

"Oral History of Lt. Gen. Marshall S. Carter," Oct. 3, 1988, approved for release Oct. 30, 2015, https://www.nsa.gov/news-features/declassified-documents/oral-history-interviews/assets/files/NSA-OH-15–88-Carter.pdf.

"Oral History Interview of Dr. Solomon Kullback," NSA OH-17–82, Aug. 26, 1982, DOCID: 4235410, declassified Aug. 28, 2015, https://www.nsa.gov/news-features/declassified-documents/oral-history-interviews/assets/files/nsa-oh-17–82-kullback.pdf.

"Oral History Interview NSA OH 23–82 with Donald F. Coffey," Nov. 4, 1982, approved for release Sept. 8, 2014, FOIA Case # 78498.

"Report for: U.S. Army-Naval Communication Intelligence Coordinating Committee. Special Report No. 1," June 9, 1944, approved for release by NSA Dec. 12, 2007, https://www.nsa.gov/news-features/declassified-documents/nsa-60th-timeline/assets/files/pre-nsa/19440609_PreNSA_Doc_3263556_USArmyNaval.pdf.

"Report of Conference Appointed to Study Allocation of Cryptanalysis," June 30, 1942, declassified July 3, 2012, https://www.nsa.gov/news-features/declassified-documents/nsa-60th-timeline/assets/files/pre-nsa/19420630_PreNSA_Doc_3983157_ReportStudy.pdf.

"Report of meeting of Standing Committee for Coordination of Cryptanalytical Work," Office of the Chief of Naval Operations, Aug. 25, 1942, declassified July 3, 2012, https://www.nsa.gov/news-features/declassified-documents/nsa-60th-timeline/assets/files/pre-nsa/19420909_PreNSA_Doc_3984124_Meeting.pdf.

Reynolds, S. Wesley. "Classified Documents in Possession of William F. Friedman," NSA, Dec. 5, 1958, A99778, approved for release May 13, 2014.

Reynolds, S. Wesley, memo, Jan. 2, 1959, approved for release May 13, 2014, https://www.nsa.gov/news-features/declassified-documents/friedman-documents/assets/files/correspondence/ACC4282/41783909082296.pdf.

Wenger, J.N, memo Aug. 16, 1937, DocRefID A72632, declassified Sept. 18, 2013.

"Wiring for E-machine, as obtained from Coast Guard," March 12, 1943, William F. Friedman Collection: Correspondence, Memoranda, and Personnel File Records—NSA/CSS, DocRefID: A4146632, Declassified and approved by release by NSA Oct. 21, 2014.

U.S. National Archives and Records Administration (NARA)

NARA College Park, MD

Coburn, Capt. M.B, memo to Col. Donovan, Dec. 24, 1941, RG 226, OSS Donovan office microfilm files, 0491, File 5–8.

Donovan, William, letter to Office of the Signal Corps, Dec. 30, 1941, RG 226, OSS Donovan office microfilm files, 0502, File 4–7–2.

Donovan, William, letter to the Secretary of War, Feb. 3, 1942, RG 226, OSS Donovan office microfilm files, 0187, File 4–13–1.

Donovan, William, memo to J.R. Hayden, Jan. 3, 1942, RG 226, OSS Donovan office microfilm files, microfilm 7–6–1, file 4–4.

Donovan, William, memo to Office of the Signal Corps, Dec. 8, 1941 RG 226, OSS Donovan office microfilm files, 0389, File 4–7–1.

Donovan, William, memos to Wallace B. Phillips, Nov. 17, 1941, RG 226, OSS Donovan office microfilm files, 0465, File 5–13–3.

Farley, J.F., letter to Commander John R. Redman, March 6, 1942, *History of Coast Guard Unit 387*, RG 38, Naval Security Group Crane, Box 57.

Friedman, Elizabeth, letter to Mr. Schwartz, Oct. 6, 1939, RG 56, Box 173, Entry 193.

"From Berlin to Argentina," Serial CG4–1544, Aug. 10, 1944, RG 38, Naval Security Group Crane, Box 79.

"From Berlin to Argentine [sic]," Serial CG3–1540, Aug. 2, 1943, RG 38, Naval Security Group Crane, Box 79.

"Historical Review of OP-20-G," RG 38, Naval Security Group Crane, Box 110, FOLDER 5750/150.

History of Coast Guard Unit 387, 1946, declassified 2008, RG 38, Naval Security Group Crane, Box 57.

Jones, Lt. Leonard (USCG), memos on "Security of Dispatch" at OSS from March 9th through April 4, 1942, RG 226, Entry 92, Box 98, Folder 22.

Jones, Lt. Leonard (USCG), memos while working at COI from March 9-April 4, 1942, RG 226, Entry 92, Box 98, Folder 22.

Kimbel, W.A, memo to Coordinator of Information, Dec. 8, 1941, RG 226, OSS Donovan office microfilm files, 0389, File 5–10.

Kimbel, W.A, memo to Coordinator of Information, Dec. 13, 1941, RG 226.

"Memo from Commandant to Mrs. Elizabeth S. Friedman," April 15, 1942, RG 38, Entry 1030 A1, Box 81, Folder 12000/3.

Memo to Colonels Clark and McCormick about German clandestine radio traffic, Nov. 17, 1942, RG 457, Entry A1 9032, Box 1279, Folder German Clandestine Radio Traffic.

Memo to Mr. Wood, Nov. 15, 1933, RG 56 Box 173, Entry 193.

Navy Headquarters OP-20-G personnel file, Naval Security Group Crane, RG 38 A1 1030, Box 1.

OP-20-G, "Plan to German landing on Argentine Coast," June 5, 1944, RG 457, Entry A1 9032, Box 1368, Folder German Espionage, Jolle Operation.

OP-20-GI-A, "THE 'JOLLE' OPERATION," Aug. 25, 1944, RG 38, Naval Security Group Crane, Box 25.

Personnel classification sheet for Elizebeth Friedman, date uncertain, but appears to be 1938 or 1939. RG 38, Entry 1030 A1, Box 81, Folder 12000/3.

Report on OP-20-G general conference meeting, March 11, 1943, RG 38, Entry 1030 A1, Box 81, Folder 5050/41.

Schwartz, Charles, letter to Elizebeth Friedman, Oct. 9, 1939, RG 56, Box 173, Entry 193United States Civil Service Classification Sheet, July 16, 1931, RG 38, Entry 1030, Box 175, Folder 12000/2 .

War diaries of OP-20-G-4–1, RG 38, Naval Security Group Crane, Box 110, Folder 5750/159–160.

Wenger, J.N. "Correction to historical review," Oct. 8, 1945, RG 38, Naval Security Group Crane, Box 108, FOLDER 5750/99 .

NARA, HYDE PARK, NY, FRANKLIN D. ROOSEVELT LIBRARY

Donovan, William, letter to Secretary Morgenthau, Dec. 14, 1941, Henry Morgenthau Diaries, Roll 127, Diary 456.

Minutes of staff meeting of Secretary Morgenthau, Nov. 5, 1941, Henry Morgenthau Diaries, Roll 127, Diary 456.

Minutes of staff meeting of Secretary Morgenthau, Dec.15, 1941, Henry Morgenthau Diaries, Roll 127, Diary 456.

Morgenthau, Henry, letter to FDR, Nov. 14, 1941, Henry Morgenthau Diaries, Roll 127, Diary 462, Franklin D. Roosevelt Library, 109–100, http://www.fdrlibrary.marist. edu/_resources/images/morg/md0625.pdf .
Notes of a telephone conversation between Secretary Morgenthau and William Donovan, June 20, 1941, Henry Morgenthau Diaries, Roll 114, 411 .
"Treasury cooperation with the Coordinator of Information," June 20, 1941, Henry Morgenthau Diaries, Roll 114 411.

NARA, New York, NY

"Docket notes," July 28, 1944, U.S. v Dickinson, CASE # C116–362, 0021 Records of District Courts of the United States.
"Indictment," Feb. 11, 1944, U.S. v Dickinson, CASE # C116–362, 0021 Records of District Courts of the United States.
"Judgment and Commitment," Aug. 14, 1944, U.S. v Dickinson, CASE # C116–362, 0021 Records of District Courts of the United States.

NARA, St. Louis, MO, Elizebeth S. Friedman Personnel Records

Affidavit signed by Elizebeth Friedman, June 23, 1941.
Appointment of Elizebeth Friedman as Cryptanalyst in Charge of the Coast Guard, June 30, 1931.
Assistant Sec. of the Navy letter to Chief of Civilian Personnel, Coast Guard, Dec. 19, 1941.
Cadiz, R.L, memo, Oct. 27, 1937.
Conference for Supervisors, March 8, 1943.
Covell, L.C. travel orders for Elizebeth Friedman, Oct. 16, 1937.
Efficiency rating of Elizebeth Friedman by Lt. Cmdr. Jones, March 31, 1943.
Efficiency rating of Elizebeth Friedman by Cmdr. Jones, March 31, 1944.
Efficiency rating of Elizebeth Friedman by Cmdr. Jones, March 31, 1945.
Efficiency rating of Elizebeth Friedman, March 31, 1946.
Federal government form for education and experience, no date.
Friedman, Elizebeth S., undated resume.
Friedman, Elizebeth S., acceptance and oath, Feb. 12, 1923.
Gorman, F.J., memo, July 18, 1931.
Gorman, F.J., memo to the chief clerk, May 11, 1933.
Gorman, Thomas, memo to the Coast Guard commandant, Jan. 11, 1938.
"Important case, Month of January, 1939," news release from Bureau of Narcotics, January 1939.
Naval Communication Service memo, Jan. 25, 1923.
Naval Communication Service memo, March 22, 1923.
Naval Communication Service memo, June 6, 1923.
Navy personnel action form, June 16, 1943.
Oath of Office, July 15, 1930.
Payroll record for Elizebeth Friedman, July 1945.
"Personal History," Oct. 21, 1927.
"Personal History," July 3, 1931.
"Personal History Statement," July 1, 1930.
Personnel recommendation, Jan. 29, 1940.
Personnel record, Nov. 20, 1920.
Secretary of the Treasury letter, Dec. 8, 1925.
Temporary duty, travel orders for Elizebeth Friedman, Jan. 11, 1938.
Time and attendance report for Elizebeth Friedman, Sept. 21, 1946.
Travel orders, April 3, 1944.
Travel orders, April 11, 1944.
U.S. Civil Service Commission appointment letter, May 5, 1927.

U.S. Civil Service Commission classification sheet, June 26, 1943.
U.S. Civil Service Commission Elizebeth Friedman personnel information sheet, June 15, 1940.
U.S. Civil Service Commission memo, Feb. 2, 1923.
Waesche, Commandant R.R., letter to Elizebeth Friedman, Oct. 15, 1938.
Waesche, Commandant R.R., memo to the GAO, July 5, 1938.
Waesche, R.R., travel orders for Elizebeth Friedman, Oct. 16, 1937.

NARA, WASHINGTON, D.C.

Avant, Grady, letter, Sept. 10, 1931, RG 26, Entry 297, Box 73, file 2.
Billard, Commandant F.C., memo to Mrs. E. S. Friedman, Cryptanalyst in Charge, Jan. 26, 1932, RG 26, Entry 297, Box 48.
Coast Guard radio dispatch from *WOLCOTT* to Pascagoula, March 20, 1929. RG 26, Entry 297, Box 73, file 2.
"Decoded messages used in 'I'm Alone' smuggling operations," RG 26, Entry 297, Box 76, file 8.
Feak, C.D., letter, April 10, 1929, RG 26, Entry 297, Box 73, file 1.
Feak, C.D., "Memorandum," March 12, 1928, RG 26, Entry 297, Box 73, file 2.
"The Former Liquor Smugglers 'I'm Alone' and 'Grace and Ruby,'" April 2, 1928, RG 26, Entry 297, Box 73, file 1.
Friedman, E.S., memo to Commander Gorman, June 9, 1933, RG 26, Entry 297, Box 48.
Friedman, E.S., memo to Lt. Cmdr. Gorman, Dec. 30, 1930, RG 26, Entry 297, Box 48, Codes and cipher file.
Friedman, E.S., "Memorandum for Commander Gorman," undated but refers to files sent in June 1933, RG 26, Entry 297, Box 48.
Gamble, A.L, memo, March 28, 1929, RG 26, Entry 297, Box 73, file 1.
Gorman, F.J., memo for A.E.S. Shamhart, June 9, 1933, RG 26, Entry 297, Box 48.
Gorman, F.J., memo, "Work of the Cryptanalysis Section of Headquarters for other branches of the Government," July 8, 1933, RG 26, Entry 297, Box 48.
Hamlet, H.G. "Effect of continued operation of the international smuggling syndicates on federal revenues," Treasury Dept., Aug. 17, 1933, RG 26, Entry 297, Box 77.
"History of the Operations of the British Schooner I'M ALONE, from 20 April, 1924." RG 26, Entry 297, Box 73, file 1.
"I'm Alone" Case, Joint Final Report of the Commissioners, Jan. 19, 1935, RG 26, Entry 297, Box 75, file 2.
Letter from unnamed intelligence officer, April 18, 1929, RG 26, Entry 297, Box 73, file 2.
Massey, Vincent. "Note from the Canadian Minister to the Secretary of State, April 9, 1929," RG 26, Entry 297, Box 74, file 2.
Matson, Melvin L. affidavit, March 27, 1929. RG 26, Entry 297, Box 73, file 1.
"Memo to Chief, Division of Foreign Control," Oct. 24, 1929, RG 26, Entry 297, Box 73, file 1.
"Memorandum, Eugene Creaser Shipping Co. Ltd," March 29, 1930, RG 26, Entry 297, Box 73, file 2.
"MEMORANDUM FOR ACTING COMMANDANT," Oct. 12, 1945, RG 26, Entry 344 (A1), Box 3, Folder 3.
"Memorandum for Mr. Hickerson," April 11, 1929, RG 26, Entry 297, Box 73, file 2.
Root, C.S. "Memorandum to Division of Foreign Control," Oct. 25, 1929, RG 26, Entry 297, Box 73, file 1.
Root, Chas. S., letter to W.R. Vallance, Oct. 5, 1929, RG 26, Entry 297, Box 73, file 1.
Root, Chas. S., "Memorandum for the Commandant," Dec. 28, 1929, RG 26, Entry 297, Box 73, file 1.
"Statement by Boatswain Frank Paul," March 27, 1929. RG 26, Entry 297, Box 73, file 1.
"Statement by Boatswain A.W. Powell," March 27, 1929, RG 26, Entry 297, Box 73, file 1.

"Statement by Capt. John Thomas Randell," March 24, 1929, RG 26, Entry 297, Box 77, file 2.

Thibadeau, William L., memo, December 18, 1930, RG 26, Entry 297, Box 48, Codes and cipher file.

Treasury Department memo, July 21, 1941, RG 26, Entry 335 (A-1), Box 2, Donovan Folder.

Unit 387 deactivation memo, Feb. 6, 1946, RG 26, Entry 338 (A-1).

Woodcock, A.W.W, memo, case number 236-S, Jan. 20, 1932, RG 26, Entry 297, Box 48.

Woodcock, A.W.W., letter to the Sec. of the Treasury, June 28, 1933, RG 26, Entry 297, Box 48.

Other Documents

"Abstract of Duty Assignments for Capt. Leonard T. Jones," USCG, Nov. 28, 1962. Courtesy Cmdr. Michael E. Bennett (USCG).

Personnel file for Leonard T. Jones, National Archives, St. Louis. Courtesy Cmdr. Michael E. Bennett (USCG).

Speeches and Videos

Atchison, Chris. Remarks at Elizebeth Smith Friedman Auditorium Dedication Ceremony, ATF National Headquarters, Washington, D.C., June 17, 2014.

Friedman, William. Transcript of "Communications Intelligence and Security" lecture, April 26, 1960, approved for release Jan. 14, 2015, https://www.nsa.gov/resources/everyone/digital-media-center/video-audio/historical-audio/friedman-audio/assets/files/Communication_Intelligence_Security_26_Apr_1960_LtCol_W_F_Friedman_Transcript.pdf.

Jones, B. Todd. ATF director at Elizebeth Smith Friedman Auditorium Dedication Ceremony, ATF National Headquarters, Washington, D.C., June 17, 2014.

Sheldon, Col. Rose Mary. "A Portrait of William F. Friedman" (Online Video), 2014, The George C. Marshall Foundation, http://marshallfoundation.org/library/digital-archive/shakespearean-ciphers-examined/.

Sheldon, Col. Rose Mary. Remarks at "Declassification and Release of William Friedman's Official Papers," (Online Video), George C. Marshall Foundation, April 25, 2015, https://www.youtube.com/watch?v=qxqgK8QCchw&app=desktop.

Sherman, Bill. Analyzes the biliteral cipher in the photo, "Knowledge is Power" (Online Video), George C. Marshall Foundation, 2014, http://marshallfoundation.org/library/digital- archive/shakespearean-ciphers-examined/.

Sherman, Bill. "A Portrait of William F. Friedman" (Online Video), George C. Marshall Foundation, 2014, http://marshallfoundation.org/library/digital-archive/shakespearean-ciphers-examined/.

Sherman, Bill. "The Friedmans on Shakespeare" (Online Video), George C. Marshall Foundation, 2014, http://marshallfoundation.org/library/digital-archive/shakespearean-ciphers-examined/.

Sherman, Dr. David, NSA Associate Dir. For Policy and Records, remarks at "Declassification and Release of William Friedman's Official Papers," (Online Video), George C. Marshall Foundation, April 25, 2015, https://www.youtube.com/watch?v=qxqgK8QCchw&app=desktop.

Smoot, Betsy Rohaly. Remarks at "Declassification and Release of William Friedman's Official Papers," (Online Video), George C. Marshall Foundation, April 25, 2015, https://www.youtube.com/watch?v=qxqgK8QCchw&app=desktop.

Tomney, Rear Adm. Christopher J. (USCG). Remarks at Elizebeth Smith Friedman Auditorium Dedication Ceremony, ATF National Headquarters, Washington, D.C., June 17, 2014.

Unpublished Works

Friedman, John R. Son of William and Elizebeth Friedman, "DIVINE FIRE, A film story by John Friedman," unpublished film script, 1994, emailed to author by Friedman.

Friedman, John R. Son of William and Elizebeth Friedman, unpublished documentary script, "Code Breaking Couple," 2006, emailed to author by Friedman.

Lyle, Katie Letcher. "Divine Fire, Elizebeth Smith Friedman, Cryptanalyst," unpublished manuscript, 1991, Center for Cryptologic History, National Security Agency.

Books

Brinkley, David. *Washington Goes to War*, Alfred A. Knopf, New York, 1988.

Budiansky, Steven. *Battle of Wits: The Complete Story of Codebreaking in World War II*, The Free Press, New York, 2000.

Clark, Ronald. *The Man Who Broke Purple*, Little, Brown and Company, Boston, Toronto, 1977.

Friedman, William F., and Friedman, Elizebeth S. *The Shakespearean Ciphers Examined*, Cambridge University Press, 1957.

Gannon, Michael. *Operation Drumbeat, The Dramatic True Story of Germany's First U-Boat Attacks Along the American Coast in World War II*, Harper & Row, New York, 1990.

Hilton, Stanley E. *Hitler's Secret War in South America 1939–1945*, Louisiana State University Press, Baton Rouge, 1981.

Kahn, David. *The Code-Breakers, The Story of Secret Writing*, Scribner, New York, 1967.

Kahn, David. *Hitler's Spies: German Military Intelligence in World War II*, Macmillan Publishing Company, Inc., New York, 1978.

Morison, Samuel Eliot. *History of United States Naval Operations in World War II, Vol. 1, The Battle of the Atlantic, September 1939-May 1943*," Little, Brown and Company, Boston, 1947.

Ottenberg, Miriam. *The Federal Investigators*, Prentice-Hall, Englewood Cliffs, NJ, 1962.

"War Report of the OSS," Sept. 5, 1947, republished 1976, by Walker and Company, New York.

Willoughby, Malcolm F. *The U.S. Coast Guard in World War II*, United States Naval Institute, Annapolis, Maryland, 1957.

Monographs

Benson, Robert Louis. "A History of U.S. Communications Intelligence during World War II: Policy and Administration," United States Cryptologic History, Series IV, World War II, Volume 8, https://www.nsa.gov/about/cryptologic-heritage/historical-figures-publications/publications/wwii/assets/files/history_us_comms.pdf.

Burke, Colin B. "It Wasn't All Magic: The early Struggle to Automate Cryptanalysis, 1930s-1960s," Center for Cryptologic History, National Security Agency, December 1994, declassified May 29, 2013, https://www.nsa.gov/news-features/declassified-documents/cryptologic-histories/assets/files/magic.pdf.

Clabby, John F. "Brigadier John Tiltman, A Giant Among Cryptanalysts," Center for Cryptologic History, NSA, 2007, https://www.nsa.gov/about/cryptologic-heritage/historical-figures-publications/publications/misc/assets/files/tiltman.pdf.

Ensign, Lt. Eric S. (USCG). *Intelligence in the Rum War at Sea, 1920–1933*, Joint Military Intelligence College, Washington, D.C., 2001.

Horsefield, J. Keith. *The International Monetary Fund 1945–1965, Vol. I: Chronicle*, International Monetary Fund, Washington, D.C., 1969, http://www.elibrary.imf.org/staticfiles/IMF_History/IMF_45–65_vol1.pdf.

Mowry, David. "German Clandestine Activities in South America in World War II," NSA, 1989, https://www.nsa.gov/news-features/declassified-documents/cryptologic-histories/assets/files/german_clandestine_activities.pdf.

Mowry, David P. "Cryptologic Aspects of German Intelligence Activities in South American during WWII," 2011, United States Cryptologic History, Series IV, World War II, Volume 11, Center for Cryptologic History, NSA, https://www.nsa.gov/about/cryptologic-heritage/historical-figures-publications/publications/wwii/assets/files/cryptologic_aspects_of_gi.pdf.

Mowry, David P. "The Cryptology of the German Intelligence Services," NSA, 1989, declassified April 13, 2009, https://www.nsa.gov/news-features/declassified-documents/cryptologic-histories/assets/files/cryptology_of_gis.pdf.

Mowry, David P. "Listening to the Rum Runners," Center for Cryptologic History, 1996 but made available by the National Security Agency in 2001.

Wilcox, Jennifer. "Sharing the Burden: Women in Cryptology during World War II," Center for Cryptologic History, March 1998, https://www.nsa.gov/about/cryptologic-heritage/historical-figures-publications/publications/wwii/assets/files/sharing_the_burden.pdf.

Wilcox, Jennifer. "Solving the Enigma: History of the Cryptanalytic Bombe," Center for Cryptologic History, National Security Agency, 2006, https://www.nsa.gov/about/cryptologic-heritage/historical-figures-publications/publications/wwii/assets/files/solving_enigma.pdf.

Articles

"Argentine Ships Will Still Sail Unguarded; Citizens of Americas Linked to Axis Spying," *New York Times*, Feb. 12, 1944.

Associated Press. "'I'm Alone' Traced to Ownership Here," Dec. 29, 1934, *New York Times*.

Associated Press. "Airliner Crashes on Utah Mountain; 19 Believed Dead," Oct. 19, 1937, *New York Times*.

Author redacted. "The Origination and Evolution of Radio Traffic Analysis, the Period Between the Wars," *Cryptologic Quarterly*, Spring 1987, declassified by NSA June 16, 2008, https://www.nsa.gov/news-features/declassified-documents/cryptologic-quarterly/assets/files/the_period_between_wars.pdf.

Bennett, Lt. Cmdr. Michael (USCG). "Guardian Spies: The Story of Coast Guard Intelligence in World War II (Part 2)," *American Intelligence Journal*, 28, no. 1 (Spring 2010).

Benson, Robert L. "The Origin of U.S.-British Communications Intelligence Cooperation (1940–41)," no date, NSA, https://www.nsa.gov/news-features/declassified-documents/cryptologic-spectrum/assets/files/origin_us_british.pdf.

Bratzel, John F., & Be Rout, Leslie. "Abwehr Ciphers in Latin America," *Cryptologia* 7, no. 2 (1983).

Brown, Capt. Raymond J. (USCG). "Coast Guard Codebreakers: Inspire Those Who Serve," *Proceedings Magazine* 124/12/1 (December 1998), Naval Institute Press, http://www.usni.org/magazines/proceedings/1998–12/coast-guard-codebreakers-inspire-those-who-serve.

Callimahos, Lambros D. "The Legendary William F. Friedman," *Cryptologic Spectrum*, Winter 1974, reprinted in "The Friedman Legacy: A Tribute to William and Elizabeth Friedman," Center for Cryptologic History, National Security Agency, 1992.

Chiles, James R. "Breaking Codes Was This Couple's Lifetime Career," *Smithsonian*, June 1987, reprinted in "The Friedman Legacy: A Tribute to William and Elizabeth Friedman," Center for Cryptologic History, National Security Agency, 1992.

Clark, W.K. "The Woman All Spies in U.S. Fear," syndicated article published in the *Miami Herald* and other newspapers in October 1939.

"Coast Guard Intelligence," *Intelligence*, Coast Guard Publication 2–0, May 2010, http://www.uscg.mil/doctrine/CGPub/CG_Pub_2_0.pdf.

"Code Expert to Get Doctorate," *New York Times*, June 11, 1938.

"Cryptologic Almanac 50th Anniversary Series, The World at the End of the War," January-February 2002, NSA, approved for release June 12, 2009, https://www.nsa. gov/news-features/declassified-documents/crypto-almanac-50th/assets/files/End_ of_the_War.pdf.

Deutsch, Harold C. "The Historical Impact of Revealing the Ultra Secret," *Journal of the U.S. Army War College*, NSA, https://www.nsa.gov/news-features/declassified- documents/cryptologic-spectrum/assets/files/ultra_secret.pdf.

"Doll Dealer Held as Japanese Spy; Was Seized in Censorship Case," *New York Times*, May 6, 1944.

"Doll Woman Enters Guilty Plea In Censor Case; Faces 10 Years," *New York Times*, July 29, 1944.

"Doll Woman Sentenced to Prison For 10 Years and Fined $10,000," *New York Times*, Aug. 15, 1944.

"Doll Woman's Trial Set," *New York Times*, July 11, 1944.

"Elizabeth Friedman Autobiography at Riverbank Laboratories, Geneva, Illinois," listed as "ESF Oral History Pt. 2" at Center for Cryptologic History, National Security Agency.

"Elizabeth Smith Friedman 1892–1980," *Cryptologic Spectrum*, December 1980, reprinted in "The Friedman Legacy: A Tribute to William and Elizebeth Friedman," Center for Cryptologic History, National Security Agency, 1992.

Friedman, William F. "A Brief History of U.S. Cryptologic Operations 1917–1929," undated National Security Agency publication, declassified July 16, 2008, https://www.nsa. gov/news-features/declassified-documents/cryptologic-spectrum/assets/files/Brief_ History_US_Cryptologic_Operations.pdf.

Friedman, William F. "Certain Aspects of Magic in the Cryptological Background of the Various Official Investigations Into the Attack on Pearl Harbor," 1957, NSA, Center for Cryptologic History, SRH-125, www.ibiblio.org/hyperwar/PTO/Magic/SRH-125/ index.html.

Friedman, William F. "Lecture V," reprinted in "The Friedman Legacy: A Tribute to William and Elizebeth Friedman," Center for Cryptologic History, National Security Agency, 2006, https://www.nsa.gov/resources/everyone/digital-media-center/video- audio/historical-audio/friedman-legacy/assets/files/friedman-legacy-transcript.pdf.

Friedman, William F. "Lecture VI," reprinted in "The Friedman Legacy: A Tribute to William and Elizebeth Friedman," Center for Cryptologic History, National Security Agency, 1992. https://www.nsa.gov/resources/everyone/digital-media-center/video- audio/historical-audio/friedman-legacy/assets/files/friedman-legacy-transcript.pdf.

Friendly, Albert. "In Memoriam Elizebeth Smith Friedman," *Cryptologic Spectrum*, NSA, December 1980, Elizebeth S. Friedman Collection, Box 16, file 24, George C. Marshall Library, Virginia Military Institute.

Hatch, David. "Enigma and Purple: How the Allies Broke German and Japanese Codes During the War," no date, http://www.usna.edu/Users/math/wdj/_files/documents/ papers/cryptoday/hatch_purple.pdf.

Helmick, Leah Stock. "Key Woman of the T-Men," *Readers Digest*, September 1937.

"The Holiday Season," *The Montreal Daily Star*, July 9, 1929, Clipping in Coast Guard files. RG 26, Entry 297, Box 77, file 12, National Archives Building, Washington, D.C.

Howell, Donna. "She Helped Break Rumrunners; Crackdown: Elizebeth Smith Friedman's code breaking upheld the law," *Investor's Business Daily*, May 19, 2005.

Hutchison, James B. "Air-Sea Safety Patrol To Be Retained IN Peace Admiral Gorman Discloses," Gannett News Service, *The Massena Observer*, Nov. 1, 1945, http://news. nnyln.net/massena-observer/massena-observer-1945-august-1946-january/ massena-observer-1945-august-1946-january%20-%200322.pdf.

"I'm Alone Apology Given to Canada" *New York Times*, Jan. 22, 1935.

"I'm Alone Skipper Describes Cruises," *New York Times*, Dec. 30, 1934.

Jenkisson, John. "The FBI vs New York Spies," *New York World-Telegram*, June 23, 1945.

Jones, Mary McCracken. "Girl Code Decipherer Learned About Ciphers From Shakespeare," *New York Sun*, Nov. 10, 1933, Elizebeth S. Friedman Collection, Box 16, file 30, George C. Marshall Library, Virginia Military Institute.

Joyce, Maureen. "Elizebeth Friedman, U.S. Cryptanalyst, Pioneer in Science of Code-Breaking Dies," *Washington Post*, Nov. 2, 1980, Elizebeth S. Friedman Collection, Box 16, file 23.

Kahn, David. "Decoding the Bard," *New York Times*, Oct. 6, 1957, http://timesmachine.nytimes.com/timesmachine/1957/10/06/91167527.html.

Lewis, Frank W. "German Agent Systems of World War II," undated, Approved for Release by NSA June 5, 2009, DOCID: 3565448.

Lunnen, Connie. "She Has a Secret Side, Breaking Codes Was More Personal in Her Day, Elizebeth Friedman Says," *The Houston Chronicle*, May 24, 1972, Elizebeth S. Friedman Collection, Box 11, file 14, George C. Marshall Library, Virginia Military Institute.

Mallon, Winifred. "Woman Wins Fame as Cryptanalyst," *New York Times*, Feb. 12, 1937.

"MILLIONS ARE SAVED TO NATION BY DECODER OF SMUGGLERS' NOTES," article in unknown newspaper, May 28, 1934, Elizebeth S. Friedman Collection, Box 11, file 15, George C. Marshall Library, Virginia Military Institute.

Mowry, David. "Cryptologic Almanac 50th Anniversary Series, William F. Friedman," National Security Agency, declassified June 12, 2009, https://www.nsa.gov/news-features/declassified-documents/crypto-almanac-50th/assets/files/William_F_Friedman.pdf.

"Open Codes," 1997, Approved for release by NSA, Dec. 1, 2011, https://www.nsa.gov/news-features/declassified-documents/crypto-almanac-50th/assets/files/open-codes.pdf.

"Radio New York: The First Civilian Intercept Station?" undated, approved for release by NSA, Dec. 1, 2011, https://www.nsa.gov/news-features/declassified-documents/crypto-almanac-50th/assets/files/radio-new-york.pdf.

Rice, William and Art Smith. "Doll Woman Yawns When Held for Trial as Paid Spy of Japs," *New York Daily News*, May 5, 1944, Elizebeth S. Friedman Collection, Marshall Library, Box 7, File 1.

"Rum Ship Captain Quits at His Goal," Oct. 5, 1933, *New York Times*.

"Seizure of Diplomatic Liquor Creates Incident," *Time Magazine*, April 1, 1929, http://www.druglibrary.org/schaffer/history/e1920/siameseincident.htm.

Sheldon, Col. Rose Mary. "William F. Friedman: A Very Private Cryptographer and His Collection," *Cryptologic Quarterly*, 2015–01, Vol. 34.

Sherman, Dr. David. "The National Security Agency and the William F. Friedman Collection," *Cryptologia*, June 29, 2016, http://dx.doi.org/10.1080/01611194.2016.1169458.

Smith, George. "Canadian Leader Denounces U.S. for 'Act of War,'" *Chicago Tribune* Press Service, May 21, 1929. Clipping from an unknown newspaper in Coast Guard files. RG 26, Entry 297, Box 77, file 12, National Archives Building, Washington, D.C.

United Press. "FOLGER AWARDS MADE," *New York Times*, April 3, 1955, http://timesmachine.nytimes.com/timesmachine/1955/04/03/88793350.html.

Weadon, Patrick. "A New Kind of Detective Work," Center for Cryptologic History, 2001, https://www.nsa.gov/about/cryptologic-heritage/historical-figures-publications/publications/pre-wwii/assets/files/new_detective_work.pdf.

"Woman Accused of Using Letters On Dolls to Convey Military Data," *New York Times*, Jan. 22, 1944.

"Woman Solves Chinese Code to Nip Opium Ring," *Washington Post*, Feb. 9, 1938, Elizebeth Friedman personnel file, National Archives, St. Louis.

Web Sources

Baxter, James Phinney. *The Greatest of Literary Problems*, Houghton Mifflin Company, Boston, 1917, https://archive.org/details/greatestoflitera00baxtrich.

Becque, Fran. "Baconian Biliteral Cipher, on the Estate of Colonel Fabayon [sic], National Security, and a Fraternity Woman," Focus on Fraternity History & More, http://www.franbecque.com/2013/08/09/baconian-biliteral-cipher-on-the-estate-of-colonel-fabyon-national-security-and-a-fraternity-woman/.

"Biographical Directory of the United States Congress," PEPPER, Claude Denson (1900–1989), http://bioguide.congress.gov/scripts/biodisplay.pl?index=p000218.

"Bletchley Park Diary, William F. Friedman" Edited with Notes and Bibliography by Colin MacKinnon, 2013, http://www.colinmackinnon.com/files/The_Bletchley_Park_Diary_of_William_F._Friedman_E.pdf.

Burke, Colin. "What OSS Black Chamber? What Yardley? What "Dr." Friedman? Ah, Grombach?" http://userpages.umbc.edu/~burke/whatossblack.pdf.

Civil War history of John Marion Smith courtesy of Gail Heiser at http://www.civilwar archive.com/Unreghst/unininf8.htm.

"Clandestine Women: Spies in American History," National Women's History Museum website, https://www.nwhm.org/online-exhibits/spies/13.htm.

"Constitution of the United States, Amendments 11–27," http://www.archives.gov/exhibits/charters/constitution_amendments_11–27.html.

Cooney, Tory. "Cracking the Code: Hillsdale alum aided U.S. intelligence during world wars," *The Hillsdale Collegian*, March 21, 2014, http://www.hillsdalecollegian.com/2014/03/cracking-the-code-hillsdale-alum-aided-u-s-intelligence-during-world-wars/.

"Cryptologic Almanac 50th Anniversary Series, Joseph N. Wenger," DOCID: 3575736, approved for release June 12, 2009, https://www.nsa.gov/news-features/declassified-documents/crypto-almanac-50th/assets/files/Joseph_N._Wenger.pdf.

"Cryptologic Excellence: Yesterday, Today, and Tomorrow," National Security Agency, undated, circa 2002, https://www.nsa.gov/about/_files/cryptologic_heritage/publications/misc/50th_anniversary.pdf.

"Elizebeth S. Friedman (1892–1980) Cryptologic Hall of Honor 1999 Inductee," NSA, https://www.nsa.gov/about/cryptologic-heritage/historical-figures-publications/hall-of- honor/1999/efriedman.shtml.

"Facts & Figures: Income and Prices 1900–1999," U.S. Diplomatic Mission to Germany, http://usa.usembassy.de/etexts/his/e_prices1.htm.

"Former Directors," National Security Agency, http://www.nsa.gov/about/leadership/former_directors.shtml.

"George C. Marshall Foundation and National Security Agency Debut," April 24, 2015, NSA, https://www.nsa.gov/news-features/press-room/press-releases/2015/marshall-foundation-and-nsa-debut-friedman-collection.shtml.

"German Espionage and Sabotage Against the United States in World War II," *O.N.I. Review* [Office of Naval Intelligence] 1, no.3 (January 1946), [declassified, formerly "confidential"], http://www.history.navy.mil/research/library/online-reading-room/title-list-alphabetically/g/german-espionage-and-sabotage.html.

"Hall of Honor Inductees: 1999," http://www.nsa.gov/about/cryptologic_heritage/hall_of_honor/1999/index.shtml.

"History of Martinique," Wikipedia, https://en.wikipedia.org/wiki/History_of_Martinique#World_War_II.

Hoover, Herbert. "Annual Message to Congress on the State of the Union," Dec. 3, 1929. Online by Gerhard Peters and John T. Woolley, *The American Presidency Project*. http://www.presidency.ucsb.edu/ws/?pid=22021.

"Interviewee: Radioman First Class Glen Boles, USCGR, World War II Coast Guard Veteran," Nov. 27, 2005, U.S. Coast Guard Oral History Program, https://www.uscg.mil/history/weboralhistory/glenboles_oralhistory.asp.

Jensen, Kurt F. "Cautious Beginnings: Canadian Foreign Intelligence, 1939–51," http://books.google.com/books?id=0YLJFlVQFoAC&pg=PA50&lpg=PA50&dq=intelligence+section+oliver+strachey&source=bl&ots=HaBhI3s4aq&sig=p6IxKVkuO96bQyUZW0f9zVeOkjg&hl=en&sa=X&ei=UVJ7U8SeNdOMyATR1oKoBg&ved=

0CFAQ6AEwCQ#v=onepage&q=intelligence%20section%20oliver%20strachey&f=false.

Military Times Hall of Valor, http://valor.militarytimes.com/recipient.php?recipientid=312360.

"National Cryptologic Museum," http://www.nsa.gov/about/cryptologic_heritage/museum/index.shtml.

"National Network of Fusion Centers Fact Sheet," Department of Homeland Security, http://www.dhs.gov/national-network-fusion-centers-fact-sheet#1.

National Security Agency photo gallery, https://www.nsa.gov/resources/everyone/digital-media-center/image-galleries/people/historical-figures/.

"NSA Observes Armed Forces Week-Coast Guard," May 15, 2015, https://www.nsa.gov/news-features/news-stories/2015/nsa-celebrates-armed-forces-week-coast-guard.shtml.

"Oliver Strachey," Wikipedia, https://en.wikipedia.org/wiki/Oliver_Strachey.

Riverbank Laboratories, City of Geneva website, http://www.geneva.il.us/riverbnk/riverpag.html.

Rules for Handling Mail and Files at Units of the United States Coast Guard, Treasury Department, 1936, http://www.archives.gov/research/military/coast-guard/1936-rules-for-handling-mail.pdf.

Sheldon, Col. Rose Mary. "The Friedman Collection: An Analytical Guide," http://marshallfoundation.org/library/wp-content/uploads/sites/16/2014/09/Friedman_Collection_Guide_September_2014.pdf.

"The Sinking of The I'm Alone," Source: Robert Thorne, Downhomer, October 2001, http://www.newfoundlandshipwrecks.com/Im%20Alone/documents/rumrunner_im_alone.htm.

Skoglund, Nancy Galey. "The *I'm Alone* Case: A Tale from the Days of Prohibition," University of Rochester Library Bulletin, Vol. XXII, Spring 1968, No. 3, http://www.lib.rochester.edu/index.cfm?PAGE=1004.

"Velvalee Dickinson, the 'Doll Woman,'" FBI Website,https://www.fbi.gov/history/famous-cases/velvalee-dickinson-the-doll-woman.

WIFLE Newsletter, March 2014, http://www.wifle.org/newsletters/march2014/index.htm.

Index

Information (or OSS) 8, 11, 114–118, 123–124, 128, 167; Cryptanalyst in Charge (or Senior Cryptanalyst) 46, 48, 69, 141; Cryptologic Hall of Honor 12, 166, 178; danger to 50, 66–67; death 9, 122, 181; discrimination 123, 126, 177; Divine Fire 21, 179; Doll Woman (Velvalee Dickinson) 10, 143–159, 178–179; domestic help 31, 38, 89, 113–114; drug cases 4, 10, 48–50, 69, 79–83, 88–99, 102, 123, 178; education 15–16, 100, 109; English roots 15; Enigma 11, 122–124, 130, 132, 135–137, 139–140, 165, 178; Fabyan, Col. George 13–14, 16–22, 23–26, 28–34, 38–39, 167; FBI work 8, 114, 127–130, 149–155, 157–159, 181; first lady invitations 86; Friedman papers 124, 171–175; Germany 8, 10–11, 25–26, 30, 102–104, 114, 120–142, 143, 151, 160, 165, 172, 178; government facilities named for her 4, 6–7, 107, 127, 177, 180–181; Hillsdale College 13, 15–16, 100; Hindu trials 25–26, 179; *Holmewood* 50, 75–79; Huntington, Indiana 14, 20; *I'm Alone* 47, 50, 52–68, 69, 104; IMF 11, 166–167, 180; international trips 87–88, 109–110, 167; interviews and press coverage 8–9, 13, 19, 23–24, 28–30, 45, 50, 69–70, 72–73, 78, 80–81, 83–84, 97–100, 104, 106–108, 162–163, 164, 180; Japan 8, 10, 79, 105, 111, 114, 128, 131, 140–141, 143–159, 161, 179; law enforcement 4–6, 12, 39–40, 44–45, 49–51, 70, 74, 78, 95, 102, 106, 162–165, 176, 181; legacy 4, 12, 173–181; Mayan hieroglyphics 109, 170–171; Military Road home 38, 70, 86, 131, 167; model or pioneer for other women 4, 6, 101, 83, 123, 176–181; naming as Elizebeth 15; NSA 123, 165, 171–174, 177; Pearl Harbor 113, 115–116, 125, 131, 144; personnel training 24–25, 28–29, 48, 74, 114–118, 175–176, 181; Pi Beta Phi sorority 16, 179; pioneer in her field 4, 6, 12, 101, 175–176, 178, 181; praising memos 62–63, 68, 74, 82–83, 85, 94–95, 141–142, 176–177; Purple cipher 110, 115–116, 179; salary 20, 32, 35–36, 40–42, 48, 86, 142; Shakespeare and *The Shakespearean Ciphers Examined* 7–8, 11, 13, 16–19, 22, 24, 30, 32, 167–170, 179, 181; spies 8, 10, 40, 104, 106–108, 114, 119, 120–142, 143–159, 160, 163–165, 178–179, 181; supervising men 175–176; testimony in cases 5, 49, 63–66, 69, 70–75, 83, 88–99, 108, 149, 164, 176; travel allowance 71, 88, 96 ; U.S. Army 7, 24–26, 28–30, 32–33, 35–37, 44, 49, 86, 100, 105–106, 108, 111, 114–115, 118–119, 120, 123, 126, 128–129, 131, 136, 141, 162, 176, 179; U.S. Coast Guard 4–6, 10–11, 40–51, 56–59,

62–63, 68, 69, 71, 73–79, 82–84, 87–89, 91, 95–96, 98–99, 100–101, 102–105, 108, 111–119, 120–142, 143, 150, 160–165, 175–176, 177–179, 181; U.S. Navy 7, 11, 25, 29–30, 36–37, 40, 48, 74, 87, 104–105, 108, 111–117, 119, 123, 126–130, 132–134, 139, 141–142, 149, 162–164, 178
Friedman, John 42, 87, 89, 106, 109–110, 113–114, 175
Friedman, Vanessa 7
Friedman, William F. 7, 11–12, 18–22, 23–34, 35–38, 40, 44, 51, 85–89, 91, 94, 100–101, 104–106, 109–111, 114–116, 123, 131–132, 137, 160–162, 164–181
Friendly, Alfred 181

Gallup, Elizabeth Wells 17–19, 22, 167, 169
Galveston, Texas 75
gangsters *see* mobsters
Gaston, Herbert 112–113, 116
Geneva, Illinois 13, 17, 28, 30, 32
Germany (or Germans) 8, 10–11, 24–26, 30, 102–104, 109, 114, 120–123, 125–128, 130–140, 143, 151, 160, 165, 172, 178
Good Housekeeping 99
Gordon, Robert 103
Gorman, Lt. Cmdr. Frank J. (USCG) 44–45, 47–48, 69, 74, 77
Government Code & Cypher School 125, 128, 131, 135
Grace, Edwin H. 72
Graves, G. Van 142
Graves, Harold N. 82
Great Depression 67, 78, 85, 87
Great Lakes 39
Gulf of Mexico 39, 43, 45, 52, 54, 70–71

Halpern, Daniel *see* Hogan, Dan
Hamburg, Germany 120, 128, 130, 132, 137, 139
Hastings, Capt. Edward 131
Hatch, David 139
Havana, Cuba (or Cuba) 43, 59
Hearn, George 60–63, 66
Hee, Ching Chun 82
Hellmuth, Oscar 137
Hillsdale College 13, 15–16, 100
Hindu conspiracy trials (World War I) 25–26, 179
Hiroshima, Japan 161
Hitt, Capt. Parker 25
Hobbs brothers 70
Hogan, Dan (alias Joseph Foran, Daniel Halpern and David Martin) 57, 60–61, 63, 66–67
Holmewood (ship) 50, 76–78
Hong Kong 82, 94, 97
Honolulu, Hawaii 82
Hoover, Herbert 50–51
Hoover, J. Edgar 127, 147, 158–159